The Islington Murder Mystery

David Barrat

Orsam Books
www.orsam.co.uk

First edition published 2012
Copyright © David Barrat 2012
Reprinted with amendments 2015
Reprinted with amendments 2017

ISBN: 978-0-9570917-0-2

Credits:

Extract from Nineteen Eighty Four by George Orwell (Copyright © George Orwell, 1949) by permission of Bill Hamilton as the Liter-ary Executor of the Estate of the Late Sonia Brownwell Orwell and Secker & Warburg Ltd.

Photographs: Alice Marie Wheatley in the dock of the North Lon-don Police Court - TopFoto; Albert Wootten portrait - © Mirrorpix; Albert Wootten outside North London Police Court - TopFoto/ © Mirrorpix; Detective Inspector Davis - TopFoto; Richard Muir - Get-ty Images; Justice Lush - Getty Images; Thomas Hedderwick - © Il-lustrated London News Ltd/Mary Evans; Alice Marie Wheatley and J.L. Pratt outside the Old Bailey © Mirrorpix; Harry & Mary Ann Wheatley and Marie in later years from private family collection, reproduced by kind permission of Simon Lawrence; Lily Wootten – Weekly Dispatch; pinfire revolver – www.northirishmilitaria.com.

Contents

Preface

'Even a god cannot change the past.'

Agathon c. 400 BC

As someone with an interest in true crime, I was amazed, while researching a completely unrelated subject, to stumble upon a major unsolved Edwardian, or rather Post-Edwardian,* English murder that fascinated and absorbed the nation in 1915 but had been completely forgotten about ever since. The more I read about the case, the more gripping I thought it was as a crime story and felt that a book was required to tell it. With no-one having written one, it seemed to fall to me to do so.

Fortunately, the story practically tells itself and I have attempted to relate it as faithfully as possible. In particular, I would like to stress that the dialogue in this book is taken directly from unchallenged witness testimony of people who were present while the conversations described took place: either listening to, or participating in, them. Where there is any dispute over what was said, I have either not used that dialogue and/or have indicated the uncertainty in the text, either in the narrative or during the later discussion. Nothing has been invented and nothing added that was not recalled by witnesses giving evidence under oath. Similarly, all questioning and cross-examination set out in this book has been reconstructed either from official court records or contemporary newspaper reports. These often do not report the exact questions asked - which is where the reconstruction part comes in - but are otherwise reproduced exactly as they were taken down or reported by the court clerks and journalists.

Although the murder in this case is unsolved, I do make an attempt at 'solving' it towards the end of the book but it goes without saying that after almost one hundred years nothing can be conclusively proved. I have tried to be as factually accurate as possible in setting out the story in order to allow proper conclusions to be drawn. In the end, it does not really matter what I think, for I cannot change the past. Even gods, it seems, cannot do that. The past is what it is and always has been.

This book has been self-published and has not, therefore, been edited by a professional editor or gone through the normal processes. I hope that the reader will ignore, if not forgive, any stylistic inconsistencies or preventable errors of grammar and will prefer to focus on the rather more interesting subject at hand – the unsolved murder of Annie Josephine Mary Wootten.

---

* The period of Queen Victoria's reign from 1837 to 1901 is called the Victorian era, the subsequent period of Edward VII's reign until his death 1910 is called the Edwardian era but then George V came to the throne and we are not allowed to refer to this as the Georgian period because that appellation is already taken by the four Georges who reigned successively from 1714 to 1820. Due to the commencement of the First World War in 1914, which created its own historical period of 'wartime Britain', the years after 1910 don't really have their own snappy title, other than 'the pre-war period' (which can only apply to the period before August 1914) and I have used the phrase 'Post Edwardian era' or 'Post-Edwardian period', which of course I did not invent, to cover them. In fact, the Post-Edwardian period can be said to have continued into the war years and beyond but it is not entirely clear when it ended. George V's reign continued until the 1930s which was an entirely different age compared to the 1910s. I suppose it stopped in 1919 after which we usually speak of the twenties and the thirties etc.

Note on Currency

In 1915 there were 12 pennies in a shilling and 20 shillings in a pound (otherwise referred to as 12d being 1s and 20s being £1). A pound was also known as a sovereign (in the form of a coin) while a guinea was a pound and one shilling. Accurate currency conversion into today's money is virtually impossible. In 1915, *The Times* newspaper cost one penny whereas it now (in 2017) costs one pound and seventy pence. So can we say that a pound and seventy pence of today's money is the equivalent of a penny in 1915? Not necessarily. Paper, printing and labour costs, as well as reading habits, are very different today compared with 1915, all affecting the price of daily newspapers then and now. It is much the same for any item or form of expenditure. There is no single conversion that works precisely but currency converter on the website measuringworth.com claims that the relative value of one penny from 1915 is twenty-three pence in today's money so that one shilling is the equivalent of £3.68 and one pound the equivalent of £73.54 - but it does also give a range of values going much higher. Bearing in mind that £2 a week was a living wage for a worker with a family in 1915, a penny in 1915 money must surely have been worth at least fifty pence in today's money and possibly more. If *The Times* newspaper test is actually correct, and a penny is the equivalent of £1.70, then a shilling would be the equivalent of £20 and a pound the equivalent of £408.

CHAPTER 1

MRS HIGSON'S FRIEND COMES

'I am not yet dead; but the Angel of Death came to me in the dusk ~, evening.'

The Thousand and One Nights, by Edward William Lane (trans.), 1838

There was nothing special about that particular afternoon in Islington on a cold Tuesday in March 1915. Everything certainly appeared normal in the Wootten household at number 114 Rotherfield Street. Little Lily returned home from school as usual at about four o'clock.[1] Her mother, Annie, made the dinner and, once that was eaten, it was time for a wash before bedtime.

Living in the small basement of a modest north London house, eight-year-old Lily had to share a bedroom not only with her parents but also with her seven-year-old sister, Ivy, her four-year-old brother, Edwin, and her little baby sister, Doris.[2] All four children were safely tucked into bed shortly after sunset at about six-thirty in the evening.[3] Having bid them goodnight,[4] Annie turned down the gas lamp in the bedroom, and, as far as the children knew, left to read a book in the only other room in the basement: the kitchen opposite the bedroom. It must have been a relief for 30-year-old Annie to sit down and relax. Her right knee was deformed and she had only just recovered from a fall in the street about a fortnight earlier which had forced her to use crutches.[5] She was now able to walk unaided and expected to go shopping with her dear friend, Cora, later in the evening.

In the bedroom, despite the increasing darkness outside, it was too early for sleep for the two older

1

..ldren and, while Edwin and Doris snoozed, Ivy
..hatted happily for a few minutes with Lily, recounting
a story her class at school had been told by one of their
teachers about a woman and a bee.[6]

Shortly after Ivy finished telling the story, the
girls were disturbed by their mother suddenly and
unexpectedly coming back into the room. Without
saying a word, Annie pulled the roller blind covering
the window to one side and looked out to the street
which, from below ground level, could barely be seen
through the glass pane. She remained at the window,
peering out into the rapidly darkening street for about
a minute after which, without any explanation, she
quickly left the bedroom, not even shutting the door
properly, and walked straight upstairs.

Alerted by this unusual behaviour, Lily and Ivy
strained their ears and were rewarded by hearing the
front door open and a foot scrape in the passage. They
heard their mother speak and another female voice
they did not recognize, although Lily at first thought it
might be her Auntie Mabel. It was certainly not Cora
Higson, the only woman who might be expected to be
visiting their mother at that time in the evening. There
was a hushed conversation which the girls could not
hear, lasting for some time – perhaps as long as an
hour.

Still the girls did not sleep, wondering who was at
the door. They managed to hear the unknown woman
say, 'I don't know the bar' but they had no idea what
it meant. Somewhat alarmingly, Ivy also heard the
woman say, 'Give me some money', and, from the
sound of it, a few coppers were handed over. Both
girls then heard the woman say: 'I'm thin and hungry,
give me some water'. After this, their mother came
down the stairs and passed by the half open bedroom
door on her way to the kitchen. She emerged from

the kitchen a few moments later and walked back up the stairs with a single glass of water in her hand. As she passed by the bedroom, Lily anxiously called out, 'Mother, who is it?' receiving the calm reply, 'Oh, it's only Mrs Higson's friend'.

Thus reassured, the two girls gave the events upstairs less attention but Ivy's ears pricked up when she heard her mother say, 'Oh don't, I've got four children downstairs' to which the woman replied, 'Oh, I would not for the world', followed by two very loud bangs like a door slamming, the girls thought. Her mother cried out 'Oh! Oh!' after each bang, and then called loudly: 'Lily! Lily!'

Both girls rushed out of bed and raced up the stairs where they found the front door of the house shut and their mother, alone, sitting on the edge of the top of the stairs in the passage with her legs lying across the landing and her unsupported back facing towards the stairs. There was blood on her face and her blue velveteen blouse was torn and burning; electric sparks were fizzing dramatically all around the material of her clothing. She wasn't speaking and appeared to be dead. The distressed little girls tried to pick their mother up but she was so heavy they couldn't do it and her limp body fell down to the half landing in the middle of the staircase. The girls did not know what to do next. There were no other adults in the house. Aware that their Auntie Lil, Annie's sister, who lived on the first floor of the building, was out visiting their grandfather and that her husband, Uncle Fred, had not yet returned from work, they decided to dress themselves and run to grandpa's house. So they rushed back down the stairs to their room in order to gather and put on their clothes.

As they were dressing, their mother's friend, Cora, appeared at the house and rapped on the door. Lily

3

ran back up the stairs and, seeing who it was, cried: 'Oh Mrs Higson, mother is dead!' Noticing Annie's prostrate body in the passage, Cora Higson rather panicked and rushed straight into the street to seek assistance from the first person she could locate.

An Irish post office sorting clerk in his mid-thirties called James Jordan was walking home from work at Mount Pleasant and was more than surprised when a highly agitated lady he did not know ran out of a house and told him a woman had fallen down some stairs and was dead or dying. Immediately offering his assistance, Mr Jordan entered the house and, as forewarned, found a woman lying on the staircase with blood covering the lower part of her face and neck. There was a small hole in the left breast of her blouse surrounded, he noticed, by an extraordinary bright red circular border, just like a ring of fire, which was smouldering. He quickly extinguished this with his hand then lifted the woman up six or seven steps into the hall. He wanted to move the body out of the passage but Lily told him the two doors in the hall leading to separate parlours were locked. He tried one of them but found it was indeed locked and correctly assumed the other one was too. He lived only a few doors away and immediately fetched his wife, Mary, who came to the house with him and saw the body on the linoleum floor in the hall. She searched for a pulse and, not finding one, realised the woman was dead.

Meanwhile, having secured Mr Jordan's assistance, Mrs Higson had again run out of the house and, not quite knowing what to do, knocked on the door of the neighbouring house at 112 Rotherfield Street. A 54-year-old maker of surgical instruments called Henry Johnstone lived there. He answered the door to be told by a now rather hysterical woman: 'Go into Mrs Wootten's, I think something has happened. I am

going to Exmouth Street'. Exmouth Street was where
Annie's father, Joseph, lived and Mrs Higson expected
to find Auntie Lil, otherwise Lily Dixon, there. As
instructed, Mr Johnstone entered number 114 and saw
Mr and Mrs Jordan, with Mrs Wootten lying prostrate
on the floor. He walked over to her and raised her
head. Blood was flowing from her nose and mouth.
He fetched a pillow from the children's bedroom and
tenderly, albeit pointlessly, placed it under her head.

At the same time, Mrs Jordan sent one of the
children for a basin of water and, when it was brought
to her, washed the dead woman's face of the blood that
was covering it. Her husband left the house to fetch
a doctor in order to certify the death. He was on his
way to Dr Madden's surgery a short distance away in
Devonshire Street but, in the road, he met his fifteen-
year-old stepson, John, and sent him for the doctor
instead. John ran as fast as he could to the surgery
and was there within two minutes. Dr Madden had a
few patients to attend to and John had to wait a short
time but the doctor was soon with the body. Following
a very quick examination he pronounced life extinct.
Seeing blood still oozing from the dead woman's nose,
and having been told by someone that she had fallen
down the stairs, the doctor assumed she had died
from a fractured skull. He was not in the house long
- less then five minutes - being impatient to get back
to his living patients. Before leaving, he instructed
Mrs Jordan to call for the nearest police constable but
decided not to wait around for his arrival.

Young John was again sent out and he ran to find
P.C. George Wood on point duty at the corner of
New North Road and Essex Road, opposite the Three
Brewers Public House. 'Will you come to Rotherfield
Street?' asked the breathless young lad, 'a woman
has fallen downstairs and broken her neck'. Showing

more urgency than the doctor, the constable made his way directly to the house and was told upon arrival by a tearful Lily: 'Mummy has fallen downstairs'. P.C. Wood saw some blood on the stairs leading from the passage to the half landing. The woman was lying on her back and he saw blood on her mouth and nostrils. He located a dark blue tapestry table cloth from somewhere in the house and covered the top half of the body. He then left the house for about quarter of an hour to telephone the police station and inform the coroner's officer of what had happened, instructing Mr and Mrs Jordan to remain inside and guard the body. While he was away, Mrs Higson returned with Annie's sister, Lily Dixon, who she had collected from her father's house. In the kitchen, the distraught woman, still reeling from the news of her sister's death, noticed an opened telegram by the mantelpiece. It had been sent from a nearby post office at shortly after six o'clock that evening and read:

```
Dickson 114 Rotherfield Street: Come at
once — FATHER.
```

She was vaguely puzzled by this. The address was correct – 114 Rotherfield Street – but her surname was wrongly spelt. She did not know what it meant - she had been with her own father all evening so he was evidently not in any trouble and would be able to spell her name correctly in any case. In the circumstances, she was not able to focus properly on the matter although she was vaguely worried that her husband's father, George Dixon, might need help of some sort.

She did not need to worry for long. Her husband, Fred, a temporary sorter for the Post Office, arrived at the house a few minutes later, shortly before nine o'clock.

Walking through the front door he immediately saw blood on the stairs leading to the basement and, in this way, became aware of his sister-in-law's sudden demise. His wife handed him the telegram, supposed to have come from either his or his wife's father, and the misspelling of his surname puzzled him too. Concerned, he went to check up on his father who lived a very short distance away, in the same street in fact, at number 84, but Mr Dixon senior knew nothing of any telegram; he would not waste time and money by foolishly sending a telegram to contact his son a few houses down the road! Fred concluded that it must simply be a wrongly addressed telegram meant for someone else.

Meanwhile, Annie's father and members of her family had been contacted and arrived at the house.

There was some discussion about what had happened. No-one had closely questioned the two distraught little girls, now exhausted and asleep in bed, about what they had seen or heard – so the adults did not know about 'Mrs Higson's friend' having called – but, from what the doctor had told them, and from their own knowledge that Annie had a weak and deformed knee, the consensus was that it must have been an accident, arising from an attempt to light the gas lamp on the ceiling in the hall, during which she had lost her balance and stumbled backwards, causing her to drop the match on her blouse and fall down the stairs, thus breaking her neck. No-one knew at the time, because the doctor's cursory and wholly inadequate examination had completely failed even to identify the entrance wound, that there was a small bullet lodged in the dead woman's spine.

Another police constable had arrived at the house by the time the family had arrived at their theory to account for the death. P.C. Walter Reeves from the coroner's office had been contacted by P.C. Wood and the two officers moved the body into the back

parlour on the ground floor. For this they needed
the help of Fred Dixon, back from his father's house,
who unlocked the door for them. The key, which was
usually kept in the lock, was missing and Fred used
his bedroom door key which did the trick. Upon
opening the door, he noticed a half full glass of water
on the table in the parlour but did not consider it of
any significance. Shortly after this, Constable Wood
spotted a key on the floor by the top of the flight
of stairs leading down to the basement; it was the
missing key to the back parlour. On the half landing
of the staircase, he also found a purse, recognised by
Mrs Dixon as her sister's, containing some silver and
copper coins.

The priority for the police officers at this stage was
to contact the husband of the dead woman, and the
father of the four children, who was a lieutenant in the
army, stationed at White City with the 10th Battalion
Bedfordshire Regiment. P.C. Wood had already sent
a communication to the White City but had been
unable to reach him. At 9:10pm, P.C. Reeves sent the
following message to Acton Police Station:

```
From Islington to Acton.  Please
inform Lieutenant Wootten of the 10th
Bedfordshire Regiment stationed at the
White City that his wife had met with
an accident at 114 Rotherfield Street
since dead.  Can he please attend at
once.  Reply.
```

However, it did not bring about the expected
arrival of the lieutenant. Joe Higson, Cora's husband,
then took on the task of contacting him. He had
returned home from work to an empty house at nine-
thirty. His wife returned at about ten and told him
all about the drama and tragedy of the evening. Half
an hour later, after having first viewed the scene at

number 114 for himself, he walked over to Essex Road tube station, where there was a public telephone, in order to call White City. He was informed by someone speaking from the Officer's Mess that it would take about ten minutes to get a message to the lieutenant's quarters. He waited on the line for more than ten minutes but the lieutenant was nowhere to be found. *Where was he?*

Although a good friend of his - someone who knew his secrets, or thought he did - what he did not know, what no-one knew, was that the husband of the late Annie Wootten was, in fact, at that very moment, in a house in Shepherd's Bush, with none other than Mrs Higson's friend.

Lieutenant Albert Wootten in 1914

CHAPTER 2

THE ROAD TO MURDER

'...The Road to Murder,
The Road to Prison,
The Road to the Gallows,
and thence through the dark regions to
Eternal Darkness and Eternal Death.'

The Juvenile Instructor and Companion by William Cooke (ed), 1869

Great Britain's entry into the war in Europe on 4
August 1914 was to change the lives of so many of
its citizens, often in unexpected ways. For Albert
Wootten, a 30-year-old insurance inspector, life at the
start of the war could hardly have been better. Having
already served in the National Reserve for nine years
as a member of the 4th Battalion Royal Fusiliers (City
of London Regiment) Wootten enlisted within the first
month, swearing his oath of attestation on 2 September
1914, and his employers at the National Union for
Insurance patriotically agreed to continue to pay his
wages of £2 a week. So he was now on two salaries:
his army pay and his inspectors' salary. Assigned to
a service battalion[7] in the 73rd Infantry Brigade of the
24th Division - the 13th Middlesex Special Reserve - his
previous experience in the reserves meant that he was
immediately promoted to sergeant on 4 September
and then to quartermaster sergeant just over a week
later, on 12 September, accompanied by a consequent
increase in pay.

Stationed at Shoreham-by-sea, about six miles to
the west of Brighton, where a huge camp of canvas
tents for over 20,000 soldiers sprung up on a golf
course and mushroomed over fields and meadows on
the Downs, Wootten was able to escape not only from

his mundane job in Islington collecting national health insurance contributions but also from the cramped conditions of 114 Rotherfield Street where he rented three rooms in a house from his brother-in-law: a ground floor parlour, a kitchen and a bedroom in the basement which he had to share with his wife and four children.

Freedom from his wife was also welcomed by Sergeant Wootten for other, rather more dubious, reasons. In October he caught the eye of a flirty 21-year-old barmaid working at the Royal George Hotel in Shoreham. She introduced herself as Marie Lanteri ('Marie' being pronounced in unusual fashion, rhyming with the last two syllables of 'Safari'), a widow from Brighton, whose Italian chauffeur husband had supposedly died in a road accident in France only four months after she had married him. She was not what one might describe as conventionally pretty. She had a slightly odd shaped, rather mousey, face and looked a little older than her age but was not entirely unattractive. The *Islington Daily Gazette* would one day describe her as a 'fresh-complexioned woman', the *Echo and London Evening Chronicle* would call her 'nice looking' while the *News of the World* would say she was 'handsome and fair-haired'. In the carefree atmosphere created by the outbreak of war, her relationship with Wootten quickly became sexual and the sergeant was a frequent, but illicit, visitor to Marie's bedroom at the hotel. It was probably not quite what the *Worthing Mercury* meant when it reported on 7 November 1914 that the soldiers camped at Shoreham 'are being well looked after by those who have gone to infinite trouble to make the men happy and comfortable in their new conditions.'[8]

Most soldiers at Shoreham's camps (a second one having been formed at the end of September) were sleeping in tents which became very chilly during the autumn of 1914 and locals sent in blankets and clothing following an appeal from the Mayor of Hove who announced that only fifty per cent of soldiers at Shoreham had any kind of overcoat and less than two hundred had received their uniforms. 'Many of them,' he said 'are in need of clothing, especially trousers and blankets, cardigan jackets, boots etc would be most welcome'.[9] The warmth and comfort of Marie's bed in her room in the George Hotel would, no doubt, also have been most welcome to Wootten and he spent a number of pleasant evenings, and probably whole nights, there.

Both Marie and Wootten would have had plenty of spare time for leisure in the evenings. The soldiers at Shoreham Camp woke up for call at 5:30am and were at the camp, training and drilling, until after tea, twelve hours later, at 5:30pm, when they were given four hours liberty. As a consequence, the town of Shoreham was full of men roaming around aimlessly during the evening. Not surprisingly, many of them ended up in the local public houses – some being arrested for minor crimes arising out of being drunk and disorderly - and it is evident that the four hour time limit was not strictly observed because at the end of September 1914, at the request of the army, and to the annoyance of local licensees deprived of increased revenues from the soldiers, the local magistrates felt compelled to decree that all licensed premises within three miles of Shoreham Bridge must close at 9pm (compared to the normal closing time of 11pm).[10] As a barmaid at the George, Marie would, therefore, have had to stop working early and it is likely that Wootten was able to stay with her, under the army's radar, at least until he had to report back for the next morning's call. He didn't exactly announce to Marie that he was married with children but some of the other soldiers in his regiment kindly decided to inform her of this fact. The relationship survived the revelation but Marie lost her position as barmaid when the hotel proprietor discovered what was going on.[11]

Following heavy rain and thunderstorms at the end of November, which turned the camps at Shoreham into a quagmire, and with the cold winter weather setting in, tents became completely unsuitable for habitation so thousands of soldiers from the camps at Shoreham, who could not be accommodated in the limited number of rapidly built wooden huts, were billeted en masse to private houses in Shoreham, Portslade and the nearby towns of Worthing and Hove in early December. This measure was not universally popular with local residents. The War Office, through the military, could compel citizens to billet soldiers in their homes and it sometimes required the attendance of the local police to ensure that admittance was allowed. The *Hove Gazette* encouraged its readers with the message that, 'householders; if approached for a billet, should recognize that this is one of the minor sacrifices by which they can help their country at the cost of a little inconvenience' and it was suggested that having a British soldier in one's house now was better than a German one later.[12] Controversy soon arose from the fact that householders in Hove were only paid by the War Office an allowance for each soldier of two shillings and sixpence a day compared to over three shillings a day in most other areas around the country and there were many other complaints and grumbles about the system.[13]

Wootten was billeted to Hove in the second week of December – there is no record as to whether his home owner was happy with the arrangement or not – and the first thing he did upon arrival was to wire Marie his new address. She came to him the same evening. The following day, Wootten began a period of seven days leave and, rather than return home to his wife and children, he brought Marie to London. They stayed in rented lodgings at 9 Gillingham Street, Pimlico, before returning together to Hove on 22 December. A month earlier, Wootten had applied for a commission in the Cavalry or, failing that, the Army Service Corps, and, although his choice of regiment was not successful, he was informed upon his return to Hove that he had been granted a temporary commission, for the duration of the war, as lieutenant in a newly formed service battalion in Kitchener's Fourth Army, the 10th Bedfordshire.[14]

Now officially an officer and a gentleman, if not exactly behaving like one, Wootten must have allowed himself a huge smile of satisfaction. Born without a legal father, in August 1883, he had grown up in poverty in Islington, being brought up by a middle-aged widow, surviving a dose of scarlet fever, and it was far from easy in post-Edwardian society for someone from a humble background like Wootten's to transform himself into a gentleman. As a young boy he had worked in a department store for Hope Brothers in Essex Road, Islington, and, when he was 16 years old, signed up for the National Reserve, joining the Royal Fusiliers, for which he would have trained and exercised for somewhere in the region of twenty-one days every year, having undergone a longer period of training at the start.[15] At the age of seventeen he was earning a living, like many in Islington at the time, as a general labourer for the Post Office at Mount Pleasant. In the summer of 1903, when he was nineteen, he made 18-year-old Annie Tilbury pregnant and did the decent thing by marrying her in October of that year. The newly married couple initially lived with Annie's parents at 28 Exmouth Street, above a butcher's shop, just across from the sorting office, but soon moved to a small rented accommodation in Rheidol Terrace, subsequently moving again to Cambridge Terrace. Five months after the marriage, Annie gave birth to a boy who Albert named after both himself and his new father-in-law, Joseph Tilbury, but baby Albert Joseph died in his father's arms of bronchitis on 19 November 1904. Two years later, when Wootten was working as an electrician's labourer, little Lily, named after Annie's sister, was born, followed quickly by Ivy in 1907 while the family was living in Edmonton and Albert was working as a store man in the Stores Department of the General Post Office.[16] Hernia problems appear to have interrupted Wootten's child producing activities, and he retired from the National Reserve in 1907, but he had fully recovered by 1911 when Edwin was born, requiring more spacious accommodation for the enlarged Wootten family.

Albert had quit his job with the Post Office and was now a manager in the wholesale clothing business but, following the passing of the National Insurance Act in December 1911, which introduced sickness and unemployment benefits to the workers of Britain, the insurance industry rapidly expanded and Albert gained employment with the National Union For Insurance as Special Sick Visitor and District Correspondent for Central London. A sick visitor's role was to check on claimants of sickness benefits in their homes in order to ensure that they were genuinely ill and not cheating the system – a controversial task considering that a sick visitor had no medical knowledge or training. However, a male sick visitor would not have been visiting ladies because the 1911 Act sensibly stated that women should not be visited at home by anyone other than female visitors.

In his new role with a fancy title, Wootten had achieved a measure of respectability, and some financial security, but he could still only afford to rent three rooms from his brother-in-law at 114 Rotherfield Street, into which the Wootten family moved on 15 December 1912. Within a couple of months, Annie was pregnant again and Doris was born in November 1913. During 1913, Wootten also appears to have fallen ill with rheumatic fever, causing him pain and swelling of his joints. There were no more Wootten children when war broke out and Albert, having fully recovered from his bout of illness, left for the seaside delights of Shoreham.

Looking resplendent and every inch the part in his khaki officer's uniform, Wootten was tall and dashing, a little under six foot in height, sporting a handlebar moustache, with pleasant hazel eyes and fair hair, and could easily have been mistaken for a member of the aristocracy. Marie was terribly impressed. Although she had been told he was a married man, she nevertheless informed her parents, who were then living in Horsted Keynes, Sussex, that she had married Wootten in London – sending her father a photograph of her 'husband' – and, when Wootten had leave from the army, the pair lived happily together as Mr and Mrs Wootten. On an officer's pay of eight shillings and sixpence a day, Wootten could afford to take a room for his mistress at 27 Coleridge Street, Hove - the landlady knowing Marie as 'Mrs Wootten' – and the two lovers enjoyed Christmas together although Marie, an asthmatic and rarely in good health at the best of times, had a short-lived cold.

During this period, according to Wootten, Marie told him: 'I can't bear the thought of you belonging to another woman. You are mine,' and she warned him, melodramatically but apparently in jest, that if she ever met his wife 'there will be trouble' and she would 'do her in'. The two lovers, as lovers do, shared intimate details of each other's lives. Wootten told Marie of the tragic death of his first son and the fact that it, and some other sad events in his life, had occurred on the nineteenth day of the month so that he regarded nineteen as his unlucky number. Marie told Wootten that she had once been arrested for aiding and abetting in a gaming transaction in London's Victoria and, in return, Wootten shared a story that he had once been assaulted by the manager of the Old Queen's Head public house in the Essex Road, Islington, leading him to issue proceedings against the man at the local police court only to have the case dismissed, being forced to pay two pounds and two shillings in costs which literally added insult to injury. He also told her that, before the war, he had worked in offices located in Colebrooke Row in Islington and that his best friend at work was a chap called Joe Higson, a clerk with whom he remained in touch.

As a token of his affection, Wootten had Marie's signet ring engraved with the initials 'M.W.' to stand for 'Marie Wootten', although as it happens 'M.W.' was, sort of, her actual initials – she had never married anyone called Lanteri and her real name was Marie Wheatley. In fact, as 'Marie' was merely an affection in place of her middle name of Mary, and her first name was Alice, she was really Alice Mary Wheatley, a name which was soon to become nationally famous and not a little notorious.

She had been born in Brighton on 21 February 1893 to Mary Ann Wheatley, the wife of Harry Wheatley, a police officer in the Brighton Police Force with a somewhat colourful career. Originally born a carpenter's son in the village of Chalk, near Gravesend in Kent, Harry migrated south to where his mother,

Alice, had been born and joined the Brighton police as a constable at the age of twenty-one on 12 December 1878.[17] He was soon in trouble. On 1 June 1879 he was found fighting in the street with another constable: his overcoat off and said to be the worse for drink. Both officers were summoned to the Brighton Borough Watch Committee, responsible for monitoring the police, which decided that Harry was to blame for the fight and fined him ten shillings. The following year, in April 1880, a police inspector was looking for P.C. Wheatley on his beat in the early hours of the morning and saw him a short distance up Hollingdean Road. Harry said he had been at a farm, taking a look round for anything suspicious, but the inspector was sure he had seen him come out of a house and Harry was reprimanded by the Chief Constable. A few weeks later, a superintendent discovered that Harry and another constable attended an illegal prize fight one Sunday morning in plain clothes but they both claimed they were just passing. The matter was referred to the Watch Committee which considered the offence not proved but Harry was reprimanded again by the Chief Constable in September 1882 when he was found asleep in a passage on his beat at 2:33am.

On the other side of the coin, Constable Wheatley was commended by the Watch Committee for his intelligence in July 1885 in apprehending a man suspiciously carrying a black bag which was found to contain stolen jewellery valued at £25. In February 1889, Harry married a local woman almost ten years his junior, the daughter of a Brighton fisherman, Mary Ann Mockford, and, in September of that same year, was promoted to sergeant. His performance in this role was evidently satisfactory because, in July 1891, he was promoted to detective officer. One of his first arrests was in August of that year when, with a colleague, he observed and detained a man passing a counterfeit florin in a local public house.[18] His career was now really taking off and it would surely not be long until he was a detective inspector and perhaps even, eventually, a superintendent. A month after Marie's birth, in March 1893, he was commended by the Watch Committee for 'courageous conduct' in helping to save the life of the Superintendent of the Fire Brigade during an attempt to rescue – unsuccessfully as it turned out – a thirteen-year-old girl from her burning bedroom in 'very dangerous and difficult circumstances'.[19] A few months later, he was commended again for helping to put out a fire at a local lodging house, following praise of his work from the grateful lodging house keeper.[20] At the time, the Brighton Police Force incorporated the local Fire Brigade, known as the Brighton Police Fire Brigade (distinguishing it from a volunteer force which also operated in the area) and a number of police officers were trained as fire fighters. Harry was one of them and had already become Chief Engineer in the Fire Brigade while still a police officer.[21]

In addition to fighting fires, as a detective he was busy surveilling and arresting various pickpockets and petty criminals around Brighton. In January 1894 he received a black eye while assisting a constable who was struggling to arrest two young, drunken, but physically strong carmen using obscene language in the street who did not wish to be taken into custody. It was a difficult situation and the policemen required the help of a passing Provost-Sergeant from the 6th Iniskilling Dragoons, based at the local barracks, in order to overpower the youths.[22] A few weeks later, Harry expressed his gratitude, and that of his fellow officers, by presenting the soldier with a suitably inscribed silver mounted riding whip, enclosed in a

plush red frame.[23] In April, Harry arrested a man for
stealing zinc and, in May, having recovered from the
death of his second daughter who had died ten
hours after birth at the end of April, he nabbed a
lady's maid accused of running off with money and
expensive items of property from her employer.[24]

Then everything went terribly wrong and Harry's
world collapsed. A scandal occurred which might
provide a clue as to what the young P.C. Wheatley had
been doing fourteen years earlier when an inspector
saw him coming out of a house in the middle of
the night. At 4:40pm on 16 May 1894, a telegram
addressed to Detective Wheatley was received at
police headquarters which read: 'Be at usual place 9:30
tonight important Sweeney'. Enquiries were made
and it was ascertained that Sweeney was Mrs Sweeney,
a woman 'of doubtful respectability', who was
supposedly living apart from her husband but with
whom Harry had been associating.[25] This did not go
down well with the Chief Constable who reported the
detective to the Watch Committee for misconduct. At a
meeting of that committee, at which Harry pleaded his
case on 23 May 1894, he was found guilty of the offence
and demoted back down to constable with seven
hundred and thirty days deducted from his period of
service for pension.[26] It must have been a crushing
blow for Harry to have reverted to the lowliest rank
and things did not get any better in November when
he was admonished by the chairman of the Watch
Committee for neglect of duty in not reporting 'certain
irregularities' which had occurred in August 1893.[27]

After this admonishment, Sergeant Wheatley seems
to have kept his head down and remained out of
trouble, at least in terms of misconduct. His left hand
and arm were severely injured from falling masonry
when attempting, in his role as Chief Engineer of

the Fire Brigade, to fight a major fire which gutted a building adjoining the Hotel Metropole in June 1897. Having recovered from this, he was then seriously wounded, with injuries to his hands, at a 'fire extinction experiment' on 25 September 1898 and was off sick on full pay for fifty-one days. The plan had been for a public demonstration by the Brighton Police Fire Brigade of the fire-fighting capabilities of a new American combination chemical fire engine in front of various invited dignitaries and hundreds of members of the public by setting alight a specially constructed wooden house and then quickly extinguishing the flames with the new engine. However, the event was poorly conceived and the combustible materials used, together with an unhelpful north-easterly breeze, immediately sent a fierce sheet of flame over the whole structure and, in attempting to quench it, Chief Engineer Wheatley's hands were badly burned, despite wearing thick fire-proof gloves.[28] Initially it was feared he might lose the use of one or both of his hands but he fully recovered from this setback and was appointed back to the rank of sergeant on 4 January 1899.

His salary was 35 shillings a week in March 1901 but this compares to over 37 shillings a week he had been earning ten years earlier as a detective.[29] A police detective of more than twenty years experience could expect to earn over 95 shillings a week in the Brighton Police Force. Had he made it to superintendent, where he might have expected to be by 1901,[30] he would have been earning over £13 a week. It must have been totally demoralising for him to be in this situation although he might have gained some comfort from a small pay rise awarded to the entire force in 1903 in response to a letter asking for more money signed by nine officers, including Harry, on behalf of all inspectors, sergeants and constables in

the Brighton police, who pointed out that they had
not had any increase in salary for more than ten years
despite increases in the cost of living and house rents
in Brighton. The rise took Harry's salary up to £2 a
week or £104 a year which was still not much to live
on (although it will be recalled that this is exactly what
Albert Wootten was earning in 1915). Nevertheless,
he diligently served his full period of service (and
more, in order to recover the seven hundred and thirty
day loss of his pension) and retired on 9 April 1906,
after nearly twenty eight years with the police, on a
pension of just over £64 per annum.[31] In June of that
year he was presented with a silver watch from his
former colleagues by the Mayoress of Brighton and
was publicly thanked by both the Mayor and the Chief
Constable for his years of devoted service.[32]

As soon as he retired from the police, Harry took
over as landlord of the 'Runt-in-Tun', an isolated rural
beerhouse situated in Maynards Green, off Horeham
Road, in East Sussex, described by a neighbour as 'a
mile from nowhere', which nevertheless did a good
trade in selling beer to passing cyclists and motorists
at a time when there was a more relaxed approach
by the authorities to drink driving.[33] The country air
must have been beneficial for Harry because he became
a father again at the age of fifty with the birth of his
only son, Walter. It was his fourth living child, having
already provided Marie with two sisters, Rose and
Lilian, in 1897 and 1904 respectively.[34] As it happens,
Harry might have been enjoying his new more relaxed
life a little too much. A note in the Brewery's files,
recording a fact finding visit to the 'Runt-in-Tun' in
1909, states: 'Landlord drunk and refused information
and access very rudely'.[35] The 'Runt-in-Tun' moved
to a new and bigger location on the same road, still in
Maynards Green, in 1912 and this is where the teenage

Marie lived until the license was transferred to a new occupier in October 1913.[36] Although her father would later say that she 'could do no hard work' due to her general poor health, it was almost certainly in this public house that Marie acquired the barmaid skills which enabled her to land the job at the George Inn in Shoreham-by-sea where she would eventually meet Lieutenant Wootten.

At the end of December 1914, Marie's mother received the following handwritten postcard:

27 Coleridge Street, Hove
28.12.14

Excuse card

Dear Mother,
No doubt you will be pleased to know Mawks is better now, to what she was, although she has still got her chest very tight. We will try and come and see you shortly. We both sincerely hope you and Dad etc are all well, so with best wishes in haste we remain,
Yours lovingly,
Bert and Mawks
A. Wootten Lieut

It was an extraordinary card for a married man with children to send to his mistress's parents, referring to Mr and Mrs Wheatley informally as 'you and Dad' and written as if he was indeed married to their daughter. He was later to explain that the card was dictated to him by Marie, that he didn't even know her pet name was 'Mawks' until that day, but he was also to wish he had never sent it.

On 30 December 1914, Wootten condescended to visit his wife and children in Rotherfield Street but he was there for only one night before joining the 10th Bedfordshire at Dovercourt, a coastal town in Essex where the new battalion was now stationed, on New

Harry Wheatley
Marie's father

Mary Ann Wheatley
Marie's mother

Year's Eve. Although separated, Marie and Wootten regularly exchanged letters but, once read, Wootten promptly put Marie's on the fire. It seems that, during this time, Marie became ill and was confined to her bed. She thought she might be pregnant but this either turned out to be a false alarm or she miscarried. On 8 January 1915, in order that Marie could maintain her room at Coleridge Street, Wootten sent her a cheque, in favour of 'Mrs A Wootten', for £2. When he obtained a week's leave on 13 January 1915, Wootten paid a short visit to his real wife and family at 114 Rotherfield Street but then, four days later, made his way to Hove to join Marie. During the four days spent with his wife, one of Marie's letters addressed to Lieutenant Wootten arrived at Dovercourt. In his absence it was naturally forwarded to him at his home address in Islington but arrived there the day after he had left to join Marie in Hove. His curious wife opened the letter and was astounded when she read the manner in which a woman she did not know was expressing her affections for her husband: the letter being signed 'Your loving Marie'. She immediately ran for help to Wootten's best friend, Joe Higson, the husband of her own best friend, who helpfully wrote a draft letter in reply for her to copy. It contained a strongly worded request that Marie should release Wootten and pointed out that, until she had come across his path, he was a loving husband and his attentions had been fully directed towards his home and children.

Wootten returned home to Rotherfield Street on 19 January, blissfully unaware that anything was wrong. As soon as he walked through the door, however, he was confronted by his wife who handed him the letter from Marie. It was useless for him to deny the relationship. There was a row and Wootten quickly agreed that he would not see Marie again. As was his usual practice, he burnt her letter. His leave being over, he had to report back to his regiment which had moved to White City, in West London, on 22 January. He was in a quandary and did not immediately break off relations with Marie. On the contrary, on 5 February he sent another cheque for £2 to 'Mrs A. Wootten' in Hove. At this exact same time, he had come down with a rather convenient illness, complaining, according to his army medical report, of 'headache, malaise, aching in limbs and laryngitis' which he claimed were the result of cold exposure while on duty at the White City. Although he had no fever, he was certified at the 2nd London General Hospital on 4 February as suffering from 'a mild attack of influenza' and given sick leave. In the circumstances, this provided a very welcome opportunity for him to repair the damage to his marriage. He returned to Rotherfield Street and, now under his wife's influence, finally wrote a letter to Marie breaking off the relationship.

This letter, dated Tuesday, 9 February 1915, was not well received by Marie. Having digested its contents, on the Thursday morning she caught the train to London. She had no idea where Wootten and the 10th Bedfordshire were based so, to his great surprise, paid a visit to Joe Higson at his workplace in Colbrooke Row. It was about 2:30pm when, carrying a small brown leather attaché case, she arrived at the offices of the National Union for Insurance asking for a 'Mr Higson' who greeted this unknown woman with some puzzlement.

'Can I help you madam?'

'I believe you are friends with Lieutenant Wootten,' stated Marie.

'Yes, that is correct,' replied Higson cautiously.

'I doubt you've heard of me.'

'Well if you tell me your name,' said Higson with a twinkle in his eye, 'I'll tell you if I have heard of you.'

'My name is Marie.'

'What? *Marie from Brighton*?'

'Yes.'

In fact, Higson already knew all about Marie, not only from the letter Mrs Wootten had shown him, but also because Wootten had told him everything about their relationship back in November.

'I want you to tell me where I can find Bert.'

'I am not Bert's keeper. I cannot tell you where he is.'

'You must tell me!'

'I'm very sorry Marie, I cannot.'

'You really must, it is very important.'

'Why?'

'I have received a letter from him stating he doesn't want anything further to do with me. Look,' she said as she handed Higson the letter. 'He mustn't talk to me like that. He cannot get rid of me so easily.'

As Higson examined the letter, she persisted:
'Tell me where I can find him. Will you help me find him?' adding woefully: 'This is a terrible mess, Annie getting to know about this.'

'You should leave Bert alone,' said Higson plainly.

'I cannot,' replied Marie.

Unable to resist any longer, and no doubt eager to be rid of her so that he could return to work, Higson agreed to meet Marie at the corner of the Angel, Islington, at half past seven that evening when he said he would attempt to help her locate Wootten.

True to his word, Higson arrived at the Angel on time and met Marie but there was something he wanted to get off his chest first. 'Before starting,' he said, 'I want to have a little conversation about this matter. Why are you running after Bert so much? You know you have no right as he has a wife and children. Pull yourself together and cast him adrift.' Marie simply responded: 'If only you knew my love for Bert, you wouldn't blame me.' Having done his best to discourage her, but unable to stop her, Higson then walked with Marie along the Essex Road to New North Road and into the Kenilworth Castle public house where he anticipated Wootten, who he knew was still on sick leave from the army, would be at this time in the evening. Upon entering the Kenilworth, he immediately saw Wootten with his wife. He called him out of the bar and they both walked across the street to where Marie was waiting.

'Marie! What are you here for?' asked a startled Wootten.

'Oh Bert, I want an understanding from you.'

'Look here, come with me, I think you need to meet my wife,' said Wootten as he and Higson, with Marie following reluctantly, returned to the Kenilworth where Wootten introduced Marie to Annie. The two women sized each other up awkwardly.

Annie, who immediately knew what Marie was up to, was the first to speak. 'Don't you think,' she asked sternly, 'you are doing a very wrong thing, trying to take a man from his wife and children?' 'Yes,' replied Marie meekly, adding 'but I can't help it. I love Bert'.

Higson suggested the two women have a conversation to try and sort things out between them. They spoke for a few uncomfortable minutes but failed to achieve anything and Wootten suggested that they all go back to his house where they could speak more freely and in more relaxed surroundings.

They made the short walk to 114 Rotherfield Street and sat in the back parlour on the ground floor. Marie sat next to Wootten as Higson took control of the situation, asking Marie: 'What is it you want?' She replied simply, 'Bert.'

'Marie, you must know it is impossible for you to be Bert's lawful wife. A woman of your intelligence should not waste her time running after a married man and should instead find someone who can make her his lawful wife.'

'Joe, I only want Bert.'

'Well then, we shall have to ask Bert what he wants. Well Bert,' said Higson, 'what do you want? Marie, or your wife, family and home?' Wootten left no room for doubt, 'I want my wife and family.'

'Well there you have it,' said Higson abruptly, 'you can't have Bert. What else do you want?'

'Well,' croaked Marie, 'I want to know if he is going to make any provision for me. I'm out of work and stranded.'

'We'll come to that in a minute,' replied Higson, 'at present, his wife and family have first claim. You knew Bert was married and had four children. Why do you hang about him so much?'

'I love Bert.' She then placed her hand on

Wootten's arm in an affectionate way but Higson put an immediate stop to this by moving her to the other side of the room. Appearing to concede her primary demand, Marie said: 'Well I think I deserve a provision, I lost my situation in Shoreham, he must do something for me.'

'You can have a provision,' said Higson, 'but it will not exist forever. Bert will help you until you find a new situation. Is that right Bert?'

'Yes, I agree with that Joe,' confirmed Wootten.

'And you must leave Bert alone and never write or see him again after getting the situation.'

'Very well Joe, I promise.'

'I'm surprised at your continuing to run after Bert. Surely there are opportunities come your way in the way of single men.'

'There is only one man I want and that is Bert.'

'You can't have Bert and there's an end to it,' said a frustrated Higson.

Higson then offered to show Marie the children, intending to verify what he had told her about Wootten's family in case she had any doubt in her mind. He took her downstairs into the bedroom where the children were all asleep in bed. The Woottens followed them down. Higson then said in a hushed tone: 'Now ask yourself the question: how can you take a man away from his wife and those four children?' An unashamed Marie turned to Wootten and said: 'Let me have them Bert!' An irritated Higson replied: 'That is impossible! We've come to definite arrangements about this matter and we're not going to start over again so there's an end of it.'

The four of them returned to the parlour. Marie, who finally seemed quite defeated, asked: 'What am I going to do tonight? I can't get back to Brighton at this hour.' Wootten asked Higson if he could put her up for the night. Higson said he would have to ask his wife and they all went over to the Higsons' home in Gibson Square. Higson introduced Marie to his wife as, 'the Marie you have heard so much about.'

Marie stayed the night at Gibson Square but removing her the next morning proved to be a more difficult task than he had imagined. She said she wanted to obtain work in London and pleaded to be allowed to stay until she did. She assured Higson that if she got a situation she would not want to see Bert again and all correspondence with him would cease. Higson relented but insisted that she could only stay until she found work and then she must leave. Finding a position was not easy, however, and she was still there a week later. Higson told her she must be out of the house by no later than Sunday 21 February, which, although he would have been totally unaware of it, happened to be Marie's birthday. He explained that the landlady of the property was unhappy with the extra inhabitant and for that reason there could be no extension of the deadline.

Marie's prolonged stay was also causing some concern in the Wootten household. On at least one occasion she wandered over to 114 Rotherfield Street claiming to wish to speak to Mrs Higson who was visiting at the time. Annie was worried that her sister and brother-in-law, also living at 114, would see Marie and wonder who she was. She did not wish the scandal of her husband's infidelity to be widely known, especially by her family, and neither, unsurprisingly, did her husband. A ruse was devised whereby Marie would be known to all and sundry as 'Mrs Higson's friend' which was intended to provide some kind of partial explanation as to why she was living with the Higsons. On Saturday 20 February, Higson explained to Marie: 'So that Mr and Mrs Dixon or any other members of the family should not know of your existence it has been agreed that you will be known as my wife's friend.' Marie merely smiled in response and said nothing.

Sunday came and Marie was still there but it was definitely agreed that she would leave the next day. With Lieutenant Wootten still on extended sick leave – his medical officer having apparently forgotten to examine him again in order to clear him to return to his unit - Higson fetched him and his wife over for a final settlement of the matter.

'Marie wants some money,' Higson informed Wootten, 'she's to leave tonight.'

Marie asked to talk to Bert alone. Annie was reluctant to agree to this and insisted that Higson should be present during any conversation. So Marie, Higson and Wootten all went outside into the street.

'I suppose I should go home, Bert.'

'Yes, I agree.'

'I shall need money for my train fare.'

'I'll give you the money but, in return, you must give me back my letters. Do you agree?'

'Okay Bert.'

'Do you promise?'

'Yes.'

With that agreement sealed, Wootten handed her the money for her fare.

'Oh Bert,' said Marie with a distinct change in manner, 'I shall never love anyone else but you! Let me have the children and we can all go and live in a secluded place together. I don't mind where.'

'But it's impossible,' replied Wootten, shaking his head firmly: 'Now please, Marie. Let me have the letters.'

Marie took Wootten and Higson to her bedroom. She opened her box and took out some letters.

Wootten held his hand out for them.

Marie hesitated: 'These are *my* letters.'

'Yes,' Higson intervened, 'but you promised to give them to him.'

'He mustn't be in such a hurry. Let me speak with Bert alone. Please Joe.'

Higson went into the kitchen where his wife and Annie were waiting. They all heard a foot stamping loudly on the floor. Higson then met Wootten at the kitchen door holding some letters in his hand. The lieutenant walked in, went over to the kitchen fire and dropped them into the flames. As the letters burned, Marie came downstairs and lay on the couch in the living room. She had still not given up on her idea of running away with Wootten: 'Bert, Bert, come with me and take the children,' she wailed. The others ignored her and continued conversing in the kitchen. About ten minutes later they all heard a loud thud. Higson rushed into the living room and found Marie lying on the floor. She had, apparently, fainted. As she came round, she asked to speak to Bert. Believing she had genuinely passed out, Higson thought he had better accede to her request and called his friend in. Marie's plea was predictable:

'I love you Bert, I love you and can never love another. Leave your house and your wife and live with me.'

'I have made up my mind,' Wootten replied coldly. 'It is an impossibility.'

After supper, the Woottens left 58 Gibson Square and a despondent Marie entered the kitchen. Being spurned by her lover and throwing a fainting fit was probably not how she had envisaged spending her twenty-second birthday. She said to Higson and Cora: 'I'll put an end to it all, I will end my life'. Higson laughed it off but Marie continued: 'Will you watch the papers and you'll see my name there'.

The next morning Marie, broken and downhearted, finally facing reality, or so it seemed, picked up her attaché case, ready to leave London. She promised Higson she would not trouble Bert anymore and boarded the train back to Brighton, although she ended up staying with her parents at 'Fir Croft', the name of their cottage in Horsted Keynes. Within a month, however, she would be back in Islington.

This time with a loaded revolver.

Harry Wheatley, circa 1914, at the gate of 'Fir Croft',
Horsted Keynes, Sussex

CHAPTER 3

IN FOR THE KILL

'I can't help feeling I know her quite well if only I could remember who she is.'

Lucy in *The Magic City* by E. Nesbit, 1910

The area which now comprises Islington was originally filled with fields and meadows at the base of a huge forest inhabited by wild beasts, bears and bulls. The Romans cleared a path through the forest and built a road through the fields to allow them to travel unimpeded into the town once called Londinium but it was not until the modern City of London began to grow in size and importance that Islington, situated within walking distance of the City, came to life as a population centre. At its very heart, since the sixteenth century, have been the two long Upper and Lower Streets which spread through Islington like two forks of lightning, travelling out from a single point: the Angel in the South, up to Highbury and Canonbury respectively in the north. Upper Street was originally known as the Long Causeway, built to allow residents to walk through Islington without their shoes being caked in mud, while Lower Street became Lower Road then Essex Road in 1864 in order to remove the pejorative nature of the description for those who lived in it: with many feeling it gave the impression they were living in poverty.[37] The new name of Essex Road was chosen because it was 'the road to Essex'.[38]

Easy access from the two causeways to Moorgate along the City Road which had been built in 1761, or to Shoreditch along the New North Road, built in 1812, turned Islington into a favourite living area for the booming numbers of clerks required to maintain the

City of London as the world's leading financial centre. The introduction of the omnibus in 1830 made travel for workers into Central London and the City fast, cheap and simple and this was largely responsible for a population explosion from a mere 10,000 inhabitants at the start of the century to over 400,000 by the end of it. When, in 1889, the General Post Office converted an old prison at Mount Pleasant, on the fringe of Islington, into their central sorting centre, requiring numerous casual labourers, it created an entirely new form of employment for local residents.

Throughout the nineteenth century, as more and more housing was required for the growing army of workers at ever increasing prices, land was acquired by developers in order to build numerous small new streets, roads, rows and avenues which were generally squeezed in haphazardly wherever there was any space near or around Upper Street and Lower Road (Essex Road). One such street was built in 1826 on land owned by James Scott Esq. of Rotherfield Park in Hampshire and was thus named Rotherfield Street. It adjoined the Lower Road at the north end and then ran parallel with the New North Road towards Hoxton. By 1860, when the housing along the road was completed, its numbers ran from number 1 in the south up to number 140 at its north end bordering Essex Road. Odd numbers were located on the west side and even numbers, including 114, on the east side of the road. Number 114 was, and remains, at the northern end with the Essex Road in sight.

The street was generally a respectable one during most of the nineteenth century, occupied originally by gentlemen and those from the well-to-do, wealthy, professional and business classes such as solicitors, physicians, landed proprietors and property dealers, the majority of whom employed their own domestic servants. There were, however, some exceptions. One Thomas Morgan of 14 Rotherfield Street was roughly evicted from his property by a gang of drunken men sent to repossess it in September 1858 and a fight ensued in the street, watched by 'a great crowd' which had gathered.[39] It was, perhaps, a sign of the neighbourhood starting to go downhill and within the next thirty years those with money had largely moved out. Developments in rail transport allowed the middle classes to live in the new leafy and spacious suburbs, commuting into London if necessary. They were replaced initially by skilled craftsmen and artisans who were themselves replaced over time by labourers and less skilled workers, with large numbers of occupants living in houses previously inhabited by just one family.

The street temporarily developed a very bad reputation towards the end of the century when a man known as 'German Fred' ran a noisy brothel in number 116.[40] His real name was Frederick Herbert and he was eventually arrested after an undercover police observation of the house. Convicted of assisting in the management of a disorderly house, he was sent to prison for three months with hard labour in August 1898. This did not cure the problem, however, because the remaining men and women living in number 116 were left untouched by the police and continued their criminal activities unabated, the men often bullying people in the street, causing one resident of Rotherfield Street to complain to the *Islington Gazette* in September 1898 that 'for months past the upper portion of the street, "Essex Road End", has been the scene of nothing but uproar' while another letter writer elaborated that: 'Quarrels are of frequent occurrence and often we are disturbed in the middle of the night with cries of "Murder!" And what is even worse, our wives and

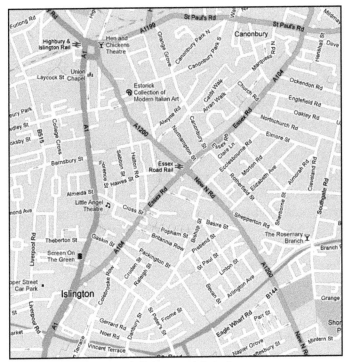

Islington as it is today
©2011 Google – Map data ©2011 Tele Atlas

daughters have in the daytime been grossly insulted
by pests of both sexes who accost them and throw
out suggestions which could only come from vile
and polluted minds'.[41] The police did eventually act,
clearing and barricading the house, which returned the
street to quiet, working class, respectability.

Cutting through the north end of Rotherfield Street
by this time was a road created by the Metropolitan
Board of Works in November 1876 which ordered that
New Norfolk Street, Suffolk Street and Marlborough
Road were to be combined into a single thoroughfare
named Ecclesbourne Road. The original plan in June
1876 had been for only New Norfolk Street and Suffolk
Street to be combined into one street called 'Blasson

Street' but residents objected to the name and a report by the Islington Vestry in July recommended it be re-named 'Newland Road'.[42] This was evidently still not deemed satisfactory hence the further change to Ecclesbourne Road.[43] If, in March 1915, as today, you wanted to find somewhere to live as close as possible to 114 Rotherfield Street without actually being in Rotherfield Street then a house in Ecclesbourne Road would have been the perfect choice. Not only does Ecclesbourne Road intersect Rotherfield Street but the side of the house numbered 118 Rotherfield Street, two doors from 114, is actually in Ecclesbourne Road, adjoining number 24. Number 36 Ecclesbourne Road, which, in March 1915, bore a card in the window announcing 'Furnished Apartments', was, and remains, five houses away from Rotherfield Street and, in distance, less than one hundred yards from 114, barely a minute's walk away.

On a cold evening at about 6:45pm on Thursday 18 March 1915, an unaccompanied woman carrying a small brown leather attaché case and wearing a long black coat and a stylish three cornered black feathered hat called at 36 Ecclesbourne Road asking for a furnished room. She had, she said, just come from Victoria and expected to be in Islington for a week, or perhaps two. The landlady, Mrs Ellen Alland, was not in the house at the time, but the maid said the front room on the first floor was available for five shillings a week and ushered the woman into the room, leaving her alone to settle in. Some fifteen minutes later, shortly after 7pm, the newly arrived guest, with her face now covered by a white motor veil (an item of headwear originally designed to protect ladies from dust while in open top motor cars), emerged from her room and left the house, informing the maid she was going 'to the post'.

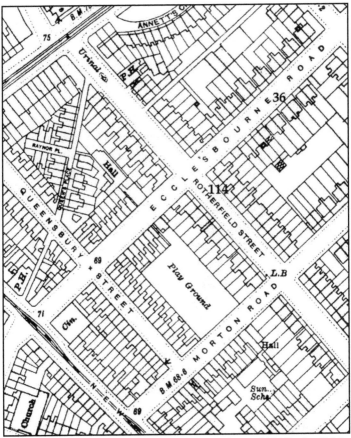

A 1914 map showing the relative positions of 114 Rotherfield
Street and 36 Ecclesbourne Road

Half an hour later, Cora Higson was walking down
Rotherfield Street on her way to visit her friend Annie,
as she did most nights of the week. Noticing a veiled
lady wearing a long black coat, standing against the
railings of the house, she initially thought it was Marie,
but it was dark at the time and she could not be sure.
Believing Marie to be back in Sussex, she concluded it
simply could not be her. She entered 114 where she
had a conversation with Annie lasting about half an
hour and then left the building in order to purchase a

bottle of stout at a nearby public house. As she exited Annie's house, she saw what appeared to be the same lady still in Rotherfield Street: now standing about two doors away from 114, although it was extremely dark – the street lamp nearest 114 had not been lit since the start of the war - so she could not be sure.

The war had plunged the whole of Islington into darkness. Fears of a Zeppelin airship raid had led to street lights being turned off across London from the early days of the conflict on the orders of the Commissioner of Police. *The Islington News and Hornsey Gazette* complained in October 1914 that 'our main streets at night are as dark as country lanes' and joked that 'the brightest places for a night stroll in London nowadays are the subways'. It pointed out that 'one accident has already occurred owing to the lack of light at a street corner' in Islington and predicted more. A meeting of the Islington Borough Council in November 1914 approved a resolution that 'the diminution of public street lighting is a source of public danger' with one alderman arguing that disasters arising from the darkness would ultimately exceed those that were likely to be suffered from the arrival of a Zeppelin fleet. 'People,' it was said, 'wanted to know what was happening that the streets should be so dark'[44]. The response of the Commissioner of Police in November was that there had been no increase in the number of traffic accidents at night in London although critics felt he had not taken into account the reduction in traffic due to the war. In fact, while the numbers for November showed no change, during December there was a significant increase in accidents in London (from 56 in December 1913 to 89 in December 1914[45]) and the *Daily Call* claimed that, 'all sensible people agree that, for reasons easily explained, the present system of reducing the lights in London is foolish.' Nevertheless, nothing was done to turn the lights back on which was why Rotherfield Street was so dark in March 1915 that Cora Higson could not identify a woman who was standing virtually in front of her.

She was not long in the public house and, when she came back out, the lady with the veil was still there, in the same place. Cora returned to 114 and descended the stairs to the kitchen where she sat talking with Annie, her sister Lil and Lil's husband Fred. About a quarter of an hour later, at around 8:45pm, there was a knock at the front door. Fred Dixon walked up the stairs from the kitchen to the door of the house which he opened to reveal, standing in the darkness on the front steps, a woman with a veil which partially obscured her face, covering her cheeks and chin, who asked: 'Can I see the lady downstairs?' Assuming she must mean Mrs Wootten, Fred walked back downstairs to inform Annie, who along with her sister, climbed up to the ground floor to speak to the woman while Cora and Fred waited in the kitchen. At the front door, Annie and Lil found a woman whose face was still largely covered by the motor veil.

'I've come about your children interfering with my children,' said the veiled lady sharply.

'I don't know who you are,' replied Annie in a calm voice. She could not see the visitor properly, the only light source in the vicinity being the gas light in the hall behind her, the veil in any case obscuring the woman's face.

'You are Mrs Wilson aren't you?'

'No, I'm not.'

'This is 14 Rotherfield Street isn't it?'

'No, it isn't.'

'I'm sorry.'

And with that, the veiled lady departed. Returning, puzzled, to the kitchen, Annie remarked knowingly to

Cora: 'How like your friend Marie's voice it was.' 'Yes it was,' agreed Mrs Higson, who had been able to hear the voice from the kitchen.

Had Annie or Cora read Edith Nesbit's *Magic City*, published five years earlier, they might have had the uneasy feeling of encountering a fictional character come to life. The anti-hero in that Alice in Wonderland type children's book was the evil Pretenderette to the Claimancy of the Delivership, a motor-veiled lady, who stole the Hippogriff and captured the Parrot in her veil before caging it and dropping it in the sea, amongst other cruel deeds. The Pretenderette could not be identified behind her veil but, towards the end of the book, she turned out to be a nurse who was horrible to children. She had accidentally followed Philip into his magic city and the motor veil she was already wearing to catch the 2:37pm train turned out to be a 'fine disguise'. Although she was not, of course, a real person it was interesting, and in some ways prophetic, that Nesbit chose an unidentified lady wearing a motor veil to represent mystery, danger and evil in equal measure for her story.

Back in the real world, at 36 Ecclesbourne Road, Violet, the maid, was wondering where the new guest had disappeared to. It was not until shortly before 10pm that she returned. The guest was, of course, none other than Marie, although she did not tell the inhabitants of the house her first name. 'We all thought you had been lost,' said the servant as she opened the door to her. 'No,' replied Marie, 'I have been to the pictures.'

The following morning, after breakfast, Marie met Mrs Alland, the landlady. She gave her name as 'Miss Wheatley' and confirmed that she would want the room for either a week or a fortnight. The landlady said that, unfortunately, the maid had wrongly informed

her of the cost of the room which would actually
be seven, not five, shillings for the week, excluding
breakfasts, and she asked for the money in advance.
Marie replied that did not have that amount of money
on her and she would have to draw a sovereign out of
the post office. She left the house, promising to return
for tea at four-thirty in the afternoon. A few minutes
after she had departed, however, the sharp eyed
landlady, upon inspecting Marie's room, realised that
Marie had taken the attaché case, her only luggage,
with her and, instinctively suspecting she would not be
coming back, dashed out of the house to find her.

It was a bitterly cold morning in Islington with the
temperature at one point having hit two degrees below
freezing and snow had fallen in the early hours.[46] The
log book for Rotherfield Street Junior School recorded
that thirty-seven pupils had been unable to make it
into school that day owing to the 'very bad weather'.
Mrs Alland was not, however, deterred by the elements
for even the briefest moment. She jumped straight onto
a car and, guessing the likely direction Marie must
have taken - towards the Angel - was highly relieved
to catch up with her at the Agricultural Hall, off Upper
Street. She tapped her on the shoulder and asked for
compensation for the previous night. 'Oh! I am coming
back,' said Marie, 'I promised to go to the post office
and I am on my way.'

'I'll come with you,' replied a still suspicious Mrs
Alland and the two women walked together to the post
office near the Angel but, three doors away from the
building, Marie opened her handbag, looked around
theatrically, and said: 'Goodness me! I have lost my
purse and bank book!'

'You cannot lose what you never had,' countered
Mrs Alland without missing a beat. She was not taken
in by Marie's amateur dramatics. 'Why don't you come
with me to the police station to give me your address?'

'I'd rather not,' said Marie pulling out one shilling and fivepence from her bag, 'look here is all the money I have, take it.'

Looking inside the case, Mrs Alland saw the money but also glimpsed a War Office envelope addressed to a 'Lieutenant Wootten' in Hove. 'Now, how can I believe your name is Wheatley?' she said. 'You won't give me any address and you have an envelope in the name of Wootten.'

'That's nothing,' said Marie as she snapped the bag shut.

'Anyway, I don't want your last penny,' Mrs Alland continued. 'If you give me your address I will be satisfied.'

'I'm going to friends in Tooting and you will get your money.'

'I would like some security first please,' declared the landlady.

Marie removed her engraved signet ring from her finger and gave it to Mrs Alland.

'This isn't valuable,' said Mrs Alland upon inspection, nevertheless holding onto it. 'Do you have some more valuable security?'

'Well, there is my brooch.'

'What is in your attaché case?'

'Only my comb and nightdress.'

'Give me the case please.'

Unable to resist the demand without an unwelcome visit to the nearest police station, Marie reluctantly handed over her attaché case. It felt surprisingly heavy to Mrs Alland as if there was rather more than a comb and nightdress in it. Marie said she would come back for the case at 4:30pm, adding: 'Please take care of my ring won't you, I value it very much,' and Mrs Alland returned to 36 Ecclesbourne Road.

Upon arrival, the landlady's curiosity got the better of her. Using a key from a case she owned with a similar lock, she managed to open the attaché case. Inside she found a white motor veil, three or four pocket handkerchiefs, a waterproof soap bag, a silver topped comb, a nightdress, some plain postcards and, wrapped up inside the nightdress, a small revolver. 'Good gracious!' she cried out as she delicately picked up the weapon, noting it was an old, dull looking thing: rusty, with a steel barrel and wooden handle but no guard around the trigger. Rummaging further she saw a waterproof soap box and, in the corner of the case, another box labelled 'Eley Pin-Fire' containing what seemed to be about fifty brand new revolver cartridges. They were unusual cartridges which all had a small pin projecting from the side of the case, revealing them to be what were known as 'pinfire' cartridges.

A typical 7mm pinfire revolver

Pinfire cartridges could only be fired from a revolver containing a cylinder with a notch at the side of each chamber at the breech end to accommodate the protruding cartridge pin. When it was fired, the hammer of such a revolver would strike the pin on the cartridge which would drive the pin into the case, exploding the primer and setting off a powder charge. The consequent release of gas inside the cartridge case would swell the case to grip against the chamber wall as the bullet would be ejected at high speed through the barrel. Pinfire revolvers were popular during the early part of the nineteenth century because they were much easier to operate than front loading revolvers but became largely redundant following the invention, in 1861, of the central fire cartridge which did not require a protruding pin. Nevertheless, as they could be bought cheaply, often second-hand, pinfire revolvers remained widely used by petty criminals. Most famously, when a starving grocer's assistant and former inmate of a lunatic asylum, Roderick Maclean, decided to assassinate Queen Victoria on the platform of Windsor Station in March 1882, it was reported to be a German pinfire revolver he used as his weapon.[47] He fired off a shot from fifteen yards but missed his target and was overpowered.

By 1915, pinfire revolvers were no longer being manufactured but there were still plenty in circulation and cartridges continued to be sold for them in ironmongers and gun/ammunition stores. Like all cartridges (and revolvers) they could be purchased without much difficulty by any adult. The Gun Licence Act of 1870 required anyone carrying a firearm outside of their house to have a licence, which could be purchased over the counter at the post office for ten shillings, but a licence was not actually needed to buy a gun. This had caused one newspaper to complain in 1889 that: 'a youth of 18 can go and buy a revolver and enough cartridges to kill a whole family with the same ease that he could buy a horsewhip or a tin of biscuits'.[48] The 1903 Pistols Act attempted to regulate the sale of pistols and revolvers to make their purchase a little more difficult but they could still be sold legally to anyone who had bothered to obtain a gun licence or, alternatively, to a householder without a licence who promised to use it only in his own property.

Mrs Alland showed the revolver and cartridges to her husband and one of the other lodgers, a clerk called Horace Mitchell, asking them what she should do. Neither knew, so Mrs Alland decided she would pay a visit to her father on the matter later in the afternoon, once she had finished her household duties.

At lunchtime on the same day, Lieutenant Wootten received an unexpected visitor at the White City. As he remembered it, the conversation went as follows:

'Marie, what are you doing here?'

'Bert, I am very sorry to trouble you but I am stranded and have no money.'

'Why, what has happened?'

'I came from home this morning, I had a few words with father, there was a quarrel and I left hurriedly. I didn't know where to go so I went to Tooting where I have an aunt. I intended to stay with her but I found she was gone out of town on a week's holiday.'

'I can't speak more now,' said Wootten, 'I have some duty to do, but here is some money for you to buy lunch and I will meet you again at four o'clock at Wood Lane Station.'

'Do you promise you will be there?'

'I promise, now I must go Marie.'

Shortly after lunch, in 36 Ecclesbourne Road, Mrs Alland put the revolver back in the attaché case and set off to see her father who owned a second-hand clothes shop in Camden Street. Not wanting to walk along the street with such a weapon, she asked Mr Mitchell to carry the case for her. The two of them had not got far when they met Marie in Essex Road, near Greenman Street. 'Where are you going?' asked Marie. 'Shopping. What do you want?' replied Mrs Alland. Seeing the case in Mitchell's hand she asked if she could have it back. 'Do you have the money?' Mrs Alland asked. 'No,' said Marie. 'Well you can't have it back then.' Mrs Alland and Mitchell carried on walking to their destination pursued by a tenacious Marie asking: 'How much do I owe you for breakfast?' 'Sixpence,' answered Mrs Alland. 'Well I can pay you sixpence for the case,' said Marie hopefully, 'and give you an address'.

'Yes, if you come to the police station with the address.'

'No, I would rather not. Here is another two shillings.'

'I'm afraid I cannot take that.'

Mrs Alland and Mitchell walked on. Marie's mind must have been working overtime at this point. She would not have failed to notice that Horace Mitchell was grimly clutching her attaché case as if it contained his life savings and Mrs Elland was speaking to her like she was a dangerous criminal. While she could not be certain of what had happened in the past few hours, she undoubtedly sensed that the landlady must have somehow opened her case and knew what it contained. A dose of disarming honesty was now what was required.

'Take care of the attaché case,' called out Marie, 'there's a revolver and a box of cartridges in it.'

'Good gracious!' exclaimed Mrs Alland, pretending she did not already know. 'You don't think I'm going to mind firearms do you?'

'It's alright, it's not loaded - the cartridges are all in the box which is unbroken, just as I bought it - I slept with it last night.'

'So would I if I had it, but not if I knew you had it!' quipped Mrs Alland. 'Do you have a licence?'

'Yes.'

'Where is it?'

'At Haywards Heath.'

'What do you want a revolver for? And why not leave it in Haywards Heath with the licence?'

'You want a revolver in a place like Haywards Heath,' said Marie laughing, 'and I can carry a revolver if I like. I had a job to get the cartridges. I could not get them at Haywards Heath and I have been to two or three shops to get them here.'

'But why do you *need* cartridges?'

'For chicken farming,' mumbled Marie.

'Good gracious! You don't want to kill chickens when farming them, you want to make them live,' responded Mrs Alland. She and Horace continued walking but they could not shake off Marie.

'Oh Mrs Alland, what do I owe you?'

'Well, let me see, it's seven shillings for the room and sixpence for breakfast.'

'Could you take half a crown off the account?' said Marie, handing over two shillings and sixpence.

'Yes, fine, so you now owe me five shillings.'

Marie walked with Mitchell and Mrs Alland as far as 29 Camden Street where Mrs Alland dismissed her by telling her she now had business to do. Marie said she would come again on Saturday. Mrs Alland told her to make it Sunday then she and Horace entered her father's shop while Marie walked off.

The sensible advice of Mrs Alland's father was to take the revolver to the police so the obliging Horace Mitchell was pressed into action once more as the case carrier and he and Mrs Alland marched off to Upper Street Police Station where they encountered two of Islington's finest, if not brightest, police officers: Sergeant Charles Hewitt and Constable John Masson. Mrs Alland told them the story about the attaché case and its contents, explaining that the owner claimed to have a licence for the revolver, and she handed over the rusty old weapon. Upon examination by Masson, the revolver was found to be fully loaded, with five chambers holding live cartridges.[49] These were removed, and a spent cartridge case in the final chamber was extracted and summarily thrown onto an open fire. Sergeant Hewitt was not only completely unfazed by the fact that an unknown woman was walking around the streets of Islington with a loaded revolver in her possession but, for reasons never adequately explained, although almost certainly due to quite unbelievable incompetence, he advised a rather surprised Mrs Alland to return it to its owner once she paid for her room.

While all this was going on in Islington, Lieutenant Wootten was meeting Marie over in West London. According to Wootten's recollection of events, Marie said:

'This is your unlucky day, Bert!'

'What do you mean?'

'It's the nineteenth, your unlucky day, the day your baby boy died.'

'Yes, so it is,' said Wootten sadly, 'but tell me what you want now.'

'I don't intend going home,' Marie replied, 'I would like to get a situation in London. But-'

'Yes, Marie?'

'I don't know where I'm going to stay Bert.'

'Well I am prepared to fund a room for you as part of the provision I promised to make but only until you find some employment.'

'Yes, I understand.'

The two of them walked over to Richmond Road in Shepherd's Bush. On the way Wootten remarked: 'You have no luggage?' 'No,' said Marie, 'I left so hurriedly, I will have to borrow a nightdress.'

'You have no rings on your fingers either I see?' observed Wootten, thinking of the signet ring he had engraved for her.

'No, indeed, they are all at the bottom of my box at home.'

They arrived at 12 Richmond Road where Wootten agreed a weekly rent with the landlady, Margaret Connor, for a furnished room. Marie asked to borrow a nightdress but Mrs Connor could only find a pink dressing jacket which was nevertheless accepted as a substitute. Wootten left Marie there at 6:30pm but returned a couple of hours later after Mess. It was decided that she would look for a situation as a barmaid.

Wootten visited Marie again at Richmond Road the next evening, Saturday, March 20, and took her out for tea. She mentioned that she had lost the reference she had used to obtain her situation at the George Hotel in Shoreham and he agreed to write her a new one. Beneath the crest of the 10th Bedfordshire Regiment, Wootten's reference read:

Two years reference

To all this may concern,
I have much pleasure in recommending Miss M.
Wheatley, as the most thorough good business woman,
honest, and respectable. I shall be pleased to answer any
questions respecting her, if referred to.

A. Wootten, Lieut
March 1915

On Sunday morning, at about eleven, Wootten met Marie again in Richmond Road. It was 21 March and, as if to signal the arrival of spring, London was bathed in sunshine on a gloriously warm day so the pair went for a ride together on an omnibus to Marble Arch. A reporter in the following day's *Daily Mirror* was in raptures about the weather in London that Sunday: 'Blue skies were sweet to gaze upon,' he gushed, 'trees that were green-tinted with buds, and the never ending antiphony of the birds were part of the glory of the day'.[50] From Marble Arch the pair walked over to

Hyde Park Corner where, according to Wootten, Marie asked him for money to send to her sister from whom she claimed to have borrowed four shillings on the morning before coming to see him. Wootten pointed out that it was Sunday so she couldn't send any money – the post offices in London were closed[51] – but Marie had an answer for that: 'No, but I can send it first thing on Monday morning.' Defeated in the exchange, Wootten compliantly handed over the required four shillings. He suggested accompanying her back to Richmond Road but she said she wanted to go for a walk on her own round Hyde Park before returning to Mrs Connor's for lunch.

Hyde Park was, at that time, regarded very much as the open air social centre of London and, with the usual Sunday Church Parade (a huge relaxed social gathering) in the park commencing at noon, people were out in numbers. According to the *Daily Mirror*, there was in the park that day, 'a pageant of pretty women and brave men. Women proudly displayed the latest spring fashions, but looked still prouder of the fact that they were being escorted by khaki-clad patriots.' Marie and the lieutenant were not, however, to be found strolling arm in arm in the sunshine amongst the happy chattering throng. Wootten left Marie at the park and, having the afternoon free, went home to 114 Rotherfield Street to visit his wife.

Shortly after one o'clock on that Sunday afternoon, there was a knock on the door at 36 Ecclesbourne Road, opened by Mrs Alland to find a smiling Marie waiting outside:

'Good afternoon Mrs Alland, I am calling for my case.'

'Do you have the remainder of the money?'

'Yes, here is the five shillings.'

Marie was invited inside to wait in the hall while

Mrs Alland, with the five shillings now safely in her hand, went off to fetch the case. When she returned she asked: 'Are you staying for the remainder of the week?'

'No,' said Marie, 'I'm going back to Haywards Heath.'

'In which case, I think I should give you two shillings back,' said Mrs Alland as she returned two coins to the grateful recipient, as well as Marie's signet ring.

About half an hour later, at around two o'clock, Joe Higson was travelling in a tram car at Old Street when, to his utter astonishment, he saw Marie, with her attaché case, walking along the City Road heading towards Bank. Unable to believe his eyes he leapt off the tram and ran after her.

'Hullo,' he said breathlessly as he caught her up, 'what are you doing here?'

'I got off at the Bank and had a walk as far as Dawson's.'

Dawson's, or Dawson Brothers to give it its proper name, was a large department store in the City Road.

'It's a funny place Islington, isn't it, to have a walk?' queried Higson sarcastically.

'I can please myself where I walk can't I?' Marie retorted.

'Yes but don't come to Islington, we don't want you,' said Higson, who nevertheless asked Marie to share a glass of wine with him.

'I see you are carrying the same luggage,' he mentioned while they were drinking. Marie just smiled as she sipped her wine. 'When did you come down?' Higson asked.

'Yesterday.'

'So where did you stay last night?'

'Gillingham Street in Victoria.'

'And what next?'

'I'm now going to Tooting to stay with my aunt.'

'Have you heard from Bert?'

'No.'

'Have you written to him?'

'Yes, twice and had no reply.'

'But what is the good of continually writing to him when he doesn't want anything to do with you?'

'I won't write to him again.'

'Good,' said Higson.

'Now I must be on my way to Tooting.'

As they parted, Marie suddenly said: 'Don't tell Bert you've seen me!'

'I won't if you wish it.'

Despite his promise of silence, Higson went straight to Wootten at Rotherfield Street. 'Who do you think I've seen Bert?'

'I don't know.'

'Marie!'

'Where?'

'In the City Road. She was carrying the usual luggage.'

'What is she doing up here?'

'She said she's on her way to Tooting.'

'Tooting?'

Wootten knew very well she was not going to Tooting but he did not tell Higson about Richmond Road or that he had been seeing Marie every day since Friday. His recollection is that he went back to visit her for about an hour that evening before returning briefly to his wife in Islington. When he left Annie late that evening to report back to the White City he did not know it would be the last time he would ever see his wife alive.

CHAPTER 4

IT'S MURDER!

'Listen to this, there has been a murder here; this is not an accident, it's murder!'

Albert Wootten (according to Frederick Dixon's recollection), 23 March 1915

On Monday, 22 March 1915, Wootten visited Marie in Richmond Road at about half past eight in the evening as usual and the two of them went out for a walk towards Hammersmith. They discussed Marie's attempts to find employment. She reported that she had written after several situations and had been to interview for two or three. Most promisingly, she had an appointment at the Surrey Arms public house in the Old Kent Road the next day at four o'clock. She had already seen the landlady who told her she had a chance of getting the position. Wootten, who gave money to Marie every time he saw her, handed over five shillings on this occasion.

Wootten was back at Richmond Road the following evening – a little later than normal because he had stopped at a barber's in Shepherd's Bush for a haircut and shave – arriving at ten minutes past nine. Mrs Wootten's dead body was now lying in the parlour of 114 Rotherfield Street. Suitably coiffured, Wootten knocked on the street door. It was opened by Marie who said: 'You're later this evening Bert.' 'Yes I know,' replied Wootten. According to his later testimony on oath, Marie looked as if she had been hurrying; she was flushed and wiped her brow with a handkerchief. In an allegedly agitated tone, she said: 'Oh Bert, I didn't get the situation I was after at the Surrey Arms.

I'm an awful drain on you. I would give five pounds
to anyone who would shoot me, if I had it.'

'Don't be silly Marie, I'm sure something will turn
up.'

Wootten, who put Marie's agitation down to her
not finding employment, stayed with her for a couple
of hours. He would later claim that she asked him
to stay the night but that he declined. He returned
to White City where he received a communication
from his Major informing him that his wife had been
involved in a serious accident. He obtained permission
to leave his quarters and made the late night journey
to Islington. Upon arriving at 114 Rotherfield Street
at about half past midnight he walked down to the
kitchen. There was a group of people in there, among
them: Joseph Tilbury, Annie's father, Albert Tilbury,
her brother, and Mr and Mrs Higson. He saw tears
streaming down his father-in-law's face.

'What is wrong?' he asked.

'Do not upset yourself Bert, Annie has passed
away.'

'What! *How?*'

'It seems that she fell over and broke her neck. The
girls heard it happen.'

Against the advice of those present, who thought
Annie's dead body was in no fit state to be viewed,
Wootten insisted on seeing it and walked up to the
parlour, unlocking the now locked door with the key
which had been left in the lock.

Removing the cloth covering his late wife's face, he
saw her nose and mouth were smattered with blood.
He then walked back down the stairs to the kitchen to
find out what had happened but no-one could tell him
very much. He assumed, like everyone else, that Annie
had fallen down the stairs. Fred Dixon showed him the
strange telegram that Lil had found in the kitchen but

it did not seem to have any connection with Annie's death, looking like it had been wrongly addressed, and he ignored it. There was nothing anyone could do and, despite Annie's dead body lying in the parlour, the Tilburys and Higsons returned to their homes, with the Dixons retiring upstairs to bed. Wootten himself went to the bedroom down in the basement where his children were all asleep. As he entered, Lily woke up and asked, heartbreakingly, 'Hello Dad, is mummy dead?' At the same time, Ivy awoke and he covered both his girls up and told them to go back to sleep. He lay down on his bed but Lily could not sleep so he asked her: 'Lily, how did mummy fall downstairs?' She replied: 'I think mummy was lighting the gas and she fell downstairs daddy.'

'Just tell me all about it. Did mummy put you to bed?'

'Yes, mummy had a little read in the kitchen and then came into the bedroom, pulled the blind to one side and looked out of the window, a lady called and asked for water and said she was thin and hungry and asked for money.'

'Who was the lady?'

'Mummy said it was Mrs Higson's friend.'

Mrs Higson's friend!

Wootten jumped out of bed and dashed up the stairs. He woke the Dixons who had fallen quickly asleep: 'This is not an accident, *it's murder*!' he cried. He brought them down to the bedroom so they could listen to what Lily had to say. She repeated the story of the woman knocking at the door, of her mother saying it was 'Mrs Higson's friend' and of the two loud bangs she had heard but Fred was not convinced. He still thought there had simply been a terrible accident. Wootten returned to the parlour to look at his wife's body, wanting to see if there was an obvious injury to her head. He could not see one and, although blood still oozed from the mouth and nostrils, there was nothing to indicate that his wife's death had been anything other than an accident, as Dr Madden had concluded. Changing his mind he told Fred: 'It can't be murder,' and everyone wearily returned to bed. Nevertheless, as Wootten drifted off for a few hours of troubled sleep he still felt that Mrs Higson's so-called 'friend', Marie, had something to do with his wife's death but he did not know exactly what.

The following morning, Wootten woke up early and prepared breakfast for the children, going over again with Lily and Ivy the story of his wife's death. On the floor in the hall he found a small pocket handkerchief which could have belonged to anyone considering the number of people who had been in and out of the house the previous evening (he later handed it to the police but it would never be identified). His next action was to walk to Colebrooke Row to have Higson released from his employment for the day. He wanted some help from his friend. There were a number of issues he needed to have sorted out in the morning; an undertaker had to be instructed to prepare the funeral arrangements while Wootten's mother also needed to be found and informed of what had happened; she was out nursing and Wootten only knew the name of the street she was working in. For the undertaker, Wootten and Higson only needed to make the short walk to 91 Essex Street where an Arthur Norton was instructed. He came round to measure the body and then provide a suitable coffin.

Meanwhile Fred Dixon was making his own investigations into the telegram addressed to 'Dickson'. He visited the post office in nearby St John Street, from where it had originated, and asked to see the original but was informed that it had been forwarded to the

Northern District Post Office in the ordinary way. The more he thought about the telegram and its arrival shortly before Annie's death the more suspicious it seemed. When he returned to Rotherfield Street soon after lunch he found Wootten and Higson conversing in the kitchen and showed the document to them. 'This is fishy work,' he said, 'I have made inquiries and come to the conclusion it is a bogus telegram. I think you should take it to the police.' Wootten was intrigued but had other ideas. Determined to track down the original, which would have the author's handwriting on it, he and Higson paid a visit to the Northern District Post Office in Upper Street but were told that the telegram would, in fact, have been sent to the East Central District Post Office, presumably a reference to the post office for the East Central District in King Edward Street. Rather than journey into the City to that office they went instead to the originating post office branch at 309 St John Street, which Fred Dixon had already visited, to see what they could find out. There they were advised to go the Post Office headquarters at St Martin's Le Grand but, equally, were told that they would not be allowed to view the original telegram without a permit so they did not bother.

Frustrated by the lack of success in uncovering any information about this mysterious telegram, Wootten decided on a more direct, but definitely ill advised, plan. With Higson as his companion and witness, he would confront Marie and force the truth out of her. Higson agreed to the plan. Hence the two self-appointed investigators made the journey across London to Richmond Road.

Meanwhile, an anonymous letter card arrived at 114 Rotherfield Street for Lieutenant Wootten, having originally been addressed to him at the White City and stamped 'North London, March 23rd 1915, 8:30pm': It read:

Have been waiting to hear your services no longer required in Army, but I see you are going to get on. Your kids come next. Sure as your name is B. Wootton. I will do you in. You ask me once to do a dirty trick for you. Now it is my turn. You passed me as if I was dirt. I ain't forgot.
L Davey turn.

Wootten and Higson knew nothing about this as they arrived in Shepherd's Bush at five o'clock for a confrontation with their prime suspect. Marie opened the door to find the two men with stern looks. According to Wootten, the colour came to her cheeks and she became flushed. Higson was the first to speak:

'Hello, you didn't expect to see me, did you?'

'No, Joe.'

'Hello Marie,' said Wootten tersely, standing by the door, as far from Marie as possible. He came quickly to the point: 'Why did you go to my house last night?'

'I did not go to your house last night.'

'You did go to my house last night, for Lily said that a lady called and it was "Mrs Higson's friend".'

Marie said nothing.

'What did you send the telegram for?' Higson held it out to her at a short distance. She glanced at it.

'I did not send that telegram. I did not know your sister-in-law's name was Dickson. I've only ever heard of her spoken of as Lil.'

'You might as well tell us the truth Marie,' said Higson. 'We have not come here for any lies.'

'I did not send that telegram, Joe.'

'Now be careful what you are saying,' said Wootten. 'Something terrible has happened. Do you know that two minutes after you left the house last night Annie was found dead at the bottom of the stairs?'

'What? Dead! Bert! What will you do with all your children?'

'Never mind what I shall do with the children.'

Higson added: 'We will look after the children. What we want from you is the truth'.

There was then some kind of discussion between Higson and Marie that things looked 'black' for her. It was never definitely established whether Marie said this herself or Higson said it and Marie agreed but, in any event, Marie denied any involvement in the death of Mrs Wootten: 'Don't drag me into this!' she cried.

Wootten broke in: 'I want to know your movements of yesterday.'

'Why don't you prove them?'

'Do you know what I believe?' Marie looked silently at Bert. 'I believe you have been to the house and you pushed Annie down the stairs.' Marie protested: 'Oh, how could I do such a thing?'

'That is my firm belief as you are the only person who my wife knew or would refer to as Mrs Higson's friend.' Marie, once more, said nothing.

Higson broke the silence: 'Surely a woman of your intelligence must know that the original telegram can be produced and we can see whether it's in your handwriting'.

'I know you can. I'm no fool Mr Higson,' retorted Marie.

'That is what I was just saying.'

'You told a lie when you came up to London,' interjected Wootten. 'You told me you had no luggage but Joe saw you on Sunday with your attaché case in City Road.'

'Well Bert I had to leave it in Tooting to get some money on it.'

'When did you get it back?' asked Wootten.

'On Sunday, after seeing you.'

'What were you doing in City Road after coming from Tooting?'

'I got off a bus at Bank and went up that way for a walk and was returning when Mr Higson saw me and spoke to me.'

Higson did not believe her. 'You couldn't get anything on your attaché case, it is only cardboard.'

'Oh indeed! It is not cardboard and you don't know what I've got in my attaché case,' said Marie enigmatically. 'Would you like to see?'

'If you care to show me.'

She brought her attaché case out from under the bed, unlocked it and pulled out a nightdress and silver comb. Higson barely glanced at it. She replaced the articles and put the case back under the bed.

Wootten was not satisfied and left the room to settle up with the landlady. Higson, sitting next to Marie on the bed, tried again:

'Now look here Marie, tell me the truth: didn't you go to 114 Rotherfield Street last night?'

'No,' said Marie firmly.

'Well then, do you care to tell me where you were last night?'

'Why should I?'

'Well, we can easily trace your movements.'

'Prove them!'

Higson realised he was not going to extract anything further from Marie. 'Do not try to get away from the house because it is being watched,' he lied. 'If you run away we shall find you.'

While this was going on, Wootten was handing over seven shillings and sixpence owing for the room and five breakfasts to Mrs Connor. He decided to continue with the investigation. 'What time did the lady come home last night?' he enquired. 'Oh I think early,' she answered. 'What, just before I came in?'

'Yes,' she said, nodding. When he returned, Wootten told Marie that he was no longer prepared to pay for her room.

'What shall I do tonight?'

'I don't care what you do tonight. I've settled all bills up to and including this present moment.'

After the two inquisitors left the house, Marie, visibly upset, and with a distinct and somewhat breathtaking economy of truth, informed Mrs Connor: 'My husband has been co-habiting with a woman in Islington and she has been found dead and I have been accused of doing it. I will have to go to back home to Brighton. Is there a pawnshop handy? I will have to pawn my ring as I have no money to get to Brighton.'

'Well,' said a sympathetic Mrs Connor, 'if I can lend you the trifle you are short of to save you from going to the pawnshop, I will do so. Let me see, I can let you have two shillings.'

Marie gratefully accepted the money and said goodbye to the landlady.

Not satisfied with Marie's protestations, Wootten finally decided it was time to go to the police with his suspicions. After returning to Islington in the evening, he met up with P.C. Reeves at Islington Police Station in Upper Street and showed him the mysterious telegram. He explained that, shortly after it had been sent, a woman showed up at his house asking for money and water and he had been to see her in Shepherd's Bush. Reeves did not enquire as to who the woman was but told Wootten to go home and await a visit from a detective who would take all the details. He knew that, earlier in the afternoon, the coroner had ordered a post-mortem into the death of Mrs Wootten, as required for all sudden or unexplained deaths. Reeves had, therefore, given instructions to the undertaker to move Mrs Wootten's body from 114 Rotherfield Street to the Islington Mortuary. This was done by Arthur Norton at about 7pm. As a result of what Wootten had told him, Reeves telephoned the Mortuary Keeper to instruct him to be extra careful when receiving the body because there might be more to Mrs Wootten's death than meets the eye.

The body had, in fact, already arrived when Reeves made this call and Samuel Maxwell, the keeper of the mortuary, was in the process of preparing it for the post-mortem. He had detected a strong smell of burning from the blouse and, after the call from Reeves, made a careful examination of the clothing of the corpse. In doing so, he noticed a very small hole with charred fragments around the lace collar of the blouse which had crumbled away. When he removed the clothes he found a small punctured wound about two and a half inches above the left breast. Upon this discovery he immediately contacted P.C. Reeves and waited for the post-mortem.

Meanwhile, Marie was not on the train to Brighton. Instead, she was making the rather shorter journey to 'The Gun', a tavern in Pimlico, arriving at about seven. Although she had not had a chance to mention it to Wootten or Higson during their meeting, she had been engaged there as a barmaid the previous morning, having responded swiftly to an advertisement in that day's *Morning Advertiser*.[52] She had originally told the licensee, Arthur Clifford, that she would like to wait until Monday before commencing work but she now informed him that it would suit her better to start tomorrow. From 'The Gun', Marie then journeyed to the much heralded Tooting, where she really did have a relative – an uncle, Henry Mockford, who was her mother's brother. She arrived at 43 Woodbury Street in Tooting somewhere between eight and eight-thirty asking to be put up for the night. While she was there she wrote the following letter to her mother in Horsted Keynes:

The Gun Tavern, Lupus Street, Victoria

My dear mother
You were very surprised to receive my letter this morning
I'm sure.
Well mum, something has occurred that I will not go back
with Bert again. I have got a job at the above so will send
you some money as soon as I get my first week's money.
He has had to join the Flying Corps so you can tell
anyone he has gone to the front which he will do in about
3 weeks time.
You are not to worry about me. I'm quite all right.
Love to you all.
Will send some money as soon as I get some.
Mawks
Miss Wheatley

don't answer any questions he may write and ask you.

The first sentence of Marie's letter, referring to a letter having been received by her mother 'this morning', is ambiguous. It is likely that Marie was referring to her mother's surprise at receiving *this* letter. Some newspapers even reported the first line as stating 'You will be surprised to read my letter this morning', conveying the impression that there was only one letter, namely the one Mrs Wheatley was reading at the time. However, while the original of Marie's letter no longer exists, an official transcript of it states 'You were very surprised to receive…' which suggests that there might have been an earlier letter from Marie to her mother. Harry Wheatley was asked about it subsequently but was unable to offer any assistance as to what it said or whether it existed. It was certainly never produced by Mrs Wheatley. If there was another letter from Marie to her mother it was probably written by Marie earlier that same day so that 'this morning' was a reference to the morning of

Thursday 25 March when Marie would have expected her first letter to arrive in Horsted Keynes. The postal service in 1915 was very efficient, with many collections and deliveries a day, and Marie might have anticipated that her second letter, posted late in the evening from Tooting, would have reached her mother during the Thursday afternoon.[53] However, the contents of the first letter, if there was one, are unknown - it must have been destroyed by Marie's mother - and it may be that it contained something which her mother did not wish the police to see, but this will never be known for sure.[54]   At the same time, no accusation was ever made that Mrs Wheatley had destroyed a letter from Marie and the likelihood is that there was only one letter. In any event, from Tooting, Marie also sent a brief postcard to Higson:

The Gun Tavern, Lupus Street, Victoria

The above is my address should you wish to see me. A.M.W.

The post-mortem was conducted the following afternoon by the renowned pathologist, Dr Bernard Spilsbury, watched by the doctor who had originally concluded that Mrs Wootten died of a broken neck, Dr George Madden. Spilsbury identified a small circular wound, a quarter of an inch in diameter in the upper part of the left chest, two inches below the middle of the collar bone. The edge of the wound was turned in but did not appear to be burned and there were no powder marks on the surrounding skin. From internal examination, a bullet track was discovered which had passed in an oblique direction downwards, backwards, and to the right, through the left lung and had then traversed the aorta, ending up lodged in the spinal column. Dr Spilsbury concluded the actual cause of death was heart failure following haemorrhage but there was now no doubt that Mrs Wootten had been shot dead and a murder most foul had been committed.

CHAPTER 5

WATCHING THE DETECTIVES

'...the real detective is by no means like the detective of fiction, who is always successful in the end.'

I Caught Crippen, Walter Dew, 1938

'I believe your name is Marie Lanteri, otherwise Wootten and Wheatley.' Thus did Detective Inspector Thomas Davis of the N Division of the Metropolitan Police announce himself to Marie at 'The Gun' at half past four in the afternoon of Thursday, 25 March 1915.

He had obtained her new employment address from 'police enquiries', the nature of which he never revealed but which might have involved the interception of Marie's letter to her mother.[55] By arrangement with the post office, the authorities routinely read private mail during the war in the hunt for German spies. It was no secret that they did so and the *Islington News and Hornsey Gazette* informed its readers in September 1914 that: 'Orders have been issued that all letters, either inland or foreign, may if it is deemed advisable, be opened and examined without question, and this is being done on a wholesale scale.' Even before the war, the police had been intercepting mail to catch criminals although this was less well known.[56] In any event, armed with whatever information he had obtained, Davis and his colleague, Detective Sergeant Charles Wesley, dashed straight from Islington to Pimlico before the post-mortem on Annie Wootten had even been conducted. As the detective inspector would have been unaware of Marie's postcard to Higson stating her whereabouts (Higson himself didn't see it until he got home from work that evening and there was no reason for the police to have intercepted Higson's mail) it is likely that he believed Marie had fled from Richmond Road and from justice. As a pursuit of a suspect, it was not quite in the same league as Chief Inspector Walter Dew's dramatic chase of Crippen across the Atlantic five years earlier, but it would not be at all surprising if Dew's exploits had crossed his mind and he thought that he too was embarked on an exercise of chasing a fleeing killer.

This was the inspector's opportunity to arrest an important murder suspect and he was not going to allow a trifling matter, such as first establishing if Marie could account for her movements at the time of the murder, to get in his way. In truth, this was not entirely his fault because, according to rules in place at the time, which will be explained in more detail later, a police officer was not allowed to question a suspect he knew he was going to arrest, even under caution, and Davis was certainly determined to arrest Marie. It is not clear if he knew about her possession of a revolver at the time but, having interviewed Wootten in Rotherfield Street for over three hours, he was certainly aware that she was known as 'Mrs Higson's friend' and that such a woman had been identified by the deceased woman to her children as having been at 114 Rotherfield Street at the time of the murder. This was more than enough for Detective Inspector Davis. A more cynical detective would have pretended he had no intention of making an arrest until he heard what she had to say for herself but, in his mind, it probably did not matter; once he arrested her for murder she would surely be so shocked that she would break down and confess everything.

Davis appears to have arrested only one person on a charge of murder before in his career, having joined the Metropolitan Police at the age of 20, in July 1892.[57]

As a detective-sergeant in November 1899, he took Karl Scholz into custody after he killed his wife at his home in Islington but a coroner's jury decided it was the result of a freak accident which occurred while Scholz was attempting to repair his rifle and he was released without a trial.[58] By contrast, Thomas' father, who had also been a police inspector (albeit not a detective), had arrested one of the most infamous murderers of the nineteenth century although, at the time, Inspector James Davis had absolutely no idea that a crime had even been committed.

It happened late on New Year's Day of 1869 at Carter Street Police Station in Walworth, South London, when William Sheward, a publican who had been born in Walworth, but lived for most of his life in Norwich where he ran the Key & Castle public house, walked into the station while Davis was on duty at the front desk and confessed to having murdered his wife nearly eighteen years earlier.[59] It was an unusual confession and an initially sceptical Inspector Davis was amazed when, in response to his enquiry as to how Sheward had managed to dispose of the body without being discovered, was told: 'The body was cut up and I believe a portion was kept in spirits of wine at the Guildhall [in Norwich] by order of the magistrates'. Davis made enquiries with the Norwich police and learnt that, back in June 1851, portions of a woman's body had been found scattered all over Norwich but the authorities had never been able to establish her identity. Some of the portions had indeed been placed in spirits to preserve them but these had now been interred.

The first discovery had been on Saturday, 21 June 1851, in suitably surreal fashion by a dwarf called Charles Johnson while he was walking his dog.[60] The dog ran home with something in its mouth which,

upon examination, was discovered to be a right hand.
Johnson went straight to the police who instigated a
search and a few more body parts, including a foot,
were found during the same weekend. Gruesome
discoveries continued to be made almost every day for
the next couple of weeks, with the last piece being the
left hand, discovered on Monday 20 July with the ring
finger cut off. A head was never found. The surgeons
who examined the body parts concluded that they
were from a young adult female aged between 16 and
26 years old who had died within a fortnight of the
first discovery. Newspapers of the day, including *The
Times*, reported that, from the appearance of the feet, 'a
person would imagine that they belonged to a girl of
15 or 16 years.'[61] The police made extensive enquiries
to locate any missing women in the relevant age group,
or even any missing bodies from graveyards of young
women who had recently died, but none were found
and the *Daily News* of 2 July 1851 boldly reported that:
'It has been clearly established that the murdered
woman, whoever she may be, was not an inhabitant of
Norwich at the time of her death'. In fact, consistent
with the search of the graveyards, opinion was starting
to gain ground that there was no murder and that a
medical student was responsible, having obtained
a body for the purposes of dissection. This seemed
unlikely to the surgeons who examined the body parts
because of the rough way they had been cut up but
it was a more comforting explanation for the general
public. It was also a reassuring thought to residents
of Norwich that it was not a local crime. The *Norwich
Mercury* of 12 July stated that: 'It is the opinion of many
criminal lawyers in London, that these remains have
been brought from a long distance by railway and
afterwards distributed by the party bringing them'.

A flurry of excitement broke out in London at the

end of July when Mrs Elizabeth Faucett reported to Lambeth police that her sister, Ann Bailey, a 25 year old housemaid, had run off in the second week of June – possibly to Norwich – with a married painter called Simon Richard Gooch and had not been seen since. Mrs Faucett said that a 'cold thrill' passed through her when she read the newspaper reports of the finding of the body parts in Norwich and she was quite sure they were the remains of her murdered sister. A week later, Ann Bailey and Simon Gooch walked into Lambeth Police Station alive and well and that was the end of the story as far as the newspapers were concerned. The Norwich murder, if it was a murder, was completely forgotten until William Sheward presented himself to Inspector Davis at the very start of 1869.

Further enquiries in Norwich established that Sheward's wife, Martha, had gone missing in June 1851 but, being 54 years old at the time of her disappearance, no-one connected her with the body parts of what was universally believed to be a young woman. Sheward was tried for the murder of his wife at the Norwich Assizes in March 1869 but withdrew his confession which was the only real evidence against him. His defence at trial was that his wife had run off with her former lover, a man with whom she used to live in Chancery Lane in London. He identified him as a carpenter called Worseldine who had, apparently, been transported to Australia but his existence was evidently doubted by the jury who found Sheward guilty and he was sentenced to death. The verdict caused considerable disquiet in some quarters. Perhaps the confession was false. How could the medical experts have so badly misjudged the dead woman's age? If she had been a teenage girl, as had originally been stated, then Martha Sheward might still be alive. The *Standard* called the verdict 'not in every respect satisfactory.'[62]

The flames were stoked when a letter with a
Brighton postmark was published in *The Times* of 5
April 1869 from someone claiming to be Mrs Sheward,
saying she was very much alive but did not want
to be found. This was undoubtedly a hoax but, the
next day, another letter was published by the same
newspaper from a lawyer, John Robert Taylor, who
claimed he once knew a carpenter called Worseldine
who had lived in Fleet Street, and subsequently ran
an oyster shop in Chancery Lane, but was now dead.
That was not the end of the matter because, on 6
April, an anonymous letter to the Chief Clerk of the
Norwich magistrates stated that Worseldine had died
on Christmas Eve in 1848 but had, for fifteen years,
despite being married to another woman, kept Martha
Sheward (when she was Martha Francis) 'in a state of
affluence.' It was not known at the time, due a lack of
any investigation, but this letter had some credibility
because, according to records at the General Register
Office, a London carpenter called John Worseldine
had, indeed, died on 24 December 1848 - in Brixton
at the age of 65. Furthermore, there is support for the
notion that he was profligate because records show
that he was made bankrupt in 1832 when he was living
at Castle Yard, near Chancery Lane, not too far from
Fleet Street, and this was not long before Martha is
believed to have met Sheward, suggesting that the lady
moved on to another man once her lover and provider
went broke. If this was the Worseldine identified by
Sheward then, clearly, as he died in 1848, Mrs Sheward
could not have run off with him in 1851. However,
John Worseldine had a son called Frederick who was
convicted of theft and transported for life in 1834 while
his brother, Henry, was a carpenter who had emigrated
to Australia at some point after 1851 and was still living
there at the time of Sheward's trial (but died in July

1870). Was it possible that Martha had left William to be with Frederick or Henry? Had Inspector Davis been taken in by a drunken fantasy invented by Sheward, reported to be an alcoholic, that he had murdered his wife?

Evidently not. On 13 April 1869, while in Norwich prison waiting to be executed, Sheward made a full confession. The reasons he gave for killing his wife are a little cryptic but it seems that his problems all started in November 1849 when, earning a living as a pawnbroker, he was made bankrupt. At that time, in an apparent attempt to avoid his creditors, he handed £400 for safekeeping to another local pawnbroker and clothier, a Mr Christie, for whom he also worked. Christie gave him a sum of about £15 a month from the capital but Mrs Sheward, perhaps not trusting Christie, wanted her husband to retrieve it all. One day - on 15 June 1851 - she told him she was going to fetch it herself. This led to what Sheward described in his confession as a 'slight altercation' but it was nevertheless serious enough for him to run his razor over his wife's throat, killing her instantly. He left the body in the house and went out to work as if nothing had happened but the corpse began to smell so, upon his return, he lit a fire in the bedroom and began mutilating it. He hacked off and carried away a few pieces, disposing of them at the various secluded locations around Norwich where they were found by local inhabitants. Martha's relations questioned William about her disappearance but he told them she had left him and gone to live elsewhere.

William later re-married and had children with his new wife but he carried around a huge sense of guilt and, when he once again got into financial difficulty, he believed he was being punished from above for his crime. He travelled to London intending to commit suicide but could not summon up the courage. When he visited the place in Walworth where he first met Martha he became consumed by a desire to confess to the murder, hence his encounter with Inspector James Davis at Carter Street Police Station. Within four months of that meeting, Sheward was dead. He was hanged at Norwich prison on 20 April 1869. It seems that the medical experts simply misjudged the age of Martha Sheward who had been of small build with fair, smooth, skin.

Undoubtedly it was the easiest arrest of his career but James Davis nevertheless goes down in history as the man who arrested the infamous Norwich murderer of 1851 at Carter Street Police Station - and it was at Carter Street Police Station that his son, Thomas, was born on 6 July 1872, presumably because James and his wife were living there at the time (it being common practice for police officers to reside at their stations). James retired from the police force a few months later and topped up his pension by becoming Inspector of Weights and Measures for the Bromley District of the Kent County Council. Thomas spent much of his own police career in Islington but his South London roots are apparent from his marriage to Annie Louisa Bassett of Bromley in April 1898. Miss Bassett was the daughter of Rowland George Bassett, the founder of *The Kentish Times*, and the nuptials at an old parish church in Foots Cray, near Sidcup, were fully reported in *The Bromley & District Times* – for whom one of Annie's brothers was a staff journalist – so we know that Thomas gave his wife a gold brooch, set pearls and bracelet as a wedding present and in return she presented him with some gold cufflinks. The newly married couple honeymooned on the Isle of Wight. By this time, Davis had been promoted to detective-sergeant. His first major success in detection work had, in fact, come shortly before the wedding, with the arrest of Mr and Mrs Pickels in a case which the defence barrister, Charles Gill, described as 'one of the most remarkable that had ever been related in any court.'[63]

On 5 November 1897, Mrs Louise Lamming, a widow who rented out rooms in her house in Amhurst Road, Hackney, was visited by Lady Audrey Pickels and her husband - a doctor - who informed her that they had come down from Yorkshire in order to commence a lawsuit to recover some thousands of pounds due to them and were looking for temporary accommodation while they did so. Impressive references were provided by their legal adviser, Sir Charles Russell, and the manager of the Bank of England. After living in Mrs Lamming's house for ten days and running up a bill of over five pounds, the couple disappeared. Over in Beresford Road, Highbury, Mrs Emily Bloxam was then graced by the presence of Lady Alice Audrey Picton Kerr, daughter of the late Admiral Kerr, and her husband, who rented rooms from her but soon vanished owing four pounds. The references they provided were discovered to be fake. Similar stories were told by Mrs Louisa Comfort of Canonbury and Mrs Isabella Tribe of Clapton, prompting an investigation which resulted in the arrest, by Davis and a detective-constable Arthur Tritton, of Alice and Joseph Arthur Pickels in January 1898.[64]

Davis' enquiries established that Alice Pickels was a boot finisher, born as Alice Hannibal, who had been convicted and bound over in 1889 at Dalston Police Court for stealing jewellery from houses to which she had gained admittance by false but plausible stories about her identity. She met Joseph Pickels who was a real doctor in his mid-twenties, educated at Owen's

College Manchester, and formerly attached to the Moorfields Ophthalmic Hospital, having convinced him that she was Lady Alice Kerr, a niece of the Marquis of Lothian, who would come into a fortune of £35,000 once she turned twenty-six (in 1895). Joseph had come into a substantial inheritance of his own of over £1,500 and 'Lady Alice' promised she would buy him a practice of his own if they married. Unfortunately, she told him, she was not on good terms with her relatives who would take steps to prevent her marrying beneath her so he could not possibly be introduced to them. On one occasion it was arranged that he would meet her aunt in Inverness but it so happened, explained Alice, that, shortly before the meeting, the aunt caught sight of her uncle, a Lord, and she left the compartment of her train to speak to him so that the planned introduction never took place. With Joseph suspecting nothing amiss, the couple married at All Saints Church, St Johns Wood, in September 1894: Alice signing the marriage certificate as Lady Kerr. While they were waiting for Alice to inherit her fortune, Dr Pickels was forced to spend his entire inheritance keeping his wife in the lifestyle to which a woman of her position, or supposed position, felt she was entitled.

By 1896, Alice had turned 26 but various 'problems' prevented her getting her hands on her fortune and the couple were now penniless. In that year, a 'Dr and Lady Pickels' had stayed at the Arundel Hotel, Victoria Embankment, but left without paying their bill. Having been tracked down and arrested by Davis and Tritton two years later, the Pickels both pleaded guilty to charges of fraud at the London County Sessions at Clerkenwell on 3 February 1898; Alice was awarded a sentence of three months imprisonment with hard labour, while her husband, who claimed that he totally

believed her story until they were arrested and he
heard the evidence against her at the police court, was
sentenced to one month in prison. Davis and Tritton
were commended by the chairman of the Sessions for
their sterling detective work.

The next year brought another commendation
for Davis: this time at the Old Bailey for apprehending
a man who broke into the Church of St Matthew in
Islington and purloined various items, including
the vicar's hood, plus the contents of the collection
boxes. Davis was on duty in Essex Road at the time
and chased the burglar, cornering one Thomas Perry
in a nearby doorway. Perry's defence in court, that
a stranger had handed him the stolen property, was
not successful and he was sentenced to eight months
hard labour. In addition to chasing criminals along the
streets of Islington, Davis had been active at home and,
in August 1899, his wife gave birth to a girl, Dorothy:
Thomas proudly describing himself as a 'Police
Detective' on the birth certificate. From Islington, in
June 1903, Detective Sergeant Davis transferred to
Holborn where he was concerned in an interesting case
of extortion.

Anton Geitel was a seventeen-year-old boy from
Austria who met commercial traveller, William
Grundon, outside the Shaftesbury Theatre during the
evening of 24 November 1903. Grundon took the boy
back to his lodgings at Gray's Inn Place for an hour.
He would later insist that he only gave him a meal
and money after the boy mentioned he was cold, out
of work, and unable to afford food. Two days later,
Geitel returned to Grundon's rooms with a letter
written by his friend, Otto Reichner, in which Reichner
reported that Geitel had told him about 'all you have
done with him at your house that night' and claimed
to be enraged 'as I hear you sent that poor starving

fellow away with having your unlawful pleasure, giving him 3s'. To remedy the alleged wrong done to poor Geitel, Reichner demanded 'sufficient money to get new clothes for him, to pay the fare to his native town…and a couple of pounds in his pocket'. After that, Reichner promised, the matter would be 'settled and buried forever'. Grundon did not pay up so the letter was followed by a personal visit from the duo who told Grundon that they wanted money or they would go straight to the police. Grundon called their bluff and went with them to Gray's Inn Road Police Station where Thomas Davis was on duty. Once Grundon explained the situation they were arrested and tried at the Old Bailey, with Davis giving evidence that Reichner was 'a very dangerous man being a well-known associate of criminals in London'. Justice Ridley sentenced Reichner to ten years in prison and Geitel to three. Mr Grundon was at pains to stress that there was 'absolutely no truth' in the suggestion of impropriety.

While at Holborn, Davis worked with Inspector Walter Dew (who would arrest Crippen) and an investigation into thefts from a transport company led to the capture of the criminals and the recovery of the stolen goods. The magistrate at Bow Street commented in August 1906: 'I consider Inspector Dew, Sergeants Davis and [others]…deserve credit for their ingenuity and care in following up their discoveries'.

After spending a year in the Commissioner's Office in 1909, then a few months at Marylebone, Thomas Davis was promoted to Detective Inspector in November 1910, transferring to Kilburn, and the Davis family moved from Stoke Newington to West Ealing where Thomas lived with his wife, daughter and mother-in-law, Jemima Sarah Bassett. In October 1911, Davis was involved in another blackmail case when he and a colleague hid themselves below a dining room window outside a house in Acton, from where they could hear 'private detectives', Herbert Marshall and William Henry Butler, demanding over two hundred pounds from a Canadian gentleman, Elijah Fader, who, they claimed, had assisted a young woman called Francis Mary Tolley in having an illegal abortion. Once Fader paid them some money, the two officers swooped and arrested the men who were tried and convicted at the Old Bailey in December 1911 before Mr Justice Avory.

The following year, Davis was involved in a murder case although he did not make the arrest. Arthur James Benbow shot his elderly landlady through the heart while she was about to prepare a pudding in her home in West Ealing on 2 April 1912 because he thought someone had performed an illegal operation on him in the night.[65] He had attempted to flee from the scene with a revolver in his pocket but had been detained by a passing doctor and who handed him over to a police constable. Benbow was recorded as saying 'I cannot think what made me do it….My head is so bad today. Can't I have my tablets?' He was arrested and cautioned by Inspector Arthur Deeks and was soon joined at the scene by Detective Inspector Davis. A bizarre tragedy nearly occurred when Deeks picked up the revolver not realising it was loaded and accidentally fired it, with the bullet passing through the clothing of Davis who thus narrowly escaped being shot dead by his colleague. Benbow was tried for murder at the Old Bailey and found guilty but insane.

Perhaps not liking being shot at in Ealing, Davis transferred back to Islington in April 1913.

Charles Wesley had joined the Metropolitan Police in 1905 and was only a few months younger than Albert Wootten, having been born on 9 December

1883.[66] His father, although born in Essex, was the Whip to the York and Ainsty hounds and, as a result, Charles was born in North Yorkshire and grew up in Lincolnshire while his father was employed as a huntsman groom to the foxhounds. The Wesley family moved down to Garston Hall in Croydon around the turn of the century as Charles' father looked after the hounds there and, as a result of living in kennels for his entire childhood, Charles developed a lifetime love of dogs.

Wesley was certainly acquainted with firearms. As a young constable, he was on duty at the Angel, Islington, on 22 March 1911 with Police Constable Henry Gerrard when one Arthur Newton emerged from the Angel public house and pulled a revolver from his coat, firing at a man standing in the street, wounding him in his cheek, before pointing the weapon at his own head. Gerrard was the first to react, rushing up to Newton and removing the revolver from his hands, passing it to Wesley for safekeeping. 'Let me do it' said Newton 'he has ruined my life'. It transpired that the man he shot, Frederick Burgess, had been living with his wife for the past five years. Newton had sent a postcard to her, asking her to meet him at the Angel, and he had taken the revolver with him to use in the event that he found her with her lover. Wesley handed the revolver with four ball cartridges to Inspector Burnham of the Finsbury Division and Newton was sentenced to 18 months hard labour at the Old Bailey.[67]

In the same year, Wesley was promoted to detective-sergeant and was part of a team of officers which raided a counterfeit coin factory on the first floor of 31 Sidney Grove, Islington, during the afternoon of 16 November 1911. One of the men in the building, William Healey, attempted to throw a plaster cast for a half crown into the fire but Wesley struggled with him and took it from his hand while other officers overpowered him. Healey was found guilty of counterfeiting at the Old Bailey and sentenced to 3 years penal servitude.[68] It was for actions such as these that Wesley received a total of fifty-seven commendations while serving as a police officer and he was, one day, to rise to become a Chief Inspector of the Criminal Investigation Department at Scotland Yard before his retirement in 1934. Two years later he would be featured in the newspapers after burglars ransacked his house in Philip Lane, Tottenham, while he was out exercising his dogs, losing property to the approximate value of £200.[69] Rather more tragically, his only son, Reginald, a photographer for the *Daily Express*, would be killed in February 1937 in an airplane crash in Scotland and Wesley himself would die five years after that.[70]

Marie had only been working behind the bar at 'The Gun' for a couple of hours when the two police officers arrived. After taking her to a private room and offering her a chair, Detective Inspector Davis got straight to the point: 'I am going to arrest you for causing the death of Annie Wootten, wife of Lieutenant Wootten at 114 Rotherfield Street, Islington, on the twenty-third of this month by shooting her with a revolver or pistol and I shall take you to Islington Police Station where you will be charged with murder.' Frustratingly for the detective-inspector, despite having omitted to inform her that she had the right to remain silent, Marie made no reply.

In fact, despite the death penalty being the mandatory punishment for murder, Marie was apparently unshaken by her arrest and when Davis left the room to make a telephone call to the police station she said to Detective Sergeant Wesley: 'It made me laugh to hear the other gentleman speaking of all my names. He has got them pat enough. What are you going to charge me with?'

Wesley, who was rather surprised by the question, considering his colleague had already explained the reason for the arrest, simply repeated the allegation: 'Causing the death of Annie Wootten, wife of Lieutenant Wootten, at 114 Rotherfield Street, Islington, on the 23rd of this month by shooting her with a revolver or pistol.' 'Well I am innocent,' said Marie, 'I have never had a revolver. What would you advise me to do?'

Unable to offer any advice, it was Wesley's turn to remain silent as Inspector Davis re-entered the room and Marie was put into a cab to be taken to Upper Street Police Station. On the way, she commented: 'I am glad it has happened like this – to have it cleared up now. I should not like to have had it hanging over my head long,' adding, a few moments later, 'It's a nice thing to be charged with. I'm only 22. I was a widow four months after I was married.'

'Where did you marry Lanteri?' enquired Inspector Davis.

'At Guildford,' said Marie but, a little later, she had a change of mind, confessing: 'I have never really been married'. Then, shortly afterwards, having evidently given her position some thought, she said, 'This is a serious matter isn't it?' and she repeated what she had earlier told Wesley: 'I have not got a revolver'. Finally, to ensure the police officer had not thought she was running from the law, she added: 'I sent a postcard to Mr Higson, telling him where I was.'

At the police station, Marie was finally asked by Inspector Davis if she would care to account for her movements on Tuesday 23 March. She stated: 'I left my room at Shepherd's Bush at 1.30pm and walked towards Marble Arch. I went to several places in

London that day.'

'Do you care to say where?' pressed Inspector Davis.

'I don't see why I should,' was Marie's extraordinary reply. One might have thought that the provision of an alibi by someone on a charge of murder would be a sensible idea but, then again, probably not if she did not have one.

.

Detective Inspector Thomas Davis (right) and Detective
Sergeant Charles Wesley outside the North London Police Court
on 26 March 1915

CHAPTER 6

PRELIMINARY HEARINGS

'…they come together like the Coroner's Inquest, to sit upon the murdered reputations of the week.'

Fainall in *The Way of the World* by William Congreve, 1700

Death was a recurring feature in Walter Schröder's life. As the coroner of Central London he naturally dealt with it every working day but, throughout his career, his direct superiors seemed to prefer dying to retirement. A humble butler's son from Hampstead, Walter left school at the age of 15 and took employment as a clerk in the Central Middlesex Coroner's Court. The work was laborious and tiresome: it being his responsibility to write a manuscript verbatim note of all the witness evidence at every inquest in the jurisdiction. He started, in 1871, as clerk to Dr Edwin Lankester, the coroner for Central Middlesex, who, three years later was embroiled in a debilitating public controversy about his expenses – mainly in respect of post-mortems – which had been calculated as being £5,195 more than the coroner's expenses in a neighbouring district over a five year period from July 1869 to July 1874.[71] Lankester was forced to write letters to various newspapers defending his expenditure as perfectly justified, even going so far as to state that he had 'no possible personal interest' in ordering post-mortem examinations – a measure of the pressure he felt under.[72] The stress did his health no good at all and he died, officially from the combination of a carbuncle infection and diabetes, in October 1874 at the age of 61. His successor, Dr William Hardwicke, lasted six and half years in the job but on Thursday

14 April 1881, having worked through seven of that day's fifteen cases at the Islington Coroner's Court, he complained to Walter, who was sitting next to him at the time, that he felt faint. Schröder, not being a medical man, sent Hardwicke to his home in Paddington but, on arrival, he was found to be insensible. A doctor was called but the next morning he died from a rupture of a blood vessel on the brain.

Following this untimely death, Schröder became clerk to Hardwicke's deputy, Dr George Danford Thomas, who succeeded him as coroner. The workload of a coroner increased after the passing of the Coroner's Act of 1887 which stated that inquests were to be held in all cases where there was a reason to suspect that death had arisen by violent or unnatural causes, or where there was a sudden death of an unknown cause, and a reliable deputy coroner was essential to share the workload. Schröder had gained a reputation as a hardworking and competent clerk and, in 1894, at the age of 39, was promoted to deputy coroner for Central Middlesex – the youngest such at that time. After a stint as deputy coroner for South West London and Surrey, he was reunited with Dr Danford Thomas, now the coroner for Central London, becoming his deputy once again in 1899. When Danford Thomas became seriously ill during the summer of 1905, Schröder took on his entire workload for almost a year until Danford Thomas resumed his duties in June 1906.[73] It was Danford Thomas, sitting with Schröder as his deputy, who opened the inquest at the Islington Coroner's Court on Tuesday, 19 July 1910, into the remains of a body found in the cellar of a 'Dr' Hawley Harvey Crippen's house at 39 Hilldrop Crescent, Camden Road.

At this time, Danford Thomas was under considerable pressure from the Public Control

Committee of the London County Council ('L.C.C.') to resign on grounds of ill health. The Lord Chancellor had even been approached to use his powers to force his removal.[74] It was believed in some quarters that the reason for this pressure was not so much because Danford Thomas was ill (although he was - and somewhat deaf to boot) but because there was resentment that he had come into office before the L.C.C. had been created, meaning that he was outside its jurisdiction and control.[75] The Lord Chancellor supported the coroner and refused the L.C.C.'s application but Dr Danford Thomas nevertheless felt the need to continue working even in poor health, partly to prove his critics in the L.C.C. wrong but also because he was not entitled to a pension, so a nice comfortable retirement was not an option. By July he had already conducted over six hundred inquests during the year and was feeling under great strain. During the first day's proceedings of the Crippen inquest, it was obvious to everyone in the courtroom that he was not well and, when the inquiry was adjourned for a month until Monday, 15 August, he mentioned his intention to take a short holiday by the sea. It was a rather shorter holiday than he planned for he died of an attack of diabetic coma on Friday, 5 August, at his sister's house in St Leonards-on-Sea at the age of 63.

After Dr Danford Thomas' death, Walter Schröder automatically became acting coroner on a temporary basis. His first major task was to re-start the Crippen inquest which was moved to the lecture hall of the Central Library in Holloway Road: the coroner's court in Islington being too small for the number of journalists and other interested parties who wished to attend.

It was a difficult inquest to manage, not helped

by the fact that Schröder was suffering from some slight throat trouble. The poor acoustics in the large hall of the library made it difficult to hear what was being said and evidence by one witness that Mrs Crippen had asked for 'a priest' a few weeks before her disappearance, was heard by many in the hall, including counsel for the prosecution and the foreman of the jury, to be that she had asked for 'the police', putting a rather different complexion on the matter. The public gallery was also rowdy. When the mortuary keeper, who had wrapped up glass jars containing the remains of the body found at Hilldrop Crescent in pieces of white paper (potentially required by Crippen's legal team to test for arsenic which might have contaminated the samples), said that he had used the remainder of the paper from which the pieces were torn to wrap up his children's lunch, Schröder was forced to threaten to have people removed by the police for laughing.[76] At one point, a member of the jury started arguing with Crippen's barrister and Schröder again had to intervene to put a stop to it. However, he managed the inquest firmly and decisively, even rejecting a personal plea by Chief Inspector Dew, who had been publicly criticised for having let Crippen flee, to be allowed to explain how this had happened. An unmoved Schröder refused the Chief Inspector permission to defend himself, explaining quite rightly that, to do so, would open up: 'a wide discussion that is outside the scope of the inquiry'. Schröder's jury found that the remains were those of Mrs Crippen and produced a verdict of wilful murder against her husband. When Crippen was hanged it was none other than Schröder who conducted the inquest into his death.[77] Once again, he was firm when the jury foreman enquired if Crippen had confessed before his execution, telling him it was not a question concerning the inquest.

After the inquest into the death of Mrs Crippen, the issue of who would permanently succeed Dr Danford Thomas as the Central London coroner needed to be resolved. It was by no means a foregone conclusion that Schröder would be selected. There were nine candidates on the shortlist for the much desired job, most of whom were experienced barristers or medical men. At the time, there was a prevailing view that all newly appointed coroners should have either a legal or medical qualification – a Bill was actually before Parliament to that effect – but Schröder had no professional qualifications at all. Furthermore, the advertisement for the role of coroner of Central London stated that it was desirable that candidates should not be over fifty years of age, yet Schröder was now fifty-five. The other eight candidates on the shortlist, one of whom included Francis Danford Thomas, son of the late coroner, were all under fifty. What Schröder did have, though, was thirty-nine uninterrupted years experience in coroners' work and had personally conducted 9,000 inquests, assisted at 20,000 others and considered 60,000 deaths reported for preliminary investigation. Since the turn of the decade he had been the Honorary Secretary for the Coroners' Society of England and Wales and, as such, had advised many coroners and been consulted by the government on important legislation affecting coroners. Furthermore, he was greatly respected by members of the medical profession, one of whom described him as a man of 'sound judgment, wide sympathies and high ability'.[78] He was also well liked by his fellow coroners. The coroner for Birmingham, when providing a reference for Schröder, described him as 'singularly well-informed, ready and capable on all occasions' while the coroner for Portsmouth said he was 'shrewd, diplomatic and discriminating'. For all these reasons, Schröder was regarded as a unique case and, despite his age and lack of qualifications, was appointed coroner for the Central District of London on 1 November 1910 with a salary of £1,250 per annum.[79]

Four years later, now well established in his role as coroner, Schröder was again involved in one of the biggest murder cases of the decade – although he did not know it at the time – when, virtually unreported, on 22 December 1914, he conducted the inquest into the demise of Margaret Elizabeth Lofty who had been found dead in her bath a few days after marrying a 'John Lloyd', the wedding ironically having taken place in Bath. His inquiry into the death of the newly crowned Mrs Lloyd (who was living within his jurisdiction, in Highgate, at the time of her fatal bath) produced a verdict of accidental death on 1 January 1915, but 'John Lloyd' turned out to be a man called George Joseph Smith whose wives had a habit of dying in the bath shortly after he purchased some form of life insurance for them or was named as beneficiary in their will.[80] Smith was arrested and charged with murder, meaning that Schröder suffered the minor indignity of being called as a witness during proceedings at Bow Street Police Court on 1 April 1915 to explain why, in effect, his inquest's verdict of accidental death could not be relied upon by Smith as a defence to the charge of murder (although in the event Smith was never tried for Lofty's death: the prosecution preferring to proceed with the death of another of his wives). Even worse, following Smith's conviction, a question was raised in Parliament by the Liberal MP for Leigh, Peter Wilson Raffan, who pointedly asked the Home Secretary to state the legal and medical qualifications of the coroners who held the inquests into the women Smith was said to have murdered.[81] Sensibly, considering that all the qualified doctors who gave evidence at the inquests had thought the deaths to have been accidental, the Home Secretary dismissed his question, claiming he could not answer while there was a pending appeal on behalf of the condemned man.

On Thursday 25 March 1915 (a few days before his appearance at Bow Street in the Brides in the Bath case), Walter Schröder opened the inquest into the death of Annie Josephine Mary Wootten in the small Islington Coroner's Court, off the Holloway Road, hidden in the tree-lined Chapel of Ease gardens of the St Mary Magdalene Church. During most of the nineteenth century, inquests in Islington had been held at various disparate and unsuitable locations, mainly local inns and taverns, but this changed in 1874 with the construction of a dedicated, purpose built, Coroner's Court with adjoining mortuary, the first of its kind in London. Almost from the start, there were grumbles about the building in the local press with the *Islington Gazette* of 27 April 1877 complaining that, 'it is evident that the court room is too small. Constant complaints reach us of the crowded state of the room: and the consequent disadvantages of bad air and insufficient ventilation.'[82] To remedy this situation, a new, bigger, courtroom was built in 1878 at the same location and the old courtroom was converted into a waiting room. A 1914 report on behalf of Islington County Council, noted that the courtroom was now 'nicely fitted, and is illuminated with electric light and gas. It is heated by a gas fire. The walls are clear and the room looks comfortable and sufficient for the district.'[83] It was also said to be 'of good size' but, at only 30 feet by 24 feet, there was not much space for the public at major hearings, hence the transfer of the Crippen inquest to the Central Library.

When the inquest into the death of Mrs Wootten

began, Marie had not yet been arrested and the fact that Mrs Wootten had been shot was not public knowledge; even Lieutenant Wootten was not aware of it. Schröder made a tight lipped statement at the opening of proceedings saying that Mrs Wootten, 'was stated to have died from injuries by falling downstairs but from further information that has come to me, a suspicion has arisen that death was due to another cause'. He said that he intended to take only sufficient evidence to enable him to adjourn the inquest to allow full enquiries to be made.

Lieutenant Wootten appeared briefly in order to state that the last time he had seen his wife alive was on Sunday and, when he left her at 11:30pm, she was very well and laughing but he had not spoken to her since. It had been his intention to visit her on Wednesday night, after Mess, but late on Tuesday his Major told him that his wife had met with an accident and he went straight home where he was given to understand that she had fallen down the stairs. He mentioned the telegram addressed to 'Dickson' and his attempts to find out more about it but there was no mention by him at this stage of Marie. He told Schröder that his wife had been 30 years old, of sober and temperate habits and that her only friends, as far as he knew, were his friends. Lily Dixon appeared next and stated that she had left her sister at four o'clock on Tuesday afternoon at which time she was quite well. When she returned home at half-past eight, her sister was lying dead in the hall. Cora Higson then told of how she had seen Annie's body at the top of the stairs at about ten minutes to eight, after little Lily had opened the front door to her. P.C. Wood told the coroner that he had been called to the house at five minutes past eight on Tuesday night and, finally, Dr Madden informed Schröder that Mrs Wootten had been dead about half an hour before his arrival soon after eight and there was nothing to indicate the cause of death.

Schröder then adjourned the inquest and Inspector Davis went off with Wesley to arrest Marie in Pimlico. So far, there had been no clue revealed to the public about what had really killed Mrs Wootten but the intrigued journalists reporting the inquest soon found out through their police contacts. The *Islington Daily Gazette* reported the next morning: 'From information which has come to hand since the inquest was adjourned, we are in a position to state that the body of the woman bears wounds which clearly indicate that she has been shot. The police are anxious to find the revolver or pistol which has probably been used. How or by whom the injuries were inflicted is a mystery: but our information is that the bullet wounds are in the chest'. The information was not quite correct, there was only one bullet wound, but the paper was quick to inform its readers that the affair was being investigated by the Criminal Investigation Department under the direction of Detective Inspector Davis and that, 'no time is being lost in seeking to elucidate the problem of the woman's death'. This might provide a clue as to the source of their story. Davis certainly had good contacts with the press through his wife's family; his brother-in-law, Herbert Henry Bassett was the city editor of *The Globe*.

Most of the national daily papers had by this time discovered that a bullet wound had been located in the chest, just below the heart, and that the police had arrested a barmaid going by the name of Marie Lanteri. It was the *Daily Chronicle*, however, which had the scoop of the day, reporting that 'Mrs Lanteri', as it called her, described as 'the widow of a chauffeur of Italian nationality', had been engaged as a barmaid at 'a well known inn at Shoreham' when she had made the acquaintance of Lieutenant Wootten. In addition, the *Daily Chronicle* reporter revealed the exclusive news that Mrs Lanteri had visited Wootten and his wife at Rotherfield Street. The paper also made an appeal on behalf of the police for anyone who had found a revolver in the district within the last few days 'or who can throw any light on the matter', to communicate with Divisional Detective Inspector Davis at Stoke Newington or Islington police stations.

Marie spent the night of Thursday 25 March in a cell at Islington Police Station where she was put under the charge of Lily Nevill, the Matron. During the night, Marie confided to her: 'I met Mr Wootten and we lived together. I didn't know he was a married man until he brought me to London to marry me when he told me he could not marry me as he was already married with four children. I was greatly upset over that and went back to my mother in Sussex and stayed there until last Friday when I came back to London'. She also stated with confidence: 'I am perfectly innocent and can prove where I was on March twenty third'.

The next day, Marie was brought to the North London Police Court in Stoke Newington. This venue had been known as the Dalston Police Court until 1890 when, in a somewhat delayed response to a remark made in the previous year by the then presiding magistrate, Haden Corser, that the name of the court was inappropriate because its business covered the whole of the north-eastern district and nearly all of the northern suburbs of London, the Home Secretary agreed to the obvious name change.[84] Now, on Friday, 26 March 1915, when Marie was brought to the court from Islington Police Station the magistrate was a straight speaking, no-nonsense, Glaswegian printer's son called Thomas Charles Hunter Hedderwick.

Hedderwick had made his mark in his very first week as magistrate of the North London Police Court five years earlier when he discharged a man who appeared before him who had severely beaten up his young daughter's boyfriend. After establishing that the 'victim', George William Downes, was a married man with two children who had not mentioned the existence of his wife to his mistress and that this was the cause of the violence against him, Hedderwick told Downes that he had behaved like a blackguard and that 'the girl's father gave you a thrashing and that is what you richly deserved,' adding to the audible approval of the public gallery, 'I cannot send a man to gaol for an offence of this description'.[85] With Marie's appearance in his court, Hedderwick was to deal again with the case of a married man with children engaged in an illicit relationship with a young single woman, although, unfortunately, it was not appropriate for him to express an opinion on the matter in this instance.

No doubt it made a welcome change for the magistrate to be dealing with a case exciting the interest of the national and local press; the headline to the story in that morning's *Daily Express* was 'MYSTERY OF AN OFFICER'S WIFE' while the *Islington Daily Gazette* called it the 'ESSEX ROAD MYSTERY'. Although a murder in North London was by no means a rarity, it was usually of the most straightforward kind and a normal day for Hedderwick involved ruling, in a cold, empty, court, on issues of petty crime, drunkenness, local disputes or trivial breaches of some regulation or another. During the war years, the police court was also troubled on a daily basis by soldiers who had gone absent without leave or simply deserted. Such matters were not of great interest and attracted little attention. Today, however, Hedderwick's court was

Thomas Charles Hunter Hedderwick, magistrate

packed, as journalists, photographers and onlookers waited to catch a glimpse of the barmaid with the exotic name who was accused of shooting an army officer's wife. Hedderwick had missed out on two famous local murderers, Crippen and George Smith - both dealt with at Bow Street Police Court after they were arrested outside his jurisdiction - but he had committed Frederick Seddon and his wife to trial at the Old Bailey for poisoning their female lodger (Mrs Seddon eventually being acquitted). More recently, he had committed to trial a man called Frederick Albert Robertson, charged with murdering his three children – subsequently found guilty and executed – and while this had not been a huge, nationally famous, crime it had excited local attention and brought crowds and journalists flocking into the police court.

So Hedderwick had some experience of dealing with cases in the glare of the media and plenty of experience in a court room, having been called to the bar in 1876. Twenty years later, having married the daughter of a wealthy brewer to become a large landed proprietor with an independent income, he was elected the Liberal Member of Parliament for Wick Burghs in his homeland of Scotland although he lost his seat in the 1900 election and was defeated again as Liberal candidate for Berkshire in January 1910. The latter blow was quickly softened when he was appointed police magistrate for North London on 4 February 1910, having been deputy chairman of the County of London Sessions for the previous few years, but beneath the surface of respectability he lived a secret life which was only revealed by his death in February 1918. Then, at the age of 67, he suddenly collapsed in a flat at 84 College Court Mansions, Hammersmith, where he had spent the evening with a widow called Annie Carter, much to the surprise of his wife who

thought he was at the Reform Club in Pall Mall.[86]
According to Mrs Carter, who said she had known
the magistrate for about two years, Hedderwick had
arrived at her door shortly after 8:30pm out of breath,
having run up three flights of stairs because he was
late for their appointment (arranged when she met him
a week earlier) and then complained of indigestion.
She suggested he should rest in her bed and left him
there overnight but, early the next morning, she heard
a thud and found him lying on the floor insensible.[87]
After his death at a nursing home the next day – a post-
mortem conducted by Dr Spilsbury at the insistence of
Hedderwick's wife having concluded his demise had
been caused by a cerebral haemorrhage - the lady was
asked by the police what the magistrate had actually
been doing there: her explanation being that he had
come to her flat to discuss a potential film of one of
Henry Wadsworth Longfellow's poems which he had
told her he wished to produce in America under a false
name and in which she was to appear. It was a curious
end to a distinguished career.

In 1915, however, Mr Hedderwick, regardless of
what he did outside of working hours, was very much
alive and in good health while the evidence of Marie's
arrest was heard for the first time in his well run
courtroom. He was a stickler for starting hearings at
the precise time listed and, unlike many courtrooms,
where members of the public could wander in and out
indiscriminately, often disturbing the proceedings,
Hedderwick ensured that the door to the court was
bolted and guarded by a police officer. Members of the
public who wanted to attend had to stand in a narrow
strip behind a barrier at the back of the court and there
was no seating available for them, thus discouraging
frivolous attendance, at least in theory because it did
not deter about a hundred members of the public (the

Marie in the dock of the North London Police Court
on 26 March 1915

maximum that could fit into the public area) from cramming into the small courtroom to see Marie. The North London Police Court was situated opposite the Alexandra Theatre in Stoke Newington Road but it was the legal drama played out in front of Mr Hedderwick that the crowds flocked to see that day.

Detective Inspector Davis, making his first public appearance in the case, revealed what Marie had said to him after he arrested her but was in for a shock when Hedderwick asked if the prisoner had been cautioned. Davis admitted he had not issued a caution and received a stern slap on the wrist from the magistrate who told him that it was customary in murder cases to caution prisoners. The inspector was to find this sharp exchange reported in almost every newspaper the following day.

At the conclusion of the short hearing, for which Wootten himself was not present, despite being in the court building, Hedderwick asked Marie – now known to the world by her correct full name of Alice Mary Wheatley – if she had any questions but she replied politely, 'No sir, nothing at all,' and was remanded in custody until 3 April. At the back of the courtroom, however, she did have something to say to Detective Sergeant Wesley – probably in response to the report in that morning's *Daily Chronicle* that she had visited Wootten and his wife at Rotherfield Street – offering him the information (which he immediately wrote down into his notebook) that: 'I have only been to Wootten's house twice, once when I saw Mrs Wootten and once when I saw Mrs Dixon,' at least that is what Wesley heard but she probably said, or at least intended to say, 'Mrs Higson' instead of 'Mrs Dixon'. Marie was then taken from the court to Holloway prison.

Meanwhile, the *News of the World* was making enquires and discovered that the police, having searched all the gardens in the vicinity of Rotherfield Street, had been unable to locate the weapon that had killed Mrs Wootten (Marie's revolver was not in her attaché case when Detective Inspector Davis had examined it) and believed it had been thrown in the Regent's Canal, although the basis of this belief seems merely to have been that the canal was near the scene of the crime. It was also reported that the bullet taken from the dead body had come from a 7mm pinfire cartridge and the police were making enquiries of ammunition stores and shooting saloons to ascertain whether any such cartridges had been sold recently.

Other newspapers were also dramatically building up the story. The front page of the *Daily Mirror* on Saturday 27 March carried the headline 'LONDON MURDER MYSTERY' with a photograph of Marie surreptitiously taken while she stood in the dock of the police court.[88] The next day's *People* headlined the story 'MYSTERY OF THE DEATH OF AN OFFICER'S WIFE' and the *Observer* called it 'THE ISLINGTON TRAGEDY'. It was the *Islington Daily Gazette* of Monday 29 March, however, that was to run with the headline 'THE ISLINGTON MURDER MYSTERY' thus creating a satisfactory name of the crime for posterity.

On Wednesday 31 March, Violet Thorn, the maid from 36 Eccelsbourne Road, was brought by police to Holloway prison where she identified Marie in a line-up of about eight women.[89] The police had now established a link between Marie and a pinfire revolver. When Marie was told the reason she had been placed in the line-up, i.e. because it was alleged that she was the woman who took a furnished room near 114 Rotherfield Street carrying an attaché case which contained an old rusty revolver and some cartridges, she replied: 'Thank you.'

Lieutenant Albert Wootten, outside the North London Police
Court, 26 March 1915

CHAPTER 7

COUNTDOWN TO TRIAL – PART 1

Inspector Gregory: 'Is there any other point to which you would wish to draw my attention?'
Sherlock Holmes: 'To the curious incident of the dog in the night-time.'
Inspector Gregory: 'The dog did nothing in the night-time.'
Sherlock Holmes: 'That was the curious incident.'

Silver Blaze by Arthur Conan Doyle, 1892

Thursday 1 April

As the police had now virtually completed their inquiries, the inquest was ready to resume before Walter Schröder and his jury. If it was decided at the inquiry that they were dealing with a case of murder, a coroner's jury had the power to identify the person or persons who they believed had committed the murder and commit them for trial at the Central Criminal Court. A magistrate in a police court had an identical power. In effect, although there were different, less rigid, rules of evidence in a coroner's court, almost the exact same procedure of one court would be duplicated by the other and Marie could, therefore, expect to face two mini-trials before her actual trial began, should she be committed. This type of situation had been criticised by *The Law Journal* during the highly publicised Crippen proceedings back in 1910 when it was stated: 'We doubt whether the double enquiry is necessary or desirable in the interests of justice' but no reform had yet been instituted.

Marie was brought back to the Islington Coroner's Court from the nearby Holloway prison in the charge of two wardresses. The papers tell us she was wearing a navy blue costume, a black hat trimmed with feathers and black furs. More importantly she now had legal

representation. She had appointed Messrs Ellis
Strange & Co as her solicitors, a firm founded in 1913
by Ellis Strange, a dubious character who evidently
liked to tell people he had been born in India - for he
recorded this on his 1911 census return - but was, in
fact, born in less exotic surroundings, in Camberwell,
south London, in 1860. Having been brought up by his
uncle and aunt in Devon he qualified as a solicitor late
in life at the age of 35, practising initially in the South
West of England, specifically in Exeter and Pinhoe,
Devon, and he established his own firm, Ellis Strange
& Co, with an office in Chancery Lane, eighteen
years later. It wasn't long, however, before he was in
trouble with the Law Society, albeit not before Marie's
arrest. In July 1916, he was suspended for two years
after the High Court ruled that he had attempted to
fraudulently misappropriate money which belonged to
his client.

It was not, however, Ellis Strange who was directly
representing Marie because he was happy to leave
this task to his managing clerk, Frederick David
Lewis - born Frederick David Levy - the son of a
notorious fraudster, Edward Lawrence Levy, a former
solicitor, debt collector and money lender who had
changed the family surname to Lewis following his
conviction at the Old Bailey of 'conspiracy to prevent
the due course of law by suborning persons to commit
perjury' in 1882, having already been struck off the
solicitors' roll by the Law Society after an earlier
conviction for forgery.[90] Once he could not practice
as a solicitor himself, he acted as a managing clerk
to existing solicitors' firms, Fisher & Co in Leicester
Square and then Micklethwaite & Co in Long Acre,
under an arrangement by which he would receive
twenty percent of the firm's profits. He tended to use
the existing partner of such firms as his puppet, in

effect controlling all the business. He was behind a number of subsequent scams and swindles and was convicted again, and sentenced to five years hard labour, for dealing in stolen goods in May 1892, dying in Wormwood Scrubs five months later at which point Frederick inherited his assets of £275.

Although Strange claimed to be paying him a salary, with a 'present' awarded if he brought in a good case, it may be that Lewis, who was also running his own business as a 'financier' out of 93 & 94 Chancery Lane, was operating a similar arrangement with Ellis Strange & Co to the one his father had operated with Fishers and Micklethwaites because he clearly had conduct of cases at the law firm. In 1914 he found himself in trouble for allegedly holding himself out as a solicitor when he was not qualified as one. This came about as the result of a highly unusual law suit commenced by a professional singer, Eileen Boyd, and her mother, Margaret - both of whom lived in Belsize Park, Hampstead - against a Mr Cunliffe, for whom Eileen sang privately in Brighton. Cunliffe had played a bizarre practical joke on them. For some reason, best known to himself, he thought it would be amusing to send a message to Eileen that her mother had been killed at London Bridge and another message to the mother that her daughter had died in a railway accident, causing both women to faint when they met each other at the railway station in Brighton as they were rushing to get to the scene of the respective bogus deaths.[91] Frederick Lewis, with whom the women were friendly, and who they believed was a solicitor, proceeded to sue the joker on their behalf for damages, winning a settlement of £75 which was paid by cheque directly to Lewis who transferred it to Ellis Strange. However, before paying out any money to the Boyds, Ellis Strange & Co put in a bill for over £44, which was deducted from the settlement money, but the Boyds claimed they had never even heard of Mr Strange, let alone instructed his firm to act on their behalf. They always believed that Lewis alone was acting for them in the litigation. The Boyds sued Ellis Strange & Co for the payment of all their settlement money and the matter reached the High Court in June 1914. It was heard by Mr Justice Scrutton, but was settled outside of the court before judgment, on the basis that the Boyds received the full £75 without having to pay any fees or costs to Ellis Strange in return for them withdrawing the allegation that Lewis had falsely represented himself as a solicitor. It was a narrow escape. When told of the settlement, Mr Justice Scrutton remarked ominously in court: 'The parties having agreed among themselves, I have no remarks to make, otherwise I would have had a good many' and it is a shame he felt unable to comment because his views would no doubt have been entertaining. Frederick Lewis did not seem to learn the lesson from the court case and, from March to June 1915, he represented himself as Marie's solicitor and was reported as such in the press. Marie even referred to him as 'my solicitor' when the proceedings were over.

To speak for Marie at the coroner's court, and in all future hearings, Frederick Lewis had instructed John Lhind Pratt from chambers in Dr. Johnson's Building in the Temple. It would turn out to be an inspired choice, albeit an unexpected one. Pratt was only 29 years old and had been practicing as a barrister for less than six years, having been called to the Bar in November 1909. He chiefly operated in the Western Circuit - covering Devon, Exeter, Plymouth and Bristol, the area where Ellis Strange used to practice (which is probably how he came to be known to Lewis) - and was virtually unknown at the Central Criminal Court, having only appeared (as junior counsel) in one case of any note: defending Jacob Peters for murder in relation to the Sydney Street siege of 1911. He had, however, been a brilliant law student. In 1907 he won a £50 prize at the Inns of Court for the best examination in evidence, procedure and criminal law and passed his final examination with a Certificate of Honour, earning a studentship of fifty guineas a year. A contemporary report in 1915 described him as having a 'well-knit athletic frame, prominent forehead, and youthful clean features which make him look a good deal younger than his age'.[92]

Mr Pratt's first contribution to the inquest was a rather curious one, at least according to newspaper reports, informing the coroner that Lieutenant Wootten, who was in an adjoining waiting room, preferred not to be in court to hear the evidence. Why it fell to Mr Pratt to deliver this message is not entirely clear although, as he was the only barrister in the courtroom, he might have regarded it as his duty to pass on the information. It may be that the newspapers got it wrong and Mr Pratt was actually telling the coroner that it was desirable, from his client's perspective, that Wootten was not in court to hear the evidence. If, on the contrary, the papers were right then Mr Pratt must have got his wires crossed somewhere along the line. Certainly, Lieutenant Wootten was annoyed by the misrepresentation. He wrote to the *Daily Call* newspaper to make clear that, far from preferring not to be in court, he was waiting anxiously outside the courtroom expecting that he was going to be called in at any minute.[93]

The issue of Lieutenant Wootten's presence or otherwise at the inquest was a relatively minor one. Mr Pratt's major tactical decision was whether to exercise his right to cross-examine the witnesses who testified before the coroner or keep his powder dry until trial. If he used his best cross-examination questions at the inquest he would lose the element of surprise for when it was really important, during any future trial. On the other hand, if he could persuade the coroner's jury that Marie was innocent, the case might never get to trial. In truth, while Mr Pratt would have taken heart in the fact that there was no eye-witness evidence and Marie had admitted nothing to anyone, the chances of the case not being sent to the Old Bailey were slim. There were, however, other reasons in favour of early cross-examination: it would allow an exploration of the weaknesses in the case against Marie and, perhaps most importantly, would force the witnesses to commit to a particular version of events. If they later told a slightly different version, or added something they forgot to mention to the coroner, this could be used to suggest their evidence was mistaken or even untruthful. Having considered the matter, Mr Pratt made the decision to cross-examine the witnesses during the inquest.

While Marie sat listening intently, only speaking occasionally to ask for a glass of water or consult with her legal representatives, the first witness of the day was Annie's sister, recalled by Mr Pratt for questioning. In response to a few initial questions from Mr Schröder, she said her sister had no enemies, lived happily with her husband and her general health was good. In cross-examination, Mr Pratt attempted to paint a picture of marital discord within the Wootten household but got nowhere. Mrs Dixon denied that Wootten's relations with other women had caused her sister unhappiness, saying she knew nothing whatever about that. It was a fruitless line of questioning but Mr Pratt was not yet aware that Annie had deliberately hidden the truth about her husband's affair with Marie from her sister. He then fished around to see whether Lieutenant Wootten possessed any firearms – if he did then perhaps he was the murderer – but Mrs Dixon told him she had never seen any in the house. Mr Pratt did, however, score one victory in his cross-examination. On the basis that her father's house in Exmouth Street was about a fifteen minute ride from Rotherfield Street, Annie's sister agreed that, had she received the 'Dickson' telegram at home at 6:30pm, she could have gone to her father's house in Exmouth Street to check he was okay and returned to Rotherfield Street by 7.00pm. It was a good point for the defence. The prosecution at any trial would presumably want to say that the purpose of the telegram was to get Mrs Dixon out of the house so that the killer would find Annie on her own. But if the murder took place some time after 7:30pm, that would have allowed Mrs Dixon plenty of time to visit her father, check he was well and get back to Rotherfield Street while Annie was still alive, undermining – but by no means disproving – the notion that the telegram was from the murderer.

A number of police witnesses followed Mrs Dixon into the witness box and the coroner became nervous when P.C. Reeves testified that Lieutenant Wootten had told him during the evening of 24 March that he had been to Shepherd's Bush to see 'a woman' about the mysterious telegram. Schröder suggested that Wootten should be in court for this evidence since he might want to deny having told Reeves anything of the sort. It was not a particularly good suggestion and Mr Pratt, showing off his superior knowledge of legal procedure, quickly put Schröder right: 'Lieutenant Wootten is not a party to the case.' he told him, 'and there is no reason why he should be in court'. However, he undertook to put the point to him when he was called, although in the event it was not controversial and there was no dispute about it. Having resolved this issue, Mr Pratt was eager to get on with his cross-examination. He had a little trick up his sleeve, asking Reeves if Wootten had said anything to him on 24 March 'about the shooting'. It was a nice try – if Wootten had mentioned a shooting the day after the murder, before the post-mortem had been conducted, he must have been the murderer – but, disappointingly for Mr Pratt, Reeves replied: 'Not at all; there was no idea then of a shooting'.

The final witnesses of the day were the medical men and there was great interest in the courtroom as Dr Spilsbury stepped into the witness box to deliver his evidence. However, this was not to be one of those cases for which Spilsbury was renowned, turning on a complicated or obscure issue of forensic pathology. The evidence that Mrs Wootten had been killed by a single bullet was clear and unambiguous. His examination of the clothing led him to believe that some scorching on it was caused by the discharge of a firearm, fired less than a foot away from Mrs Wootten's left shoulder and probably a few inches from it. He thought the weapon used had been a revolver and death would have followed inside three minutes but it would have been possible for Mrs Wootten to have cried out or spoken a word. Mr Pratt attempted a strange line of cross-examination, asking him if the injury could have been self-inflicted. Spilsbury was unable to rule out such a possibility but stated that he was of the opinion that it was not suicide. He explained that, if it had been self inflicted, the weapon must have been held in the left hand (evidence was later adduced that Mrs Wootten was right handed). This was all he could say from a medical perspective but it was a futile line of cross-examination bearing in mind that no weapon had been found with, or near, the body.

Overall, it had not been a particularly good day for Mr Pratt and he would have plenty of time to reflect on his performance because the next day was Good Friday and Schröder adjourned the inquest to Monday. Before that, however, he and Marie were back for a brief appearance at the North London Police Court.

Saturday 3 April

The courts did not close on Saturdays in 1915, even over the Easter holiday weekend, and Mr Pratt had his first hearing before Mr Hedderwick in the morning. The only issue of the day regarding Marie's case was when the coroner's inquest would finish so that the committal proceedings could begin. Nevertheless, the public gallery was crowded with 'a large number of fashionably dressed women' according to the *Islington Daily Gazette*. Lieutenant Wootten was also in court. Marie herself was again dressed in black and said to be looking very pale but composed. As to the timing of the coroner's inquest, Inspector Davis thought it would be completed by the end of the week but Mr Pratt did not think this possible and, after some discussion, Hedderwick decided that the case against Marie would be opened on Tuesday 13 April. She was remanded in custody until the following Saturday. Mr Pratt asked for permission for Marie's father to visit her in prison which was granted by the magistrate.

Monday 5 April

The drama of the inquest really began at the resumed hearing on Easter Monday when little Lily, described by the *Daily Express* as 'a pretty fair-haired child', told her story for the first time.[94] In a hushed room she spoke of the woman she heard at the door and of her mother saying it was 'Mrs Higson's friend'.[95] She told of the subsequent two loud bangs and her mother calling out her name. She was asked a number of questions by the coroner and impressed everyone in the courtroom by answering him clearly and intelligently. Perhaps the most important question was what kind of voice she had heard at the door that evening. She said it was a 'nice voice'. Pushed to say whether it was a deep voice or a soft voice, she said 'soft voice'. Replying to Mr Pratt, who was particularly interested in fixing the time of death, wanting to make it as late as possible, Lily said she always went to bed at 6.30pm and her mother was talking for nearly an hour with the woman at the door. She also confirmed that she had told her father the story about the visitor later that night. An alert member of the jury asked if she had heard a knock at the front door after her mother had left the bedroom but Lily said she had heard nothing at all. Asked further questions by the coroner she said that her bedroom window looked into the street across the garden and one could see the path that leads from the street to the steps up to the door but her mother looked out of the window at the side furthest from the path.

Her young age only really showed in two of her answers. At one point she said that she heard her mother shut the front door after the two bangs. 'How did you know it was mother?' asked the coroner. 'Because when the person went, mother was all right' replied Lily. 'How do you know?' followed up the coroner. 'Because after she had shut the door she called me,' (by which she meant the cry of 'Lily, Lily'). It was an understandable assumption for a little girl who, at the time, had absolutely no idea her mother had been shot, but it seems more likely that it was the murderer who closed the door. Her other slip came when she told Mr Pratt that Mrs Higson knocked at the door about three quarters of an hour after the two bangs; it could only have been a matter of minutes.

Ivy followed her sister and, when asked by the

coroner if she knew what an oath meant, showed
remarkable composure for a seven-year-old by telling
the coroner: 'It means to tell the truth. I read the Bible
and am taught that it is wrong to say anything that
is not true. I am taught at Sunday School that it is
wrong to tell a lie.' But she was so small she needed
a footstall in order for her head to be visible over the
rail of the witness box. When she was finally in a
position to speak, she told essentially the same story
as Lily although she remembered more of what the
visitor had said than her sister, such as her asking for
money. She also thought that the woman had said she
was 'thin and hungry' after having received the glass
of water whereas Lily had said it was before. But most
importantly, like Lily, she remembered her mother
saying it was 'Mrs Higson's friend' at the door.

Once Ivy had stepped down from her footstall, it
was Cora Higson's turn to explain who her 'friend'
was. 'I have no friend in London except one,' she
said. 'Who is that?' asked the coroner. The courtroom
was silent. 'Marie Wheatley,' replied Mrs Higson. It
was a dramatic moment. Everyone looked at Marie
but there was no reaction from her at all. During his
cross-examination, Mr Pratt asked: 'Is Marie Wheatley
your friend?' to which Mrs Higson confused just about
everyone in the courtroom by replying: 'No, not at
all.' Mr Pratt resolved the contradiction by eliciting
from Mrs Higson the explanation that calling Marie
'Mrs Higson's friend' was for Mrs Wootten's sake
because Annie did not want her family to know who
Marie was. By way of explanation as to why this was
necessary she said: 'Because Mr Wootten had been
carrying on with her I suppose.' This was the first
public mention of an affair between Marie and the
married officer although it was undoubtedly what
everyone had suspected.

Mrs Higson also told of her sighting of the veiled lady outside 114 Rotherfield Street five nights before the murder. Mr Pratt asked why she did not speak to her. 'Because I was not sure it was her,' came Mrs Higson's reply. That was a good answer from his client's point of view but Mr Pratt, perhaps showing his inexperience, asked one question too many on the subject, prompting Mrs Higson to elaborate by saying: 'I did not want to speak to her,' which was not quite as helpful. Furthermore, when asked how she could be sure the woman who knocked at the door was Miss Wheatley, Mrs Higson replied: 'I think I should have known whether it was Marie as she has rather a peculiar voice.' Unfortunately she did not elaborate on this so we do not know in which way Marie's voice was believed by her to be so peculiar.

Thursday 8 April

Anyone in the small coroner's court who had been left unmoved by the sight of the two little girls recalling the death of their mother in Rotherfield Street must have been a hard hearted person indeed and perhaps Marie herself was affected for when the hearing resumed on Thursday morning she was not there. 'I notice that Alice Mary Wheatley is not present,' said Mr Schröder immediately after taking his seat in the courtroom. 'As she had not arrived five minutes ago, my officer telephoned to the prison. He was informed she did not intend coming here today'. Mr Pratt then told the coroner that Marie was unwell, although why that message had not been conveyed to the coroner's officer by Marie via the prison governor is unclear. In any event, Mr Pratt said he did not require an adjournment and the evidence continued in her absence.

James Jordan, the post office sorter who had been asked by Mrs Higson to help on the night of the murder, was the first witness of the day. His most significant contribution was to confirm that he had not seen anyone leaving Rotherfield Street in a hurry when he was walking home that night. However, he had some more information to offer the inquest. As a neighbour of the Woottens – he lived at 108 Rotherfield Street – he knew there was a very noisy dog at No. 114, yet it had not barked during the night of the murder. This caused a buzz of interest in the court. It seemed there might be some kind of Sherlockian mystery attaching itself to the case. Jordan's wife added to the mystery by describing it as a 'wicked' dog and saying that she had heard it bark at No. 114 a day or two before the murder but, like her husband, not on the night of the murder itself. Henry Johnstone, who next gave evidence, confused the issue by saying that 'Mrs Wootten's dog', which he saw in the house on the night of the murder, was 'not a noisy one' although he confessed he was a little hard of hearing, which might have explained the contradiction. Fred Dixon finally appeared to clear the matter of ownership up by revealing that the dog was, in fact, *his* dog. It was a cross between a Fox Terrier and a Pomeranian and, he said, would bark if there was a stranger at the door.

The most important evidence of the day came during Mr Dixon's evidence. Asked by the coroner whether the veiled lady who knocked at the door of No. 114 during the evening of 18 March was wearing a light or a dark veil, Mr Dixon said 'It looked dark.' It was a crucial answer. Although the evidence of the maid at 36 Ecclesbourne Road had yet to been given to the inquest, when Marie left the house on the evening of 18 March she had been seen wearing a white veil and was still wearing it when she returned later than night. So, if the veiled lady at No. 114 had her face covered by a dark veil, it could not have been Marie, or at least that is what Mr Pratt would argue. An obvious answer to the point was that it was a very dark night and there was no street lighting which meant that the white veil looked dark. But obvious answers were not as important as witness testimony and it was the first major piece of good news for Marie.

Saturday 10 April

A resumed hearing at the North London Police Court where Detective Inspector Davis informed Mr Hedderwick that the Director of Public Prosecutions would be prepared to proceed with the case on Tuesday. However, the magistrate quite rightly said that it would be a mistake to have two inquiries running at the same time and the inquest did not look like it would finish by Tuesday. It was suggested that if it had not concluded by Tuesday, only immaterial evidence would be heard by the police court. Marie, who was at the court dressed in a blue costume, was remanded until Tuesday.

Monday 12 April

A dramatic day in the Islington Coroner's Court as Lieutenant Wootten gave evidence and was cross-examined by Mr Pratt. First into the witness box, however, was Joe Higson who told the story of how Marie had turned up at his place of employment and had pleaded to be taken to see Wootten. He told of the arrangement reached between the Woottens and Marie at 114 Rotherfield Street that evening and of how Marie then stayed at his house where she threatened to commit suicide. He also told of his surprise meeting with Marie in the City Road on Sunday 21 March and then the story of the interview with Marie at Richmond Road the day after the murder.

Originally from Chorlton, near Manchester, Higson was a confident and eloquent witness with a remarkable memory for the exact words spoken during every conversation he was involved in. It was, perhaps, *too* good a memory for he became slightly unstuck in his evidence over the issue of what had been said at Richmond Road about the attaché case. He first claimed that Wootten said to Marie: 'You have told me a lie. You said you hadn't your attaché case. You had left it at Tooting,' to which Marie replied: 'Well Bert I had to get some money on it.' He then corrected himself, saying 'I now remember that Lieutenant Wootten said: "When you came up last Friday you said you had not got your attaché case". Miss Wheatley then said: "I had to leave it at Tooting to get some money on it."' Despite this slip, Higson's evidence was quite damning against Marie, especially in relation to the telegram. Higson pointed out that, when shown the telegram, Marie had said she could not have sent it because she did not know that Mr Wootten's sister-in-law was called 'Dixon' (or 'Dickson' as the telegram stated) yet nothing had been said to Marie about the telegram having been sent to Wootten's sister-in-law. It was a dangerous point and, with Higson's questions during the interview with Marie clearly indicating that he believed Marie was guilty of the murder of Mrs Wootten, Mr Pratt was not going to give the witness an easy time. He was particularly focused on Higson's claim that, during the interview at Richmond Road, Marie had said, 'Things look black against me,' to which Higson replied 'yes.' Although it was merely a statement of the obvious by Marie, Mr Pratt did not like the implication that Marie had seemed to be suggesting that she was guilty and he sought to undermine this. His first line of questioning, however, was to draw attention to the important fact that Wootten had not told his friend that Marie was staying at 12 Richmond Road until after his wife's murder:

Pratt: You are friends with Mr Wootten?

Higson: Yes.

Pratt: At the time of the occurrence you were in a close friendship with him?

Higson: Yes.

Pratt: Did he consult you on many occasions for advice?

Higson: Yes.

Pratt: Including the question of his relationship with Miss Wheatley?[96]

Higson: Yes.

Pratt: When did you first know Miss Wheatley was staying at 12 Richmond Road?

Higson: Not until I went there on Wednesday, 24th March.

Pratt: What happened then?

Higson: I asked Lieutenant Wootten if he knew where Marie was and he said he did and I suggested we should go and see her.

Pratt: When did you first see her?

Higson: When she called at my place of business.

Pratt: She knew you were his intimate friend?

Higson: Yes.

Pratt: And you would know where he was?

Higson: Yes.

Pratt: This was after you had drafted the letter you mentioned for Mrs Wootten to write to Miss Wheatley?

Higson: Yes.

Pratt: On February 11th, you all met at 114 Rotherfield Street?

Higson: Yes.

Pratt: You then discussed the relations between Mr and Mrs Wootten and Miss Wheatley?

Higson: Yes.

Pratt: Was it definitely decided that night between

Miss Wheatley and Lieutenant Wootten that they should release each other?

Higson: Yes, it was.

Pratt: What was the reason she came to your house?

Higson: Because she could not get back to Brighton that night.

Pratt: Yet she stayed there more than a week?

Higson: Yes, that was to try and get a situation.

Pratt: While staying at your house, was Miss Wheatley visited by the deceased?

Higson: Yes, once.

Pratt: At whose request was that visit?

Higson: Mine.

Pratt: How many times did Mrs Wootten see Miss Wheatley at your house?

Higson: Twice.

Pratt: What was the other occasion?

Higson: That was on a visit to my wife.

Pratt: Were you present on both occasions?

Higson: I was.

Pratt: On the first occasion what conversation took place between the deceased and Miss Wheatley?

Higson: None.

Pratt: What was the reason for that visit?

Higson: That was on the occasion when Mrs Wootten came to see my wife and myself.

Pratt: There was no conversation at all?

Higson: No, they would not speak to each other.

Pratt: Was it a case of Miss Wheatley not wanting to speak to Mrs Wootten or vice versa?

Higson: I think it was a case of both being of the same mind.

Pratt: And the second occasion?

Higson: There were a few words exchanged in respect to Miss Wheatley being in my house.

Pratt: And the day after that she went to Sussex?

Higson: Yes.

Pratt: What was the purpose of referring to Miss Wheatley as 'Mrs Higson's friend'?

Higson: The thinking was that if Mrs Dixon knew who Miss Wheatley was she would carry the information down to her people.

Pratt: So an arrangement was made that she should be known as 'Miss Higson's friend' and not Miss Wheatley?

Higson: Yes.

Pratt: How was calling Miss Wheatley 'Mrs Higson's friend' going to conceal Lieutenant Wootten's relations with Miss Wheatley?

Higson: I do not know.

Pratt: Was any arrangement made as to giving up letters?

Higson: Yes, on Sunday, February 21st an arrangement was made whereby all the letters Miss Wheatley received from Lieutenant Wootten were to be given up.

Pratt: Did she give them up willingly?

Higson: There was a certain amount of hesitation, but they were given willingly.

Pratt: How did she give them?

Higson: She went to the box and handed them to Lieutenant Wootten.

Pratt: There was no force employed to get the letters?

Higson: Not in my presence.

Pratt: You say you met Miss Wheatley on Sunday 21st March at about 2pm?

Higson: Yes.

Pratt: Have you since learnt that Lieutenant Wootten was staying with her on 21st March?

Higson: No.

Pratt: You had suspicions there had been foul play on 24th March?

Higson: No.

Pratt: Did Mr Wootten suggest there had been foul play?

Higson: No.

Pratt: What was the other business you were going to attend to on 24th March?

Higson: To find Lieutenant Wootten's mother. She was out nursing. And about going to an orphanage.

Pratt: Did you not, in fact, devote the day to amateur detective work?

Higson: No.

Pratt: What were your suspicions when you went to see Miss Wheatley on March 24th?

Higson: We had suspicions that she was connected with the death of Mrs Wootten.

Pratt: What do you mean by 'we'?

Higson: I mean Lieutenant Wootten and myself.

Pratt: What did Mr Wootten tell you?

Higson: He told me that he had spoken to the children and they had told him that a lady had been to the house and asked for a drink of water and food and coppers and that Mrs Wootten had said that the visitor was 'Mrs Higson's friend'. The telegram together with the information Wootten had given to me, led me to the conclusion that we should visit Miss Wheatley.

Pratt: You thought a crime had been committed from what Lieutenant Wootten told you?

Higson: Yes.

Pratt: Did you know of the telegram on the night of the occurrence?

Higson: No, not then.

Pratt: At that time did you have any idea of any shooting?

Higson: No.

Pratt: And the two bangs did not arouse any suspicion?

Higson: No.

Pratt: So from that information you decided a crime had been committed and suspected Miss Wheatley had committed the crime?

Higson: Yes.

Pratt: When did you first know of the telegram?

Higson: In the afternoon of that day when I went to 114 Rotherfield Street.

Pratt: You considered a crime had been committed after seeing the telegram and hearing what the children had said?

Higson: Yes.

Pratt: You concluded the case looked very black against Miss Wheatley?

Higson: I concluded this after she suggested it.

Pratt: I put it to you that you suggested it.

Higson: No, she suggested it and I agreed.

Pratt: What were your thoughts at the time?

Higson: I cannot say.

Pratt: You said it looked black against Miss Wheatley?

Higson: I did not say that.

Pratt: Miss Wheatley knew there was a sister-in-law of Lieutenant Wootten's living in 114 Rotherfield Street?

Higson: Yes.

Pratt: And you had just shown her the telegram addressed to 'Dickson'?

Higson: Yes.

Pratt: It did not take much for Miss Wheatley to conclude the sister-in-law's name was Dixon?

Higson: I suppose not.

Pratt: Was Miss Wheatley surprised to hear of the death of Mrs Wootten?

Higson: By her expression, she was surprised.

Pratt: Did you make a note about this conversation?

Higson: No, but my recollection is clear today that I can give you word for word of it.

Pratt: You can give me word for word about the attaché case?

Higson: Yes, after refreshing my mind a little.

Pratt: Who mentioned the word 'Tooting' in reference to the attaché case?

Higson: Both Mr Wootten and Miss Wheatley did.

Pratt: How can you be so sure if you made no note?

Higson: I made a careful mental note of the doings the whole afternoon of 24th March.

Pratt: What was the second article in the attaché case?

Higson: Some article of clothing.

Pratt: What about the rest of the contents of the attaché case?

Higson: I did not interest myself further in that.

Pratt: Miss Wheatley always said she had not been to Rotherfield Street?

Higson: Yes.

Pratt: The whole purpose of your visit was to get her to admit she had been to Rotherfield Street and sent the telegram the night before?

Higson: Yes.

Pratt: I suggest you tried to bluff her into making an admission?

Higson: No. I pressed my questions, I did not consider my reference to the telegram was bluffing her.

Pratt: Why did you ask her questions while Lieutenant Wootten was out of the room?

Higson: I wanted to see if she would admit it to me.

Pratt: If she had, would it have been in confidence?

Higson: No.

Pratt: What would you have done if she had?

Higson: I would have gone to the police.

Pratt: But she stoutly denied it again?

Higson: Yes.

Pratt: When you told her not to go away she said if she did she would let you have her address?

Higson: No, I did not know if she was going away.

Pratt: Did you have any actual evidence to say that the deceased had not fallen downstairs?

Higson: No.

It was an effective cross-examination. Mr Pratt scored a good point by describing Higson and Wootten's activities the day after the murder as 'amateur detective work' and he had managed to induce Higson to agree that Marie could have guessed that the telegram had been addressed to Wootten's sister-in-law. He clearly discomforted him with his failure of recollection over the issue of the attaché case and Higson slipped up again by saying that both Marie and Wootten mentioned 'Tooting' whereas his final position during his evidence-in-chief had been that only Marie had done so. Yet the central theme of Mr Pratt's cross-examination, namely that Higson and Wootten had dashed to Richmond Road to accuse Marie of murdering Mrs Wootten without any reasonable basis, only worked if one ignored the facts that (a) Marie was known as 'Mrs Higson's friend' and (b) Mrs Wootten had told her daughter that 'Mrs Higson's friend' was the woman who was in the house moments before she died. It must have seemed to the coroner's jury that Higson had every reason to suspect Marie, who had then only increased suspicions by refusing to reveal her whereabouts at the time of the murder. Furthermore, Mr Pratt had not challenged any of Higson's evidence save for the rather irrelevant issue of whether he or Marie had said that the case looked black against her. The rest of Higson's evidence, including everything that had happened during Marie's visit to London in February, the meeting at Bank and the rest of the conversation at Richmond Road, appeared to be accepted as accurate and truthful by Mr Pratt on behalf of Marie.

The highlight of the day was the cross-examination of Lieutenant Wootten by Mr Pratt. Before this, however, there was drama in the court during Wootten's evidence to the coroner as Marie, who had been silent until now, called out: 'Oh, you liar!' while Wootten was telling the coroner that, towards the end of 1914, Marie had showed him a cardboard target which she said was the result of her shooting with a Morris tube rifle at Shoreham. It was quite common in wartime Britain for women to practise shooting at rifle ranges. The *Daily Mirror* of 17 August 1914, for example, reported that 'Women are becoming more and more enthusiastic about learning to shoot, and each day large numbers of women are taking rifle practice.' Wootten claimed the cardboard showed marks of 'excellent shooting' by Marie, thus prompting the outburst from the dock. Perhaps more significantly, Wootten said that, when he saw her shortly after 9pm on the night of the murder, Marie: 'appeared in rather an excited manner and appeared to have been hurrying.' It was an obviously prejudicial comment, made with the aim of suggesting that Marie had rushed back from murdering his wife in Islington to make the meeting. Mr Pratt then got to work:

> **Pratt:** When did you first meet Miss Wheatley?
> **Wootten:** In October last year.
> **Pratt:** Did you tell her point blank that you were a married man?

Wootten: No, but she quickly found out.

Pratt: When?

Wootten: Very quickly in October. Our friendship was then well advanced. She knew I was married before she left the George Hotel in Shoreham.

Pratt: You have told us that, while at Gillingham Street, Miss Wheatley said that if she ever met your wife she would 'do her in'?

Wootten: Yes.

Pratt: Are you suggesting that remark has any bearing on the crime?

Wootten: No, it was said in jest.

Pratt: Did you regard it as a threat?

Wootten: No, I regarded it as silly, foolish talk.

Pratt: You denounced Miss Wheatley to the police?

Wootten: I did.

Pratt: As the murderess of your wife?

Wootten: You have no right to make such a suggestion Mr Pratt.

The Coroner: Please just answer the questions put by the gentleman.

Wootten: I am as much a gentleman as he.

The Coroner: You must obey my ruling.

Wootten: Yes sir, I am sorry.

Pratt: I will ask it again. Did you denounce Miss Wheatley to the police as the murderess of your wife?

Wootten: I denounced her to the police but not as the murderess of my wife.

Pratt: In what way did you denounce her to the police?

Wootten: In the course of conversation with Inspector Davis I told him of her existence and he took down details. I told him all that had happened and what our relationship had been and the next I heard was that she had been arrested.

Pratt: When was this conversation?

Wootten: It was about 8:30pm on 24th March and lasted until about midnight.

Pratt: Did you know that your wife had been shot at this time?

Wootten: I had no knowledge of that at all.

Pratt: Murder seems to have suggested itself to your mind at an early stage of this occurrence?

Wootten: After the conversation I had with my daughter, and seeing the telegram and taking particular notice of the attitude of Miss Wheatley when I went there on 24th March, I came to the conclusion that Miss Wheatley had been to my house and that something foul had happened.

Pratt: What do you mean by that?

Wootten: I thought Miss Wheatley had pushed my wife downstairs. My wife had a defective leg which had been operated on at one time and the knee was weak so this could easily be done.

Pratt: When you visited Miss Wheatley at Richmond Road, you had that impression in your mind?

Wootten: Yes.

Pratt: Why did you go to see her?

Wootten: I went to know what had happened when she came to my house the previous evening.

Pratt: Did you go with an open mind?

Wootten: No, I would say not.

Pratt: Why not?

Wootten: I thought that after my little girl had said somebody had called at the house and asked for money and said she was thin and hungry and asked for water and then my little girl was relating to me about the slamming of the door, and my wife exclaiming 'Oh, oh', it appeared to me that there was a possibility of somebody calling and banging my wife on the head. And that was my object in going a second time to look at my wife's head. As soon as I heard it from my daughter Lily I called down Mr Dixon and said – I think I said – 'This is no accident, I think it's murder'.

Pratt: Do you disagree with Mr Dixon's words which were 'Listen to this there has been a murder here, this is not an accident, it's murder'?

Wootten: Yes I do disagree. I said 'I think it's murder'.

Pratt: Are you positive you used the words 'I think it's murder'?

Wootten: Yes.

Pratt: You thought it was murder?

Wootten: Yes.

Pratt: And the evidence for that was the statement that Lily had made to you about a woman calling and a banging of the door and 'oh oh' being exclaimed by your wife?

Wootten: That is so.

Pratt: Was it not until the first hearing in this inquest that you were convinced it was murder?

Wootten: No, on early Wednesday morning I thought it was murder.

Pratt: And the foundation for that was nothing more than the statement that had been made to you by Lily?

Wootten: That is correct.

Pratt: When you visited Miss Wheatley at Richmond Road in the afternoon of 24th March what was the first thing you asked her?

Wootten: I said 'Why did you go to my house?'

Pratt: And the second?

Wootten: 'Why did you send that telegram?'

Pratt: Why jump to the conclusion that she had sent the telegram?

Wootten: Marie often sent telegrams.

Pratt: And for that reason you thought she had sent the telegram?

Wootten: Yes.

Pratt: Combining the facts all together you started by assuming she was a guilty woman?

Wootten: Yes, and it was confirmed in my mind by her lies.

Pratt: Had she told you any lies?

Wootten: She lied to me in reference to her luggage on the previous Friday.

Pratt: So the lying was in reference to the attaché case?

Wootten: Mostly, yes.

Pratt: She used to carry luggage in the attaché case?

Wootten: Yes.

Pratt: What is the importance of the attaché case?

Wootten: To anyone connected with the matter the circumstances of the attaché case seemed important.

Pratt: What importance did you attach to it?

Wootten: I attached importance with reference to her lying.

Pratt: During the interview, she did not pause or hesitate in her answers?

Wootten: She paused on several occasions.

Pratt: Was it a pause or a pause of hesitation?

Wootten: A pause which appeared to me that she was too frightened to answer.

Pratt: Did the landlady also pause after answering your questions?

Wootten: Yes, with one or two she was not certain.

Pratt: What kind of pause was it with Miss Wheatley?

Wootten: The pause was the fright a guilty woman experiences.

Pratt: Was there a look of satisfaction on her face when you told her your wife was dead?

Wootten: No.

Pratt: How long did the conversation last?

Wootten: Half an hour.

Pratt: Did you leave her without saying goodbye?

Wootten: Yes.

Pratt: And was she still in an agitated state?

Wootten: Yes.

Pratt: Was she agitated before you accused her?

Wootten: Yes.

Pratt: What was the first thing you said to her?

Wootten: 'What did you go to my house for last night?'

Pratt: Was that very different from the usual way you greeted her when you went to Richmond Road?

Wootten: Yes.

Pratt: She agreed to give you up on February 11th?

Wootten: Yes.

Pratt: She agreed that it was very wrong to take a man from his wife and children?

Wootten: Yes, but she expressed her love for me.

Pratt: She ultimately agreed to give you up?

Wootten: Yes.

Pratt: What were your feelings for her at that time?

Wootten: Very cold.

Pratt: Have they become any warmer since?

Wootten: No.

Pratt: Have you ever promised to marry Miss Wheatley?

Wootten: Never.

Pratt: You never led her to suppose you would marry her?

Wootten: No.

Pratt: So she would gain nothing by your wife's death?

Wootten: I suppose not, no.

Pratt: You had agreed to assist her to obtain a situation and to provide for her until she did obtain one?

Wootten: Yes.

Pratt: With that she went down into Sussex and you did not see her again until 19th March?

Wootten: Yes.

Pratt: Did you reply to any of her letters there?

Wootten: No.

Pratt: Do you still have any of those letters?

Wootten: No.

Pratt: Why not?

Wootten: I burnt them as soon as I received them.

Pratt: How do you feel you had treated her?

Wootten: In my mind I thought I had been very kind. I had given her cheques and money and kept her in the proper way. There had been a second arrangement that she should go home. At the Higsons of course she had money as well.

Pratt: Your promise to provide for her which was made on 12th February was kept up until Sunday 20th February?

Wootten: Yes.

Pratt: A whole week your promise was kept?

Wootten: Yes, the next thing was I gave her two shillings or so for lunch on 19th March. And in pursuance of that agreement I paid the landlady 7/6 at Richmond Road.

Pratt: How did you refer to Miss Wheatley?

Wootten: As Marie Lanteri.

Pratt: Was she always known to you as Lanteri?

Wootten: Yes.

Pratt: Did you not take the room at Richmond Road for Mr and Mrs Wootten?

Wootten: No, I said it was for the lady I had with me.

Pratt: And while she was there she tried to get a situation?

Wootten: Yes.

Pratt: You gave her a reference to enable her to get a situation?

Wootten: I gave her a letter of recommendation.

Pratt: It is for a 'Miss Wheatley' although you say you knew her as Marie Lanteri?

Wootten: Yes.

Pratt: You did not object to indulging in this bit of deceit?

Wootten: No.

Pratt: How far was 12 Richmond Road from White City?

Wootten: Not very far.

Pratt: How often did you see her?

Wootten: On several occasions.

Pratt: Most evenings while you were at White City?

Wootten: Not most evenings.

Pratt: What was the usual time you called to see her in the evening?

Wootten: There was no usual time. If I came straight from the Mess it would be about 8:30pm.

Pratt: On the Tuesday night did you leave White City after Mess?

Wootten: Yes.

Pratt: Yet you did not get to 12 Richmond Road until ten past nine in the evening?

Wootten: Yes, I went to a shaving salon and got a hair cut and shampoo.

Pratt: How long were you at the shaving salon?

Wootten: Nearly an hour.

Pratt: Where was it?

Wootten: Just past Shepherd's Bush station?

Pratt: Can you tell us the name of it?

Wootten: I believe it was called 'Everett'.

Pratt: What time did you leave the Mess at White City?

Wootten: About five past eight.

Pratt: When you saw Miss Wheatley at 9:10pm was she not despondent about finding a situation?

Wootten: Yes.

Pratt: Did you say to the coroner last month: 'I then left'?

Wootten: Yes.

Pratt: What time did you leave?

Wootten: Not much before 11pm.

Pratt: Can you be positive about that?

Wootten: No, I cannot be.

Pratt: How do you know what time you arrived at Richmond Road?

Wootten: I fancy Miss Wheatley said to me 'You're later tonight'. That was why I saw it was ten past nine, I looked at the clock.

Pratt: No further questions.

Lieutenant Wootten stepped down from the witness box at 8:30pm. He had been in there for seven hours. It had been a very long day. Mr Pratt had not, however, achieved a great deal. Wootten's admission that Marie did not have a motive because he had not promised to marry her was not worth much; that she did had a motive in eliminating a rival was fairly obvious to everyone. However, he had laid the foundation for future questions and he had kept some surprises up his sleeve. It would not be the last confrontation between Mr Pratt and Lieutenant Wootten. Certainly, if the lieutenant walked out of the coroner's court feeling satisfied with himself in the belief that was as difficult as it was going to get, he was very wrong.

Tuesday 13 April 1915

All parties returned to Stoke Newington for the

start of the committal proceedings at the North London Police Court with the addition of a new face: Edward Charles Percy Boyd, junior counsel to the Treasury who was appearing for the prosecution. As the inquest had not concluded, only three uncontroversial witnesses were called, among them Mr and Mrs Jordan which meant that the subject of the dog which had not barked in the night came back to life. James Jordan admitted that he had made a mistake during the inquest and that the 'noisy dog' was actually a dog which lived next door to the Woottens! That was not an end to the issue, however, because Mary Jordan then said: 'I know that the Wootten's dog is a very cross dog. Whenever a stranger goes to the door he is very cross. He shows his crossness by making a good deal of noise. They sometimes have to lift him by the collar.' Young John Reddin, Mr Jordan's stepson who had fetched both the doctor and the constable, caused some amusement in court by giving his full name as John Joseph Peter Paul James Reddin (causing Mr Hedderwick to point out to laughter in the courtroom that he had 'all the names of the apostles'). He was the final witness of the day before everyone, except Messrs Boyd and Hedderwick, returned to Islington.

Thursday 15 April 1915

Both George Dixon and Joseph Tilbury, the fathers of Mr and Mrs Dixon respectively, appeared at the coroner's court to confirm they did not send any telegram on the night of the murder. Mrs Connor, the landlady at 12 Richmond Road appeared next. She gave some important evidence that Lieutenant Wootten claimed that he took the room for 'his wife' for a fortnight and told her that the amount of time the room was needed would 'depend on how things went at the White City'. She confirmed that she saw Marie on the night of the murder at twenty minutes to nine although she said: 'I fancied I heard her come in a little time before'. Helpfully for Marie she said that she did not seem excited or exhausted when she saw her that night.

The next witnesses were those from 36 Ecclesbourne Road, commencing with the maid, Violet Thorn, who Mr Pratt severely aggravated by questioning closely on every point of her evidence. However, he could not shake her strong recollection that Marie arrived at the house shortly before seven on the evening of 18 March, left fifteen minutes later and returned shortly before ten. He appeared to challenge her evidence that, when doing the dusting, she had picked up Marie's attaché case while Marie had been out that evening and felt it was quite heavy, and also that she saw the revolver when Mrs Alland removed it from Marie's attaché case the next day, but she stood her ground on both points. The only success Mr Pratt achieved from his cross-examination of the maid was to induce her to agree that the motor veil she had seen Marie wearing when she left Ecclesbourne Road was white and not an unusual item of clothing, there being 'plenty about'.

By contrast with his treatment of the maid, Mr Pratt did not cross-examine the formidable Mrs Alland, the landlady from 36 Ecclesbourne Road, at all, save to ask her if she knew the Woottens, which she said she did not. It now appeared to be accepted by the defence that Marie, who Mrs Alland identified as the woman who had given her the attaché case, did have a loaded revolver with her while staying at Ecclesbourne Road and that Mrs Alland's detailed account of her conversations with Marie about the revolver was true.

Saturday 17 April 1915

The final day of the inquest produced emotion in court as Marie broke down in tears while her father, now working in his retirement as a jobbing gardener, gave evidence. He did not mention that he had once been a police officer but confirmed that for over thirty years he had owned an old rusty revolver which had been kept in a toy box while he lived at the 'Runt-in-Tun' public house in Heathfield and had been played with by his children, including Marie. He had not seen the weapon since September 1914, when he and his family moved to Horsted Keynes, and he did not know what had become of it. It was not clear what he said that caused Marie to start to cry but she was reported as being red-eyed and tearful, sobbing bitterly into her handkerchief virtually throughout his stint in the witness box.

Other witnesses of the day included Gertrude Taylor, a postal and telegraph clerk, from the St John Street post office who had received the original telegram addressed to 'Dickson' of 114 Rotherfield Street at just after six o'clock in the evening of 23 March but could not remember who had brought it in. 'I think it was a boy,' she said 'but I am not certain.' The sender's name on the telegram was 'Laker' of 6 Popham Street, off Essex Road, and the bemused actual resident of 6 Popham Street, one Edward Green, appeared before the coroner to confirm that he had not sent the telegram and no-one by the name 'Laker' lived at that address.

The final witnesses were the detective police officers who arrested Marie: Inspector Davis and Sergeant Wesley. Inspector Davis attempted to defend his failure to caution Marie by saying that he did not think it was necessary to caution a prisoner if a question was put to the advantage of the prisoner. When he asked Marie to account for her movements at the time of the murder, he claimed he was doing it for her own benefit and that, if she had given him a satisfactory answer, she would have been freed. To Mr Pratt's evident disbelief, he said that when he put the questions to her he had not considered the possibility of her declining to give information nor had he considered that any refusal would be likely to be used against her.

Once the police officers had given their evidence, Mr Schröder asked Marie if she wished to go into the witness box. Mr Pratt replied: 'No. She will not give evidence at this inquiry,' but Mr Schröder countered that he needed to hear it from the prisoner herself and Marie said: 'No sir. I do not wish to give evidence.' After an hour's adjournment, the coroner then addressed the jury, telling them that the time had arrived for them to consider the facts of the case. He informed them that they were inquiring whether there was a prima facie case against some person or persons of causing Mrs Wootten's death. A coroner's inquisition was not, he said, a trial. It was only for the jury to consider whether, on the whole of the facts given in evidence, death was natural, accidental or whether a person came to their death by murder, manslaughter or suicide. The coroner continued:

> The evidence which you have before you is that the deceased woman died from the infliction of a wound. You have the evidence that Lieutenant Wootten was known to Alice Mary Wheatley – that she had threatened, if ever she met his wife, that she would 'do her in'. She is introduced to Mrs Wootten. At a later date, a woman answering the description of Miss Wheatley takes lodgings in a street near to where the Woottens resided, and while there she is known to have in her attaché case a revolver. Where that revolver came from is not clear, but you have it in evidence that it was an old one, and you have had evidence today

from Mr Wheatley that he did possess a revolver – an old rusty one which had been allowed to lie about and which his children played with. Also that the last time he saw it was in a box and it had been kept in one of the rooms which Alice Mary Wheatley had occupied, and that he had not seen it for several months. You have it in evidence that deceased died from injury inflicted by a bullet. There was no weapon found in the house. The person who entered the house on March 23rd was described by deceased as 'Mrs Higson's friend'. Mrs Higson's friend was Miss Wheatley. The name of 'Mrs Higson's friend' was a name agreed to by Lieutenant Wootten and his wife, and others, so that when speaking of her it should be known who was meant. She was the person of whom deceased said to her children, 'It is only Mrs Higson's friend' and she, so far as we know, was the only person who has been mentioned in this case as being in possession of any weapon.

If one person kills another, the law assumes it is murder, unless the facts in evidence reduce it to manslaughter. In the present case, you have only one person mentioned, but you must bear in mind one very important thing, that an inquest is not a trial and that if you find a verdict against any person it is not a condemnation. It is rather a formal accusation, sufficient to place such person on trial, and no more. There may be answers to all the points which have been put before you in evidence. We are simply inquiring whether there is a prima facie case against any person causing the death of the deceased Annie Josephine Wootten. If you think there is enough in the evidence sufficient to place a person on trial – enough to call upon the person for a defence – it is your duty to find a verdict accusing that person. The only person against whom suspicion has been directed, the only person mentioned, the only person known to have uttered any threat, the only person known to have had a revolver in her possession, is Alice Mary Wheatley. If she is not associated with the death of the deceased, then no other person is before you. If you think there is enough in the evidence, sufficient to place her on trial, or anything to call upon any person for a defence, it is your duty to find a verdict accusing that person.

Listening to this speech, Mr Pratt must have been frustrated that the coroner referred to Marie's alleged threat to kill Wootten's wife as evidence of intent to murder, despite Wootten's concession in the witness box that this had been said in jest and had no bearing at all on the crime. After retiring for ten minutes the jury returned.

Coroner: Have you agreed to your verdict?
Forman of the jury: Yes.
Coroner: What do you find?
Foreman of the jury: We find that Alice Mary Wheatley was the cause of the death of Annie Josephine Wootten.
Coroner: You find that she died from the cause described by Doctor Spilsbury?
Foreman of the jury: Yes.
Coroner: You find that that was caused by the act of Alice Mary Wheatley?
Foreman of the jury: Yes sir.
Coroner: And that she is guilty of wilful murder?
Foreman of the jury: Yes, that is right.
Coroner (to Inspector Davis): I will give you a warrant committing her to trial for murder at the next session of the Central Criminal Court.

Walter Schröder was notorious for making it clear when he disagreed with a verdict of his jury. In January 1911, for example, when the jury at his inquest into the death of Emily Esther Kent, a 42-year-old widow whose body had been recovered from a pond in Hampstead, pronounced as the verdict for her death: 'Found drowned' (instead of murdered), he replied: 'What! Very well, it is your verdict not mine', thus clearly disassociating himself from it. One of the jurors defended the verdict by pointing out that there was no evidence of foul play to which Schröder retorted 'I hope that in the next case you will give close attention to the evidence': appearing to have in mind the evidence of the deceased's sister that she had seen Emily 'running for her life' down the street on the night of her death. However, the foreman did not care for Schröder's opinion, bluntly informing the coroner: 'We don't want to have to be told that we are here to do our duty' and the jury stubbornly adhered to their verdict.[97] They might have had in mind that Emily had recently been depressed and probably thought it was either a case of suicide or an accident.

Similarly, a few months later, in response to a verdict of 'death by misadventure' at an inquest into the death of a 54-year-old labourer, Thomas Robson, who had been punched a number of times in the ribs – causing two of them to break – by a neighbour called Robert Burgess, in revenge for having been accidentally cut by shards of a bottle Robson had thrown at some cats the night before, Schröder said: 'Well gentlemen, it is your verdict not mine'. The medical evidence had been that death was caused by heart failure due to peritonitis and disease of the liver and kidney but that Robson's fractured ribs accelerated death, so Schröder was evidently of the view that manslaughter was the appropriate verdict. Once again the jury disagreed with their coroner: the foreman explaining to Schröder that they considered the blow was inadvertently given by Burgess.[98]

Following the verdict in respect of Annie Wootten's death, however, there were to be no barbed comments made by the coroner. To the jury, Schröder said, 'I very much appreciate the careful attention you have given to this case,' and he also thanked Detective Inspector Davis and Detective Sergeant Wesley for their assistance. The official verdict of the inquest was: 'Wilful murder against Alice Mary Wheatley'.

Lily Wootten, aged 8

CHAPTER 8

COUNTDOWN TO TRIAL – PART 2

Tuesday 20 April 1915

Now that Marie was committed to trial at the Old
Bailey, the magistrate's hearing might seem to be
redundant. After all, its sole purpose was to decide
whether a prisoner should be committed for trial.
However, it was quite possible, albeit a very rare
occurrence, for a coroner's jury to commit a person for
trial while the magistrate at the committal proceedings
decided against doing so. Such an outcome invariably
meant that the case would not be proceeded with at
trial. In 1906, for example, an unlicensed midwife,
Amelia Hollis, had been arrested for the murder of
baker's wife, Bertha Doel, who died shortly after
a botched illegal abortion. Although a coroner's
inquisition had committed her for trial, the magistrate
in the South Western Magistrate's court dismissed the
charge. When her case appeared before Mr Justice
Darling at the Old Bailey, the prosecution offered no
evidence and she was discharged. Thus, even though
the verdict of the coroner's jury verdict had gone
against Marie, that was not necessarily the end of the
matter and there was still everything to play for in
front of Mr Hedderwick at the North London Police
Court.

With Marie listening carefully from the dock, and
another large crowd in the public gallery, Mr Boyd
opened the case for the prosecution but did so with
one hand tied, metaphorically, behind his back. The
magistrate had ruled that the evidence of the two
girls - that their mother had told them the woman
who visited 114 Rotherfield Street on the night of the

murder was 'Mrs Higson's friend' - was inadmissible; due to the fact that they were reporting what a third party had told them, which was considered hearsay. For anyone not familiar with the rules of evidence it was a strange ruling in view of the fact that Mrs Wootten herself was unable to give evidence by virtue of having been murdered. It seemed to give an advantage to the murderer – assuming the murderer to be 'Mrs Higson's friend' – by having killed the one person who had openly identified her before the crime was committed. In many ways it was a travesty of justice by excluding such crucial evidence. At the same time, it is fair to say that there can be serious problems with hearsay evidence, whereby someone is simply reporting what they have been told by a third party, and reliance on it can obviously lead to miscarriages of justice. The first person Lily had spoken to about the visit of 'Mrs Higson's friend' was her father. Perhaps, it could be said, he had put the idea into her head by asking her if her mother had told her that 'Mrs Higson's friend' had called and, being at such an impressionable age, she had agreed and incorporated it into her story. However, Lily had immediately repeated her story to Mr and Mrs Dixon in the early hours of the morning after her mother's death and Ivy had subsequently corroborated it in the witness box in the coroner's court. It is highly unlikely that the notion could have been accidentally implanted into the minds of both children. In theory, they could have been deliberately lying on the instructions of their father but, in reality, the idea that Wootten could have coached his young daughters to falsely implicate Marie is inconceivable and, despite their young age, there can be no doubt at all that they were telling the truth about being informed by their mother of the visit of 'Mrs Higson's friend'. Mr Pratt had the opportunity

to cross-examine the girls about their evidence, as
he had done at the coroner's court, and if there was
any weakness in their story it would have emerged
that way. Nevertheless, there was a clear legal rule
that hearsay statements were not allowed and, in
the absence of direct testimony by Mrs Wootten, the
evidence that Mrs Higson's friend was the woman
at the door on the night of the murder was hearsay.
Ironically, if Mrs Wootten had managed to say to her
children before she expired 'Marie Wheatley shot me',
or even 'Mrs Higson's friend shot me', that evidence
might well have been admissible because statements
of a dying person were allowed in evidence as an
exception to the hearsay rule.

Lily and Ivy were the only two witnesses of the
day, both dressed in black to mourn the death of their
mother. The newspaper reporter from the *Weekly
Dispatch* described them as 'such little girls, pretty,
rosy-cheeked, blue-eyed, little girls with the most
winning of smiles who look up shyly when they are
spoken to'.[99] When they were brought into court there
was a murmur of sympathy from the public space at
the back of the court which had attracted about a dozen
women wearing hats with huge feathers and old men
wearing glasses. As a result of the magistrate's ruling,
Mr Boyd carefully enquired of Lily if she had asked
her mother a question which her mother had then
answered. Lily confirmed this had happened but was
not allowed to elaborate. Mr Pratt then closely cross-
examined her on her evidence and it is worth setting
out some of that cross-examination here to show how
thoroughly she was questioned:

> **Pratt:** How long was it after your mother left your
> room that she came down for a glass of water?
> **Lily:** I can't say, sir.
> **Pratt:** Do you remember saying it was about

an hour afterwards when you were asked that question before?

Lily: No, I don't remember, sir.

Pratt: Do you remember being asked how long there was between the two bangs?

Lily: Yes, sir.

Pratt: Do you remember saying that you didn't know?

Lily: No, sir.

Pratt: Do you remember saying it was 'a minute'?

Lily: No, sir.

Pratt: Can you say now why you said it was a minute?

Lily: No, sir.

Pratt: Did anyone tell you it was a minute?

Lily: No, sir.

Pratt: Was it before or after your mother came down that you heard someone say 'thin and hungry'?

Lily: It was before she came down.

Pratt: Did you say last time that you heard your mother shut the door after the person went?

Lily: Yes, I think that was a mistake.

Pratt: Who made you think it was mother who shut the door?

Lily: I don't know, sir.

Pratt: How long were you with your mother before Mrs Higson came?

Lily: I can't say. I think it was about two minutes.

Pratt: What were you doing when Mrs Higson knocked?

Lily: I was downstairs dressing myself.

Pratt: What were you wearing when you ran up to your mother?

Lily: My nightdress.

Pratt: Did you then go down and start dressing?

Lily: Yes, sir.

Pratt: What were you wearing when Mrs Higson knocked at the door?

Lily: I only had my stays [corset] on.

Pratt: When your father came home were you awake?

Lily: I think so.

Pratt: Did you tell him about the two bangs?

Lily: Yes, sir.

Pratt: Are you sure you told him that?

Lily: Yes, sir.

Pratt: Was it at night or the next morning when you told him about seeing sparks around your mother's blouse?

Lily: I don't know.

Pratt: Did you tell your father that your mother was lighting the gas?

Lily: No, sir.

Pratt: What time did your father come into your room?

Lily: I think it was one o'clock as it was a long time after.

Pratt: A long time after what?

Lily: A long time after he came to the house at about twelve.

Pratt: Has anyone told you to say these things?

Lily: No, sir.

Pratt: Did you have a clock in your room?

Lily: No, sir.

Pratt: Do you remember saying before that Mrs Higson knocked at the door about three quarters of an hour after the bang?

Lily: No, sir.

Pratt: Do you know how long it was?

Lily: No, sir.

As Lily had been cross-examined by Mr Pratt about her conversation with her father after the murder, Mr Boyd was now allowed to ask for more details during his re-examination and Lily said: 'When I spoke to daddy at about one o'clock I said I'd heard two bangs and that I heard someone come in and that I'd asked mummy who it was and she said "Mrs Higson's friend".' So the visit of 'Mrs Higson's friend' did become admissible but, in true Alice in Wonderland style, only as an account of what Lily had said to her father, not of what her mother had said to her!

Friday 23 April 1915

There was only limited time at the police court in between its normal daily round of summonses to squeeze in the evidence relating to the death of Mrs Wootten and it was not until the end of the week that the hearing resumed. It was another day with only two witnesses: Dr Madden and Police Constable Augustus Langridge. The latter gave evidence regarding the layout of 114 Rotherfield Street. He was asked whether it would have been possible for the killer to have escaped out of the back of the house but he said that anyone trying to leave that way would have needed to have climbed a wall topped with chicken wire which was intact when he inspected it the day after the murder. Langridge said that he could not have climbed the wall himself without displacing the supports or breaking the wire.

Tuesday 27 April 1915

Lily Dixon returned to give evidence and corroborated what her husband had told the coroner about the veil worn by the lady who visited Rotherfield Street on the evening of 18 March: 'The veil looked dark to me' she said during her evidence-in-chief and then told Mr Pratt: 'As far as I can recollect it looked like a dark veil'. Mr Boyd, during re-examination, elicited the evidence that, 'it was very dark outside the door', but it remained a damaging point against the prosecution's desire to prove that the veiled lady was Marie.

Friday 30 April 1915

After Mr Hedderwick had disposed of a number of private summonses, the hearing of the charge against Marie continued with the evidence of Dr Spilsbury. Mr Pratt persisted with his line of questioning directed at the possibility that Mrs Wootten had committed suicide, despite the absence of a weapon near the body. He attempted to force Dr Spilsbury to concede that the wound could have been self inflicted if fired by the left hand of Mrs Wootten but Spilsbury said that due to the 'very oblique direction of the course of the bullet and the difficulty of holding a weapon in that direction at a short distance from the garment' it was quite improbable.

Fred Dixon was next into the witness box and he once again said that the veil worn by the lady who visited 114 Rotherfield Street on the evening of 18 March 'seemed dark'. The matter of his silent dog was returned to by Mr Pratt who asked him if it had barked when the veiled lady had knocked at the door but he said he could not remember. At the same time, he told Mr Pratt that it was 'a good watchdog and usually barks when strangers come to the door'. In re-examination he put an end to the issue of why no-one had seen the dog after the murder of Mrs Wootten by saying that it was 'hiding away upstairs', adding that he thought it had been 'frightened' by all the people in the house. In the end, the dog that did not bark was something of a red herring.

The undoubted comedy highlight of the day was the evidence of Gertrude Taylor from the St John Street post office. During her evidence-in-chief she said that

she did not remember who handed in the telegram
addressed to 'Dickson' at 114 Rotherfield Street
and, in cross-examination, agreed that she had no
recollection of ever having seen Marie Wheatley until
she was asked to identify her in a line-up. However,
in re-examination by Mr Boyd, she confirmed that she
had, in fact, picked out Marie from the line-up. For
a moment, it seemed that the evidence finally existed
to prove Marie had sent the telegram. This belief
did not last long as, in further cross-examination, Ms
Taylor confessed that the only reason she had picked
Marie out from the identity parade was because
she had previously seen a photograph of her in a
newspaper! She told the court she had no recollection
of having seen Marie on 23 March or any other day.
Mr Hedderwick then asked about her evidence at the
coroner's court that she thought a boy had handed in
the telegram. She agreed that she remembered a boy
handing in a telegram on 23 March but stated: 'I cannot
say if this is the one.' She pointed out that she took in
between fifteen and twenty telegrams a day.

During the evening, after the court's business had
concluded, Detective Inspector Davis and Sergeant
Wesley went travelling. They wanted to time the
journey from Rotherfield Street to Shepherd's Bush to
see if Marie could have killed Mrs Wootten at quarter
to eight and been safely back in Richmond Road by
twenty to nine when she spoke to Mrs Connor. They
departed from Rotherfield Street at 7:46pm and made
the short walk to Essex Road tube station where they
boarded a G.N. & City train to Moorgate Street & Bank
station changing onto the Central London Railway for
a train to Shepherd's Bush. There were no delays on
the journey. From Shepherd's Bush tube station they
walked to 12 Richmond Road, arriving at 8:34pm, a
total journey time of 48 minutes. It was tight if the

murder had been committed at or just before a quarter to eight, leaving Marie just six or seven minutes to remove her outdoor clothes, compose herself and speak to Mrs Connor, but it was do-able.

Tuesday 4 May 1915

Lieutenant Wootten dominated the day's proceedings as he spent most of the day in-chief telling his story. It was reported that, while he gave his evidence, Marie took many notes, using the gaoler's record book as her desk. When not writing or passing notes to her counsel she kept her eyes fixed on the lieutenant. Wooten was allowed to state that he told Marie during the interview with Higson at Richmond Road on 24 March that Lily had told him that his wife had said 'Mrs Higson's friend' had visited the house. Mr Pratt reserved his cross-examination.

Friday 6 May 1915

Mr Pratt was unable to attend the court so evidence-in-chief only was heard from Mr and Mrs Higson and Violet Thorn. As a result of another ruling by the magistrate, Mrs Higson was not allowed to mention the fact that Mrs Wootten had remarked that the veiled lady's voice had sounded like Marie's on the night of 18 March. However, she was allowed to give evidence that she herself thought the woman sounded like Marie.

Wednesday 11 May 1915

Finally it was time for the cross-examination by Mr Pratt of Lieutenant Wootten. If, having survived Mr Pratt's questioning in the coroner's court, Lieutenant Wootten thought he was in for an easy ride he had a shock coming:

Pratt: When did you first meet Miss Wheatley?
Wootten: I first met her in October.
Pratt: And when was the first time you took her

154

out?

Wootten: I think that was on 14th October.

Pratt: Tell me, Mr Wootten, when did misconduct first take place?

Wootten: That would have been on 22nd October.

Pratt: When did you tell her you were married?

Wootten: She knew I was married the first day I went out with her.

Pratt: Are you sure it was the first day?

Wootten: I think I told her definitely I was married the next Saturday.

Pratt: The fact is you did not tell her before misconduct took place?

Wootten: I did.

Pratt: Did you not tell her you were single when you first knew her?

Wootten: No. She asked me if I was married. She had been told I was married and had four children.

Pratt: Did she not tax you with being a married man in December?

Wootten: No, she had taxed me with that much earlier.

Pratt: Did you deny it?

Wootten: No.

Pratt: Isn't the truth that you did not tell her you were married until December?

Wootten: No, that is not true.

Pratt: Now, did you ever write to her parents?

Wootten: No, never.

Pratt: Are you sure.

Wootten: I feel certain I did not.

Pratt: You only 'feel' certain?

Wootten: I definitely think I did not write to them.

Pratt: I understand the police have a postcard. Can the witness be shown 'Exhibit 20'?

Wootten: Yes, I have it.

Pratt: That is a postcard from you to Miss Wheatley's mother is it not?

Wootten: Yes.

Pratt: Is it in your handwriting?

Wootten: Yes it is.

Pratt: It is?

Wootten: Yes, well, it is some time ago since October.

Pratt: Do you remember writing it?

Wootten: No.

Pratt: Did you write it?

Wootten: Yes, I did. I didn't remember doing so. I now recollect her asking me to write a card to her mother when she was indisposed. That is the only letter or card I ever wrote to her parents. I wrote the card to 'Dear mother' at Miss Wheatley's dictation while I was staying with her at Coleridge Street, Hove, in December. Practically the whole of the card was dictated to me. I did not know that Miss Wheatley was known as 'Mawks' until she dictated the card to me.

Pratt: Did you understand when you wrote it that she had written to her parents saying she was married to you?

Wootten: Yes, I did.

Pratt: Did you write to her father or send him any photograph of yourself?

Wootten: No.

Pratt: Did you write to him as 'Dear Dad'?

Wootten: No.

Pratt: Now, what was the date she left her employment at the George Hotel in Shoreham?

Wootten: I cannot say.

Pratt: Did she tell you why she left?

Wootten: Yes, she suggested to me that misconduct was the cause. She gave me as the reason that the proprietor said she was getting too familiar with soldiers.

Pratt: Was your name mentioned?

Wootten: No.

Pratt: I put it to you that Miss Wheatley was discharged from her situation without a reference because of her relations with you?

Wootten: I do not know what was in the mind of the proprietor of the hotel.

Pratt: Did you give her a reference?

Wootten: No, not a reference, but I gave her a testimonial because she told me she'd lost the reference that she got the George Hotel situation with.

Pratt: Did Miss Wheatley end up living with you?

Wootten: Yes.

Pratt: How did that come about?

Wootten: I wired her my address the first night I was at Hove and in consequence she came to see me and I lived with her from the 22nd to 30th December. I stayed with her at Gillingham Street for seven days. The day after that I left Hove and returned to Coleridge Street.

Pratt: Was Miss Wheatley in the family way when you went to Gillingham Street?

Wootten: No, she wasn't unwell then. She was ill in January.

Pratt: What was the illness referred to in the postcard?

Wootten: That was only a cold. In January she was confined to her bed while I was in Dovercourt.

Pratt: When were you at Coleridge Street?

Wootten: From the 17th to the 19th or 20th January.

Pratt: Did Miss Wheatley have a miscarriage about then?

Wootten: I can't say. I knew she had a flooding or something like that.

Pratt: Did you enquire?

Wootten: No.

Pratt: You were not interested?

Wootten: No, I suppose not. She did not tell me. Soon after I went to see her she got well.

Pratt: She had told you she was in the family way had she not?

Wootten: No, she told me she didn't know whether she was or not.

Pratt: Did you prescribe medicine for her?

Wootten: No, not at all. I had recommended chlorodyne[100] for her chest.

Pratt: Did you buy medicine for her?

Wootten: No, never. I gave her money to buy chlorodyne and tooth paste.

Pratt: Did you give her money to buy anything else?

Wootten: I don't remember doing so.

Pratt: How often were you at home during this period?

Wootten: I believe I spent the night of 30th December at home and I was home again on 13th January and again either 19th or 20th January.

Pratt: Are you a man of independent means Mr Wootten?

Wootten: Not exactly, I am dependent on my pay.

Pratt: Which is what?

Wootten: I had £104 a year apart from my pay as a soldier. My insurance company paid me my full pay while on active service.

Pratt: Were you giving Miss Wheatley considerable sums up to the end of January?

Wootten: No, I would not say so. I was giving her cheques for £2 but not every week.

Pratt: How often would you give her a cheque for £2?

Wootten: I can't say.

Pratt: Did you keep an account of it?

Wootten: No.

Pratt: I put it to you that your wife and children were the sufferers for this little pleasure of yours?

Wootten: Not at all. My wife had the £104 a year from the insurance company paid direct to her. Moreover I sent her money from time to time and gave her money when I went home.

Pratt: Do you mean to say you paid your mess bills, your personal expenses and kept this other establishment going in Brighton all on your pay as a second lieutenant?

Wootten: I am a first lieutenant.

Pratt: I beg your pardon. You managed to do all this on your lieutenant's pay?

Wootten: Yes.

Pratt: When did your wife discover your relations with Miss Wheatley?

Wootten: On 19th January. I resolved then to cease the relationship.

Pratt: When did you write a letter breaking off the relationship.

Wootten: That was on 9th February but I think I wrote to her before that saying she would have to leave and she must get a situation.

Pratt: When was that?

Wootten: I can't say, it was soon after my talk with my wife.

Pratt: This is the first time you have mentioned that letter is it not?

Wootten: No.

Pratt: When did you mention it before?

Wootten: I said I wrote letters.

Pratt: Did you mention the contents?

Wootten: No.

Pratt: Why not?

Wootten: I wasn't asked.

Pratt: Did you offer in either of those letters to make provision for Miss Wheatley until she got a situation?

Wootten: No, but when she saw me on 11th February she said I must do something for her.

Pratt: Did she say she'd lost her situation through you?

Wootten: No, my misconduct was never mentioned in that context.

Pratt: Why did you feel she had a claim on you?

Wootten: Because of the misconduct.

Pratt: Was it not because you had deceived her as to being a married man?

Wootten: No, it was because of the misconduct.

Pratt: Turning to the 11th February?

Wootten: Yes.

Pratt: You met her outside the Kenilworth and asked her to go inside?

Wootten: Yes.

Pratt: What part did your wife play in the conversation?

Wootten: Very little. She was a quiet woman.

Pratt: And very upset?

Wootten: Yes.

Pratt: What did she say?

Wootten: All she said at the Kenilworth is what I've given in evidence.

Pratt: Which is hardly anything?

Wootten: Well, at the interviews with Marie she was a mere spectator leaving the talking to Mr Higson and myself.

Pratt: I suggest that when Miss Wheatley came into the Kenilworth your wife said: 'What are you two going to do about it? I'm sick of it all' or words to that effect?

Wootten: She said nothing of the sort.

Pratt: What was the effect of the arrangement made on 21st February?

Wootten: That Miss Wheatley was to go away and not trouble me any more.

Pratt: Before that an arrangement was come to that you should provide for her until she obtained a situation?

Wootten: Yes.

Pratt: You had promised that on 11th February?

Wootten: Yes.

Pratt: When you last saw Marie on 21st February she was perfectly willing to break off relations with you was she not?

Wootten: No, she was not.

Pratt: Mr Wootten, she was perfectly willing wasn't she?

Wootten: No, she was not perfectly willing, she made several requests for me to take the children and go with her and provide a home for her.

Pratt: So you say she was not perfectly willing but she did agree to break off relations?

Wootten: Yes.

Pratt: You said when you gave your evidence last week that you did not live with Miss Wheatley again after 20th January, is that so?

Wootten: Yes.

Pratt: Turning to the moment you took back the letters you had written to Miss Wheatley?

Wootten: Yes.

Pratt: Did she want to give them up?

Wootten: No, she expressed she did not want to.

Pratt: Did you use force to obtain them?

Wootten: No, none at all.

Pratt: Where was Mr Higson at the time?

Wootten: He was at the kitchen door which was

open.

Pratt: Did he have a full view?

Wootten: I can't say.

Pratt: But he would have heard all that went on?

Wootten: Yes.

Pratt: Did Miss Wheatley stamp her foot?

Wootten: She may have done.

Pratt: Why did she do this?

Wootten: I do not know. I can't remember if she did.

Pratt: There was a struggle wasn't there Mr Wootten?

Wootten: No, there was no struggle.

Pratt: Were the letters to Miss Wheatley signed 'Your loving husband'?

Wootten: I could not tell you. Some of them may have been. I don't remember signing that. I mainly signed them 'Bert' or I might say 'With love, Bert'.

Pratt: Now, you lived with Miss Wheatley at Richmond Road in Shepherd's Bush?

Wootten: No, I never lived with her.

Pratt: Did you take the room for her as your wife?

Wootten: No.

Pratt: Did you tell the landlady she was your wife?

Wootten: No. The landlady showed us a small room, not big enough for two. She said, 'It is not a double bedded room'. I said, 'No, it's for the lady only'.

Pratt: Did you say: 'I only want it for my wife'?

Wootten: No, I didn't mention her as my wife.

Pratt: Are you positive?

Wootten: Yes.

Pratt: Why did you avoid using the word?

Wootten: I didn't avoid using the word, there was no need to.

Pratt: You visited her that same night at Shepherd's

Bush?

Wootten: Yes, after Mess.

Pratt: And there was misconduct that night wasn't there Mr Wootten?

Wootten: No, absolutely not. There was no misconduct between us after 19th or 20th January.

Pratt: Did you then visit her on Saturday 20th March?

Wootten: No, I took her out for tea that day.

Pratt: Did you take her back to Richmond Road?

Wootten: I don't think so.

Pratt: And there was misconduct wasn't there?

Wootten: No.

Pratt: And the next day you gave her some money?

Wootten: Yes.

Pratt: How much?

Wootten: Four shillings.

Pratt: That was for her to get her attaché case wasn't it?

Wootten: No, she said nothing about it. I knew she had not come up with it. I gave her four shillings as she said she'd borrowed it from her sister.

Pratt: You were in the room for an hour?

Wootten: No, not for that long.

Pratt: You knew she had been at Ecclesbourne Road?

Wootten: No, I did not know that.

Pratt: On 22nd March you went to her room after Mess?

Wootten: Yes.

Pratt: And you were there a couple of hours?

Wootten: No, we went for a walk very nearly as far as Hammersmith. I'm almost certain we weren't in the room an hour.

Pratt: What were you doing?

Wootten: That night we discussed her situation

and she told me she was going to the Surrey Arms, Surrey Square, Old Kent Road, next day at 4pm. She said she'd seen the landlady who told her she had a chance of getting the place.

Pratt: Is that when you gave her the reference?

Wootten: I had given her a testimonial before this, I think I gave it to her on 20th March.

Pratt: It was a reference wasn't it Mr Wootten?

Wootten: No, it was a testimonial. I have already said so. You keep jumping around from one subject to another and then going back on it.

Mr Hedderwick: The learned counsel is entitled to conduct his cross-examination any way he pleases.

Pratt: Do you see at the top where it says 'Two years reference'?

Wootten: Yes.

Pratt: Did you intend it to be understood that you were giving her a two years' reference?

Wootten: That was not my intention.

Pratt: Mr Wootten, it was a reference was it not?

Wootten: I don't want you to speak to me in that tone of voice, I am a gentleman as well as you.

Pratt: Could you look at 'Exhibit 21' please?

Wootten: Yes.

Pratt: Could you read the first line?

Wootten: 'To all this may concern'.

Pratt: And the next please?

Wootten: 'I have much pleasure in recommending Miss M. Wheatley as a thorough good business woman, honest, and respectable.'

Mr Hedderwick: It appears to me to be both a testimonial and a reference.

Pratt: It is in the name Wheatley?

Wootten: Yes

Pratt: When did you know that was her maiden name?

Wootten: I knew this sometime in October. I

believed up to her arrest her name was Lanteri.

Pratt: Why did you give her a reference, or testimonial if you like, in the name of Wheatley?

Wootten: Because she asked me to.

Pratt: When did you have the ring engraved for her?

Wootten: I can't say. It was while we were staying at Hove in the latter part of December.

Pratt: Did you stay there as Mr and Mrs Wootten?

Wootten: Yes.

Pratt: What did the initials 'MW' on the ring mean?

Wootten: I had the intials put on for both our names. 'M' for Marie and 'W' for Wootten. I wore it myself for a time.

Pratt: On the night of your wife's death when did you rise from the Mess table at the White City?

Wootten: I believe it was before 8pm, between 5 to 8 and 8.

Pratt: Yet you didn't call at Richmond until 9:10pm?

Wootten: Yes, in the interval I had gone into the lounge for coffee, I may have been there 10 minutes. I then went to Wood Lane Station from there to Shepherd's Bush and then straight to a hairdresser.

Pratt: What is the distance from there to Richmond Road?

Wootten: About half a mile.

Pratt: Did you go straight there from the hairdresser's?

Wootten: Yes.

Pratt: Were there any customers at the hairdresser's?

Wootten: No, I was the only one.

Pratt: How many assistants did you see there?

Wootten: Two.

Mr Hedderwick: Really, Mr Pratt, is that a matter

of importance?

Pratt: I must test the accuracy of the witness. Mr Wootten, did you have a haircut?

Wootten: A haircut and shampoo (laughter in court) and a shave.

Pratt: In your evidence-in-chief you said that when you got to Richmond Road 'Miss Wheatley was flushed when she opened the door and appeared as if she had been hurrying, she appeared to be agitated, in a state of nervous excitement'.

Wootten: Yes.

Pratt: What was the first thing she said?

Wootten: 'Oh Bert, I haven't got that situation'.

Pratt: Did she not speak to you at the door about you being late?

Wootten: Ah, yes she did.

Pratt: What was your usual time of getting to Richmond?

Wootten: Between 8 and 9.

Pratt: So she would have been expecting you at the earlier time that night?

Wootten: Yes, she would have been.

Pratt: Had you told her the previous night you were coming the next night?

Wootten: I can't say I did; I think she took it for granted I would see her that night.

Pratt: Did you stay the night?

Wootten: She asked me to but I refused.

Pratt: Were you not in the bed then?

Wootten: No.

Pratt: Did you not undress and get into bed with her that night?

Wootten: No, I did not.

Pratt: What time did you leave her that night?

Wootten: It was before 11pm.

Pratt: Might it have been after 10:30pm?

Wootten: It might have been.

Pratt: Did she then say: 'I'd give anyone £5 to shoot me'?

Wootten: Yes, I think it was that day.

Pratt: Had she threatened to shoot herself?

Wootten: She had several times threatened to take her life by taking poison or by drowning herself.

Pratt: But did she not threaten to shoot herself?

Wootten: I don't remember that.

Pratt: When were those threats made?

Wootten: On occasions previous to this, when staying at Gibson Square she threatened to take her own life.

Pratt: Did she do so before that?

Wootten: I don't remember.

Pratt: You knew she had a revolver in her possession?

Wootten: No, I never knew that.

Pratt: Between 19th and 24th March when did you see the attaché case?

Wootten: I never saw it between those dates.

Pratt: Yet you had been in her room every day from 19th to 24th March?

Wootten: Yes.

Pratt: And had not seen it?

Wootten: Yes.

Pratt: Did you see inside it on 24th March?

Wootten: I saw something like a nightdress in it. I glanced in the case when it was open, nothing more than a glance.

Pratt: During the early hours following your wife's death did you believe your wife's death was accidental?

Wootten: No.

Pratt: But you had an idea?

Wootten: Yes.

Pratt: You thought something foul had happened?
Wootten: Yes.
Pratt: You had an idea that your wife's death was due to foul play?
Wootten: Yes, the idea was brought up in this way that when I went into my bedroom my daughter Lily said something, this idea was strengthened by the production of the telegram and the enquiries I made about it.
Pratt: What were your thoughts when you went to bed finally on 23rd March after your conversation with the Dixons?
Wootten: My thoughts were varied, I was thinking the whole thing out.
Pratt: So, let me see, did you say to the coroner: 'feeling convinced it was an accident I went to bed'?
Wootten: I don't remember saying it.
Pratt: So if you said it, it was untrue?
Wootten: No, I wasn't convinced either way.
Pratt: And what were the fresh facts that came to your knowledge between going to bed and seeing Miss Wheatley the next day?
Wootten: The only fresh fact was the telegram and what Ivy said.
Pratt: Did you not speak to Lily before going to bed?
Wootten: Both my children told me next morning what had happened.
Pratt: Did you accuse Miss Wheatley of murder?
Wootten: No, when I saw her I told her what I believed. I didn't accuse her. I gave her the grounds of my belief.
Pratt: Which were what?
Wootten: What Lily had told me about the two bangs and 'Mrs Higson's friend.'
Pratt: Did you tell the coroner you had told Miss

Wheatley that?

Wootten: I believe I did.

Pratt: The truth is you did not tell Miss Wheatley on 24th March about Lily's statement did you?

Wootten: I did.

Pratt: Why did you not tell the coroner that?

Wootten: I thought I did tell the coroner.

Pratt: When you asked her if she went to your house and sent the telegram she replied at once didn't she?

Wootten: Yes.

Pratt: She replied at once that she did not go to your house and send the telegram?

Wootten: Yes.

Pratt: No hesitation?

Wootten: No.

Pratt: You said in evidence that on the 24th you said to Miss Wheatley: 'I want your movements on the 23rd' and she replied 'You prove them'.

Wootten: Yes.

Pratt: In fact, what she actually said was: 'I had been after a situation'?

Wootten: No, she did not say that.

Pratt: When you asked her why she went to your house last night did she reply at once: 'I did not go to your house last night'?

Wootten: Yes.

Pratt: And she denied sending the telegram?

Wootten: Yes.

Mr Hedderwick (to Mr Pratt): I am not at all sure that you have not let in the statements of the children to the witness which would not otherwise have been evidence.

Pratt: I submit not. I have been very careful on that point. (To the witness): Did Miss Wheatley say to you: 'The case looks black against me, but don't drag me into this'?

Wootten: Yes.

Pratt: You did not say a word of this before the coroner?

Wootten: I meant to if I did not.

Pratt: I put it to you that it was Mr Higson who said 'The case looks black against you'?

Wootten: No, she said 'The case looks black against me and you're not going to drag me into it'.

Pratt: When you came away from that interview you were still suspicious?

Wootten: Yes.

Pratt: You paid the landlady's bill?

Wootten: Yes.

Pratt: Did you know Miss Wheatley was then left with only a few shillings in the world?

Wootten: No, and I did not care much.

Pratt: You were quite content for her to be turned out and left to starve?

Wootten: Exactly.

Pratt: Was your married life a happy one?

Wootten: Yes, it was a very happy one.

Pratt: Even after your wife discovered your relations with this girl?

Wootten: Yes. We had a conversation about it and it was agreed that the whole thing should be dropped.

Pratt: She did not reproach you about it?

Wootten: No, she was not of a quarrelsome disposition.

Pratt: Didn't you have trouble before this with another girl?

Wootten: No.

Pratt: With a girl connected with the post office?

Wootten: No, there was no trouble at all.

Pratt: You know the girl I refer to?

Wootten: No, I do not. If you have a name to

suggest let me hear it.

Pratt: I do not propose to mention this girl's name.

Wootten: No, because you cannot.

Mr Hedderwick: Was there such a girl?

Wootten: There was not.

Pratt: At the time of the murder did you receive a letter-card threatening you?

Wootten: Yes, the day after.

Pratt: Could the witness be shown 'Exhibit 22'?

Wootten: Yes.

Pratt: Where did you receive it?

Wootten: At 114 Rotherfield Street.

Pratt: What is the postmark?

Wootten: 8:30pm, posted in North District.

Pratt: Do you know the writing?

Wootten: No, I don't recognize it.

Pratt: Do you know what 'L Davey turn' means?

Wootten: No.

Pratt: Do you notice that your name is spelt 'Wootton'?

Wootten: Yes. Could counsel see how it is spelt on the cover?

Pratt: Still with an 'o'?

Wootten: Yes.

Pratt: Were you in love with Miss Wheatley?

Wootten: Not exactly.

Pratt: There was never love at all?

Wootten: No.

Pratt: Did you ever promise to marry her?

Wootten: No, I did not.

Pratt: Did you lead her to think you would marry her if you were free?

Wootten: No, sir.

Pratt: Do you think you led her to believe you were in love with her?

Wootten: I don't think so. I did not personally express my love for her. I never said it and never wrote it.

Pratt: What do you mean by 'not exactly' and 'personally'.

Wootten: I mean what I say. If you have not the common sense to understand –

Pratt: Do not be impertinent sir!

Wootten: You asked for it!

Pratt: Was it you who gave information to the police about Miss Wheatley?

Wootten: Yes.

Pratt: Did you denounce her as the murderer of your wife?

Wootten: I said before the coroner that I denounced her but not as the murderer of my wife. I gave information to the police of my suspicions, not of her having murdered my wife. I didn't then know she had been murdered. I told the police my suspicions of Miss Wheatley having pushed my wife downstairs.

Pratt: No further questions.

Mr Pratt could feel very satisfied with this cross-examination. His production of Wootten's postcard to Marie's mother had unsettled the lieutenant from the start and he had cleverly undermined his credibility by asking him if he had sent such a card (which he originally denied) before producing it as an exhibit. Having flourished this postcard he then introduced, for the first time, the possibility that Marie had been made pregnant by him, and miscarried, before revealing his third surprise: the possibility that Wootten had been having an affair with another, unidentified, woman. Wootten did not help himself by his quibbling over whether he had written a testimonial or reference for Marie and his willingness to have entitled it a 'two years reference' was very damaging for him, having known Marie for only about six months. On one

question, however, Mr Pratt had been quite unfair.
His challenge to Wootten's denial that he had seen
the attaché case by pointing out that he had been in
Marie's room 'every day between 19 and 24 March'
was disingenuous for it was clear that the attaché case
was being held as security by Mrs Alland between 19
and 21 March and Higson gave evidence that it had
been hidden under the bed during the interview on 24
March (and, of course, both he and Wootten did see it
once Marie produced it). So there were, in fact, only
two days – 22 and 23 March – when Wootten could
possibly have seen the attaché case in Marie's room
before she produced it on 24 March and his failure to
have spotted it was rather less suspicious than it might
otherwise have been.

Friday 14 May 1915

Mr Boyd attempted to repair some of the damage
caused by Mr Pratt's cross-examination when
Lieutenant Wootten was recalled to the witness stand
for re-examination. He asked if the lieutenant had
really been willing to let Marie starve. Wootten replied
that the idea had never entered his head and he had
only answered in the way he had because of the way
the question had been put by counsel. In fact, he had
been led into a well baited trap by Mr Pratt. While
it might seem logical that a refusal to give someone
money means that one is willing for them to starve
to death, that is not the usual thought process and,
in this case, Wootten would have known that Marie
could have relied on her family for assistance before
the possibility of starvation even arose. Wootten also
clarified that he had never had any discussions with
Marie about her being pregnant or about her having a
miscarriage except that she had once asked him if he
would look after her if she was pregnant and he said
he would. Finally, he corrected his evidence that he

did not know an 'L. Davey' by recalling his altercation with a publican of that name about which he had told Marie (although that man's name was actually William Davy). In the end, Mr Boyd was not allowed to ask Wootten what his children had told him which made him suspect Marie of murdering his wife.

Stepping into the witness box after Wootten's departure was Joe Higson for his second bout of cross-examination by Mr Pratt:

Pratt: What did Miss Wheatley ask you to do to help her on 11th February?

Higson: She told me that she wanted an understanding as to what Lieutenant Wootten was going to do for her.

Pratt: What did you take that to mean?

Higson: Providing money for her.

Pratt: What was the effect of what took place at subsequent conferences?

Higson: Lieutenant Wootten told Miss Wheatley that it was impossible for him to go away with her or live with her.

Pratt: Are you sure he told her that?

Higson: Yes, he made it very clear that he had no desire to go away with her.

Pratt: What was the arrangement that you mentioned to her on 11th February which had been made in the back parlour?

Higson: The arrangement was that Lieutenant Wootten should make a provision for her until she got a situation and that she should refrain from worrying him by correspondence or personally.

Pratt: Did you have any discussions as to Lieutenant Wootten refraining from writing to her or seeing her?

Higson: No.

Pratt: What steps did Mrs Wootten take to obtain a

promise from Lieutenant Wootten not to see her?

Higson: None, she left the matter in my hands.

Pratt: She told you that or that is the impression you got?

Higson: Her exact words were: 'I'll leave it to you Joe to pull this thing through'.

Pratt: Did you get Lieutenant Wootten to promise that he would have nothing more to do with Miss Wheatley?

Higson: No.

Pratt: Well, why not?

Higson: I didn't think it necessary. I don't think the thought ever entered my head. I took it the arrangement applied to both parties.

Pratt: Did Mr Wootten agree to that arrangement?

Higson: I believe so.

Pratt: And Miss Wheatley, did she agree to that arrangement?

Higson: Yes, I believe so. I reminded her of that promise on 22nd February, the day she went away, and then she gave me her promise that she wouldn't worry Mr Wootten any more.

Pratt: Were you present when she handed her letters to Wootten?

Higson: No, I was standing outside at the kitchen door.

Pratt: Were the letters not exchanged in the bedroom?

Higson: The kitchen and bedroom doors both join on an angle.

Pratt: Were you in a position to hear any conversation between them?

Higson: Yes, but I did not hear anything when the letters were supposed to be handed over.

Pratt: Was this the day she threatened to take her life?

Higson: Yes.

Pratt: Did you ever hear her threaten to do that on any other occasion?

Higson: I can't say that I did.

Pratt: You have said when giving your evidence to this court that when you met her in City Road you asked her when she came to London and she said 'yesterday'?

Higson: Yes.

Pratt: That would make it Saturday?

Higson: Yes.

Pratt: Did you say that before the coroner?

Higson: I can't say if I did.

Pratt: You say you asked her where she'd stayed the Saturday night and she told you Gillingham Street?

Higson: Yes.

Pratt: Did you mention that before to the coroner?

Higson: I don't believe I did.

Pratt: Did you say before the coroner that she said she was going to Tooting?

Higson: I believe I did mention that.

Pratt: Did you see Lieutenant Wootten between 19th and 23rd March?

Higson: Yes, I saw him after seeing Marie in the City Road.

Pratt: Did you relay the conversation to him that you had with Marie?

Higson: In a nutshell, yes.

Pratt: Did he tell you that he'd seen Marie?

Higson: No.

Pratt: Did he tell you anything about Richmond Road?

Higson: No.

Pratt: Before you called on Marie on 24th March did you believe a crime had been committed?

Higson: Yes.

Pratt: What did you believe Mrs Wootten's death was due to?

Higson: To her having been pushed down the stairs.

Pratt: Throughout the interview you pressed Miss Wheatley to tell the truth?

Higson: Yes.

Pratt: By the 'truth' did you mean that she had pushed Mrs Wootten down the stairs?

Higson: No, I asked her to tell me the truth in reply to the particular question I put to her.

Pratt: She did not say 'Things look black against me' did she?

Higson: Yes, she did.

Pratt: You said it and she said 'yes' in reply?

Higson: No, I said 'yes' in reply to her.

Pratt: But you thought things looked black against her?

Higson: No, it never entered my head.

Pratt: But the substance of your thoughts was that it looked black against her?

Higson: It may have been. I wasn't thinking about my thoughts at the time. I was asking questions.

Pratt: Are you sure it was not you who said 'things look black against you'?

Higson: I am sure.

Pratt: Where was the attaché case?

Higson: It was taken from the floor under the bed.

Pratt: Did you not say at the coroner's court that the first thing said in the conversation about the dispatch case was: 'Lieutenant Wootten then said to Miss Wheatley: "you told me a lie when you said you hadn't the attaché case and that you had left it at Tooting".'

Higson: I can't say if that was what I had said.

Pratt: But you did correct it?

Higson: Yes.

Pratt: When cross-examined you said that both Lieutenant Wootten and Miss Wheatley mentioned Tooting?

Higson: Yes.

Pratt: Did you not say at the coroner's court that you could repeat the conversation word for word?

Higson: Yes, but I meant the bulk of the conversation.

Pratt: What is the correct version?

Higson: The correct version is that Mr Wootten never mentioned Tooting at all. He said, 'you told me a lie when you came up on Friday, you said you hadn't got your attaché case with you'. Miss Wheatley replied, 'Well Bert, I had to leave it at Tooting'.

Pratt: Was this the first time Tooting was mentioned?

Higson: Yes.

Pratt: Did Mr Wootten ask Miss Wheatley when she recovered the attaché case?

Higson: No.

Pratt: Are you sure Mr Higson?

Higson: I don't believe he did, I don't recollect him saying that.

Pratt: Isn't the truth that Miss Wheatley said that she had got it on Sunday after seeing him?

Higson: No, I don't remember her saying that.

Pratt: Are you quite sure?

Higson: She did not say it in my presence.

Pratt: When was she in your presence?

Higson: During the whole of the interview.

Pratt: Had you seen what Miss Wheatley carried in her attaché case when she was in your house in February?

Higson: Yes.

Pratt: Did Lieutenant Wootten inform Miss Wheatley he believed she had pushed Mrs Wootten downstairs?

Higson: Yes.

Pratt: On what basis did he give her to understand he believed this?

Higson: From what his daughter Lily had told him.

Pratt: Did you say this before the coroner?

Higson: I can't say, probably I wasn't asked.

Pratt: Did you say it when you gave evidence here last week?

Higson: I don't believe so.

Pratt: Why not?

Higson: I wasn't asked it.

Pratt: Were the two main things you charged Marie with on 24 March: going to 114 Rotherfield Street the previous night and sending the telegram?

Higson: Yes.

Pratt: And she denied them both?

Higson: Yes.

Pratt: Thank you. No further questions.

Ernest Ashdown, an engineer employed by ammunition manufacturers, Eley Brothers, gave evidence next as an expert witness. He had weighed and measured the bullet removed from Mrs Wootten's body by Dr Spilsbury and stated that, while its shape was distorted, in weight, diameter and length it corresponded to a 7mm cartridge made by Eley Brothers for pinfire revolvers. He further stated that Eley Brothers did not make central fire cartridges of that type. In cross-examination, he confirmed there was sufficient demand by consumers for 7mm pinfire cartridges for Eley Brothers to manufacture them and asked by the court how many were made he said 'a large quantity' adding that 'a good many' pinfire revolvers were sold in England. Although his evidence was accepted by Mr Pratt, there was a fundamental flaw in the prosecution calling someone from Eley Brothers as an expert witness. The only reason for any suspicion that Mrs Wootten had been shot with an Eley bullet was the fact that Marie had been found to have a box of cartridges in an Eley box in her possession a few days before the murder. So asking an Eley employee to confirm the bullet removed from Mrs Wootten was consistent with being an Eley bullet had only limited evidential value. Perhaps an employee from another manufacturer would have found it consistent with one of their bullets. It was a prosecution mistake which was to have dire consequences later. Mrs Higson was then recalled for cross-examination and it is worth repeating it in its entirety:

> **Pratt:** When did you first see Miss Wheatley?
> **Mrs Higson:** On 11th February, when my husband introduced her to me as the Marie I'd heard so much about.
> **Pratt:** How did you hear of her before she arrived at your home?
> **Mrs Higson:** I'd heard about her from my husband and Mrs Wootten.
> **Pratt:** When was this?
> **Mrs Higson:** About a few weeks before 11th February.
> **Pratt:** On 18th March, what time was it when you first saw the woman with the veil in Rotherfield Street?
> **Mrs Higson:** It was about 7:30pm.
> **Pratt:** Were any street lights on near the house?
> **Mrs Higson:** No, it was very dark.
> **Pratt:** Was the woman stood on the same side of the street as you or on the other side?
> **Mrs Higson:** She was on the same side as me.
> **Pratt:** How close were you to the woman who wore

the veil?

Mrs Higson: I passed right by her, a few yards away, there wasn't the width of the footpath between us.

Pratt: 'A few yards', so quite a distance?

Mrs Higson: I beg your pardon, I mean feet, there were only a few feet between us, not yards.

Pratt: Did you speak to the woman?

Mrs Higson: No.

Pratt: Why not?

Mrs Higson: Because I was not sure who it was.

Pratt: What was the colour of the veil?

Mrs Higson: It looked dark to me.

Pratt: What else was she wearing?

Mrs Higson: A long dark coat.

Pratt: Did you see the features of her face?

Mrs Higson: I did, just the side of her face.

Pratt: It was light enough for you to see that?

Mrs Higson: Yes, but not light enough for me to be sure it was Miss Wheatley.

Pratt: How long had she been staying at the same lodgings as you?

Mrs Higson: Ten days.

Pratt: When did you see the woman again?

Mrs Higson: About 45 minutes later.

Pratt: How far away from you was she?

Mrs Higson: A good way off – about two doors away.

Pratt: Did you see her clearly?

Mrs Higson: No I just saw a dark form of a woman down the street.

Pratt: Did you face her?

Mrs Higson: No.

Pratt: Did you pass her?

Mrs Higson: No.

Pratt: Could you say it was the same woman?

Mrs Higson: No, she was too far away for that.

Pratt: When was the knock at the door?

Mrs Higson: About 15 minutes later.

Pratt: Which would make it what time?

Mrs Higson: About 8:30pm.

Pratt: What did you do?

Mrs Higson: I remained in the kitchen while Mrs Dixon followed Mrs Wootten to the door and Mr Dixon and I were listening.

Pratt: Could you hear the words spoken?

Mrs Higson: No, I didn't hear Mrs Wootten's voice; it's rather difficult to hear from the kitchen what goes on at the front door.

Pratt: Could you hear the other woman's voice?

Mrs Higson: Yes, it was louder than Mrs Wootten's.

Pratt: Yet you heard no words?

Mrs Higson: I only heard the sound of the voice. I thought it was Miss Wheatley's voice.

Pratt: Are you positive about that?

Mrs Higson: I would not like to be positive; I thought she was at home at the time. I thought the voice was like Miss Wheatley's.

Pratt: What time did you arrive at 114 Rotherfield Street on the night of 23 March?

Mrs Higson: It was about 7:50pm; that is as near as I can put it now.

Pratt: How do you fix the time?

Mrs Higson: I looked at my watch just before.

Pratt: Was the garden gate open or closed?

Mrs Higson: I can't say.

Pratt: Did you open it?

Mrs Higson: I don't remember.

Pratt: Where did you come from when you entered Rotherfield Street?

Mrs Higson: Essex Road.

Pratt: Did you walk down the road on the same

side as 114?

Mrs Higson: Yes.

Pratt: Was it dark?

Mrs Higson: Yes.

Pratt: Did you notice any street lamps lit?

Mrs Higson: No.

Pratt: Did you notice anybody in the street?

Mrs Higson: No.

Pratt: Are you saying there was no-one in the street?

Mrs Higson: I can't say that. There may have been people there.

Pratt: When Miss Wheatley was staying with you at Gibson Square did she ever visit 114 Rotherfield Street?

Mrs Higson: Yes, she went on Saturday afternoon to find me.

Pratt: No further questions.

Mr Boyd stood up quickly to clarify with Mrs Higson that the 'Saturday afternoon' she was referring to was Saturday 20 February but that, while at 114, she did not see Marie who later explained that she had gone there to see Mr Wootten but had only seen his wife.

Mrs Alland also repeated her detailed account of her conversations with Marie on 19 March and, once again, Mr Pratt declined to cross-examine her at all. Her recollection of events was supported by both her husband and the lodger, Mr Mitchell, who also gave unchallenged evidence to the court.

Saturday 15 May 1915

Mr Pratt continued his pointless attack on the maid at the Ecclesbourne Road lodgings by attempting once again to challenge her recollection of the timing of events of the evening of 18 March. Why did she happen to notice the time when Marie arrived? Did she always make a mental note of the time of a knock at the door? Did she, as a rule, time lodgers in and out? Ms Thorn answered these questions with ease so Mr Pratt moved swiftly on to the helpful part of her evidence, namely that Marie had left the house wearing a *white* motor veil and was still wearing it when she came back. She agreed that the white veil showed up 'very clearly and distinctly' against her black coat. Mr Boyd attempted to limit the damage by asking her if the hall in which she had seen Marie was well lit and she agreed it was.

The other important witness to appear in Stoke Newington on the Saturday was Mrs Connor from 12 Richmond Road. Mr Pratt's main strategy was, of course, to destroy Lieutenant Wootten's credibility and Mrs Connor, despite being a prosecution witness, supplied some very helpful evidence for the defence. Wootten had been firm in his testimony that he had not introduced Marie as his wife when booking the room in Richmond Road but, during her evidence-in-chief, Mrs Connor stated: 'Mr Wootten said it was for his wife'. Curiously, she also said that she asked Marie her name two days later and Marie said 'Wootten'. If she had believed from the start that Marie was Mrs Wootten such a question would surely have been unnecessary but Mr Boyd was not allowed to cross-examine his own witness, even if he had noticed the discrepancy. Naturally, Mr Pratt returned to the issue in cross-examination and, when asked about it, Mrs Connor said: 'I'm quite sure Lieutenant Wootten said he wanted the room for his wife; he introduced her to me as his wife'. Her second helpful piece of testimony for the defence was her confirmation, as she had told the coroner, that Wootten had said that the amount of time he would require the room for 'would depend on

how he would be placed at White City', not on how
Marie was placed. This was damaging for Wootten
because he was only meant to be paying for the room
until Marie found a situation; it was not supposed
to be for his own convenience. Thirdly, Mrs Connor
said that there was nothing strange in Marie's manner
when she saw her at twenty minutes to nine and she
didn't appear excited, tired or exhausted: her manner
and appearance being the same as always. This, of
course, undermined Wootten's evidence that she was
out of breath and flustered when he saw her fully half
an hour later. Finally, she told Mr Pratt that Marie's
attaché case was 'generally kept on the dressing table
most times'. This was important for the defence
because Wootten had claimed not to have seen it in
her room during any of his visits to Richmond Road;
indeed when he learnt from Higson that she had it
with her on Sunday he accused her of lying to him
about it during their confrontation on the Wednesday.

At the end of the day, Sergeant Hewitt, who had
examined the revolver presented to him by Mrs Alland
in Upper Street Police Station on 19 March, explained
how he had thrown the spent cartridge removed
from the revolver into the fireplace. He was told by
Mr Hedderwick that it was 'a very silly thing to do'
although advising Mrs Alland to return the weapon to
Marie was probably even sillier.

Sunday 16 May 1915
There was no court hearing on the Sunday but
Detective Inspector Davis and Sergeant Wesley
were busy again on their travels. This time they left
Rotherfield Street at 7:30pm and decided to catch a
bus to Kings Cross Metropolitan Station. From there it
was possible to take a train direct to Shepherd's Bush
Metropolitan Station. Again, there were no delays or
long waits for the trains, and the entire journey took

just 40 minutes, meaning they arrived at Richmond Road at 8:10pm. There was, therefore, plenty of time for Marie to have made it back before 8:40pm, even if she had not left Rotherfield Street until ten to eight.

Tuesday 19 May 1915

It was the very last day of evidence at the North London Police Court and it began in shambolic fashion. When the proceedings were ready to commence at 11:20am there were no witnesses available in the courtroom. Detective Inspector Davis said he had seen some of them in the court but they had gone out again. In what might be considered a barbed comment against the officer, Mr Hedderwick suggested that 'an experienced detective' be sent to the nearest public house. Detective Davis replied that he had warned the witnesses to be ready at quarter past eleven to which the impatient magistrate countered that they should have been warned to be there at eleven o'clock and he angrily stormed from the court.

A few minutes later, Harry Wheatley appeared in court after his name had been called several times. The hearing then resumed at 11:30am and Mr Hedderwick, back in his chair, asked the witness why he had not been there at the proper time. Mr Wheatley replied that he had been elsewhere in the building chatting to his brother-in-law, Henry Mockford, who was another prosecution witness. The magistrate told Wheatley he ought to be punished for not being there at the proper time but, added dryly, 'it is punishment enough for you to be here at all' and left it at that. When he eventually got round to giving evidence, Mr Wheatley revealed that, when his daughter left for London on 18 March, she told him that she had a letter from Wootten enclosing a money order for seven shillings and she was going to see him. Yet Wootten had sworn that the last time he had written to Marie was in February.

Another potentially crucial statement by Mr Wheatley was that there was 'a flaw in the barrel' of his missing pinfire revolver which 'might explode if fired'. In cross examination he expanded on this by saying that there was 'a rusty flaw or crack extending half way up the barrel which I think would make it dangerous for anyone to fire it.' Obviously, if the revolver could not be fired without exploding then it could not have been the murder weapon. Less helpfully for Marie, her father also revealed that she had told him that she was married to Wootten.

Detective Inspector Davis' day went from bad to worse as he received a stern ticking off from the magistrate about his failure to caution Marie when he arrested her. He annoyed the magistrate by initially saying that Marie had not been cautioned 'in the orthodox way'. 'Was she cautioned at all?' asked Mr Hedderwick. 'No sir,' replied Davis. 'Then why not say so?' came the inevitable response. Hedderwick then went on to lecture the detective by saying: 'when an officer arrests a person on a criminal charge it is proper, and moreover, it is the duty of that officer to caution the person arrested that whatever is said might be used in evidence, especially when a person is arrested on a charge of such gravity as this. It is obvious that a person suddenly charged with a very serious offence might, in the distress and agitation of the moment, blurt out something which, however innocent in itself, might from the unconsidered nature of the utterance, tell heavily against the person upon trial. I hope the police will bear this in mind in the future'. It was music to Mr Pratt's ears. Not that Marie had said anything terribly incriminating to the police but her comments such as 'I am glad it has happened like this' and 'I should not liked to have had this hanging over my head' could have been taken to be admissions of guilt as opposed to someone pleased to prove her innocence after the accusations made by Wootten and Higson. The barrister did not let Inspector Davis off lightly and he put him under sustained pressure over his failure to caution his client:

Pratt: When was Miss Wheatley formally charged?
Davis: It was the next day, at 12:30pm – as near as I can remember.
Pratt: Was she cautioned then?
Davis: No.
Pratt: Was she cautioned any time before that?
Davis: No.
Pratt: When she was put in your charge what questions did you ask her?
Davis: Those I have said in my evidence.
Pratt: You said 'Would you care to give me an account of your movements'?
Davis: Yes
Pratt: Did you use that form to avoid putting a question?
Davis: No.
Pratt: Why did you not caution her?
Davis: I had in my mind that if she could give her movements I might be justified in liberating her. I felt the questions to her about her movements were for her own benefit.
Pratt: Did you contemplate the possibility of her declining to give that information?
Davis: No, that never crossed my mind.
Pratt: You never contemplated her answers being used as evidence against her?
Davis: No. I was anxious to help her if I could.
Pratt: What was the effect of using the words: 'Would you care to give me an account of your movements?' and 'Will you give me an account of your movements?'?

Davis: I would say it is much the same.
Pratt: Did you have it in mind that it was improper to put questions to a person under arrest?
Davis: No, or I should not have done it.
Pratt: Is it proper to put questions to a prisoner under arrest without a caution?
Davis: I would say so, but only when the questions are for the prisoner's own benefit.

Although the inspector's answers might seem breathtakingly ignorant today, it was in some ways understandable, if not excusable, that he might be confused about the proper procedure. A caution by a police officer, informing a suspect of his or her right to silence, was not, strictly speaking, required under English law which had not been updated since the first half of the nineteenth century.

When the century began, it was envisaged that an arrest would be initiated by a magistrate who would issue a summons against a named individual. A constable would then be sent to arrest that person who would be brought before the magistrate. At this point, as codified in the Administration of Justice Act 1848, the prisoner would formally be told by the magistrate that he or she did not have to say anything but that whatever they did say would be taken down in writing and could be used in evidence against them. It was not originally anticipated that police constables would be making their own decisions about who to arrest so there was no standard procedure to assist them.

By the second half of the century, police officers, whether constables or detectives, were frequently making independent investigations of criminal offences and there was total confusion among police forces about whether and when a suspect should be cautioned. This came to the surface in 1906 when the Chief Constable of Birmingham felt compelled

to write to the Lord Chief Justice to ask for advice
after one judge had criticised a member of his force
for cautioning a prisoner while another had criticised
one of his constables for not doing so. However, the
issue was not resolved and when Chief Inspector Kane
of Scotland Yard arrested a former butler, George
Wooltorton, for extracting money at gunpoint from his
former employer in October 1907, he freely confessed
in court to not cautioning the prisoner by warning him
that what he said might be used against him, adding to
the surprise of many present that he had never in his
life done so with any prisoner. 'I tell the prisoner who
I am and what I charge him with', he was reported
as saying, 'and then I keep my mouth shut'. *John
Bull* commented sniffily that while the inspector may
be justified in this procedure in law, 'he is certainly
violating the well-known rule commonly acted upon
by other officers'.[101]

Similarly, when Steinie Morrison made a voluntary
statement at Leman Street Police Station, while under
arrest, regarding the murder of Leon Beron in January
1911, he was not cautioned beforehand by Divisional
Detective Inspector Alfred Ward to whom he made
the statement.[102] At a subsequent inquiry set up by
the Home Secretary to enquire into the circumstances
surrounding Morrison's arrest and detention, Inspector
Ward said that it was no part of his duty to warn
Morrison before he made his statement. Contrary to
general practice, he suggested that, 'If a man made a
voluntary statement to a police officer he did it with his
eyes open'.[103]

In October 1912, as a result of all the confusion, so
called 'Judges' Rules' were issued by the judges of the
King's Bench, at the request of the Home Secretary,
providing guidance to police officers when making
arrests. These rules stated that, although an officer

could question any person in order to establish if an offence had been committed, once an officer had reasonable grounds to suspect that a person had, in fact, committed an offence, and had made up his mind to initiate criminal proceedings, the suspect should first be cautioned before being asked any further questions. The caution would normally be in the form: 'You do not have to say anything but anything you say will be taken down and may be used against you at your trial'.[104] Although not having the force of law, any police officer who ignored the rules would run the risk of any evidence they obtained from a suspect being ruled inadmissible.

The obvious weakness of this system was that the point at which an individual officer decided to make an arrest was only within the knowledge of that officer and many arresting officers asked whatever questions they wanted and subsequently informed the court that they had not made up their minds to effect an arrest until they received an unsatisfactory answer from the suspect. The problem here for the officer was that if the suspect said nothing in answer to any questions, which was their right, there would be no legal justification to then go ahead with an arrest, having obtained no new information. And if they simply arrested them and asked them questions *after* arrest there was always a danger that the answers would be ruled inadmissible, even under caution, because some judges did not approve of police officers questioning a prisoner in custody. Mr Hedderwick certainly did not. In February 1913, he told a police officer who questioned a man in prison that: 'It is no part of a police officer's duty to do anything in the way of examination or cross-examination of a person who is to be charged'.[105] According to Hedderwick, such examination should only occur in open court and he offered the view that, if such questioning by police of prisoners in custody should be tolerated, 'we should be under the same system as the French, where a prisoner is brow-beaten'. Later in the same year when, refusing an application of the police to interview a prisoner, he said that it would be 'outrageous' for police to question a person in custody.[106] However, this was a personal opinion of Hedderwick's. Other magistrates and judges might allow such questioning. A police officer almost needed to be a lawyer to understand what he could and could not do. Having said that, the Judges' Rules had been in existence as a guide for well over two years by the time of Marie's arrest and Detective Inspector Davis should have known of them.

As soon as the prosecution closed its case, Mr Pratt submitted that Marie ought not to be committed for trial on evidence which, he said, 'basically consisted of statements alleged to have been made by the dead woman and it would have to be decided whether these statements were admissible'. He also pointed out that there was no evidence at all that Marie was at 114 Rotherfield Street on the night of the tragedy. While he did not mention it – being so obvious - the other point in Marie's favour was, of course, that there was no fingerprint evidence against her at all.

Fingerprints had only been used in criminal trials since the early part of the century and the first conviction for murder as the result of a fingerprint being found at the scene of a crime had been in 1905 when two brothers, Albert and Alfred Stratton, were convicted for the murder of an elderly shop manager, Thomas Farrow, and his wife, in Deptford High Street.[107] This case also set a legal precedent because police had been allowed to take fingerprints of the Stratton brothers after their arrest and use those prints (or at least those of Alfred, whose right thumb print matched a mark left on a cash box) against them in evidence, as opposed to comparing them with fingerprints already registered at Scotland Yard, which was a major step in a legal system designed to protect the rights of those under arrest. The use of fingerprints as evidence by the police increased steadily and, within only a few years, criminals either wore gloves or took care to wipe their prints from any weapon they carried.[108] Indeed, it was the suspicious fact that a professional burglar called John Williams had wiped fingerprints from a revolver, before burying it the morning after the fatal shooting of a police inspector in Eastbourne, which played a major part in his being convicted and executed for the murder in December 1912 even though there was no actual fingerprint evidence against him.[109] So the prosecution could, in theory, have used fingerprint evidence against Marie but, initially believing Annie's death to have been a tragic accident, the police had simply not made any search of the inside of 114 Rotherfield Street for prints.

Having said this, with Marie known to have previously been inside number 114, the discovery of her fingerprints might not have been of any significance. The murder weapon was obviously missing so no fingerprints could be extracted from that, even if it could be proved that the bullet which killed Mrs Wootten was fired from Marie's revolver. Of course, it would not have been at all surprising if Marie's prints had been found on the revolver but it might still have been significant if they had turned out to be the only prints on it (excluding those of the Allands and the two police officers who had held it). But that is theoretical only - there was no murder weapon and there were no fingerprints.

Mr Hedderwick commented that Mr Pratt had made his submission very carefully adding, somewhat cryptically, that he would rather not say anything about the evidence one way or the other. He stated that the case was essentially one for a jury so Marie Wheatley was formally charged for the murder of Annie Wootten and committed for trial at the Central Criminal Court. Marie, as usual, said nothing.

CHAPTER 9

THE NEW BAILEY

'Defend the children of the poor & punish the wrongdoer'

Inscription above the door of the main entrance of the Central
Criminal Court, opened by King Edward VII on 27 February 1907

It was a warm and sunny day in London – the
hottest of the year so far - as Mr Pratt walked up
Fleet Street towards the Old Bailey for the start of
Marie's trial on Monday, 21 June 1915. 'Old' is a
misnomer because it was a new building, having
been completed just eight years earlier on the site of
the now demolished Newgate Gaol, replacing the
former Sessions House as the new Central Criminal
Court. For the first few years of its life, it was, in fact,
widely known as 'the New Bailey' but this did not
really seem to work and everyone just slipped back
into calling it the Old Bailey, as it had always been.
Designed by Edward Mountford at a cost to the City
Corporation of nearly four hundred thousand pounds,
it was an impressive four storey addition to London's
architecture. Looking down on Mr Pratt, at the top of
a huge green dome, was a twelve foot high bronze cast
statue, covered with gold leaf, of the Lady of Justice,
a three foot sword brandished in her right hand and
the scales of justice in her left. Mr Pratt would have
been hoping that those scales would balance out in his
client's favour over the coming week but it was the
sword which was metaphorically hanging over Marie's
head; the only penalty for murder was death; although
it would, of course, be a rope which would administer
the punishment if she was found guilty. And it was
not going to be a lady who decided Marie's fate; a jury
in 1915 would be filled exclusively with men because

women were not allowed to serve on one. They would also be men who lived in a house with at least fifteen windows to ensure that poor people could not sit in judgement on anyone.[110]

A week earlier, on 15 June, a grand jury at the Old Bailey had returned a true bill for murder against Marie. This was an archaic procedure which, on the advice of the recorder, usually rubber stamped the magistrate's finding. While it was not unknown for a grand jury to throw out a murder charge, it did not happen on this occasion, despite the fact that it was recognised that there was only circumstantial evidence against Marie. Although Mr Pratt had failed to prevent his client from facing a murder trial, he would have been reasonably pleased with what he had achieved so far on her behalf. Leaving aside the crucial issue of the admissibility of Lily and Ivy's evidence – which would be decided by the judge – he had neutralized most of the remaining parts of the prosecution case. The veiled lady was important to the prosecution because her existence suggested Marie was planning the murder but all three witnesses who saw the mysterious lady in Rotherfield Street said her veil was a 'dark' one, whereas the maid at 36 Ecclesbourne Road had, of course, seen her leave the house wearing a white veil. In any event, there was no evidence that the veiled lady had anything to do with the murder. To the extent, therefore, that Mr Pratt had failed to undermine the maid's recollection as to Marie's comings and goings, which matched the comings and goings of the veiled lady, it probably did not matter.

In a similar vein, there was nothing to connect Marie to the 'Dickson' telegram which was not obviously in her handwriting and no-one had seen her hand it in at the post office. Wootten's belief that Marie had sent it because she liked to send telegrams was hardly going to impress a jury. Similarly, the 'L Davey' letter card could not be linked with Marie and the wrong spelling of Wootten's surname was very unhelpful to the prosecution considering that Marie knew how to spell it correctly; the lieutenant's request for Mr Pratt to read the spelling on the cover, only for that to contain the same error, was the kind of performance to give a prosecutor sleepless nights. In the event, the prosecution abandoned any reliance on that letter card at the trial.

As for Wootten's evidence, there was very little that had survived Mr Pratt's two cross-examinations which was harmful to Marie's life and liberty. Wootten himself had admitted that Marie's threat to kill his wife had been said in jest and could not be taken seriously. His claim that Marie had been agitated and flushed when he saw her on the night of the murder was contradicted by the landlady's evidence and could, in any case, be interpreted as her being upset after failing to get the position she had been hoping for as a barmaid. The suggestion that Marie had hidden her attaché case containing the revolver from Wootten, and lied to him about not having it, was undermined by the landlady's testimony that it was on open display on the dressing table in her room but, even without that, Wootten's credibility on any issue was in tatters. He had absolutely denied on oath ever having written to Marie's parents only to withdraw that denial moments later when such a communication was produced. And that postcard, albeit probably dictated by Marie, left the quite false impression that Wootten and Marie were married. Furthermore, Wootten had grudgingly admitted to 'deceit' in preparing a reference for Marie as if he had known her for two years. It was going to be hard for a jury to believe anything he said.

Mr Pratt's strategy of presenting Marie as a victim

of the lieutenant's philandering had also not been entirely unsuccessful. The picture he had painted of a young woman losing her job through the inconsiderate actions of an older, married, man who had then abandoned her, barely supporting her financially, despite an agreement that he would do so, was not so wide of the mark. Then, on the mere basis of the word of an eight-year-old girl, the two amateur detectives, Wootten and Higson, had dashed across London to accuse a startled and upset Marie of murder (quite wrongly suggesting that she had pushed Mrs Wootten down the stairs) before denouncing her to the police who had then arrested her during her first day in her new position without even informing her of her rights.

At the same time, Mr Pratt had in no way disposed of Mrs Alland's evidence which proved that Marie had been carrying in her attaché case a loaded pinfire revolver, which fired 7mm cartridges, only days before her rival for Wootten's affections had been shot dead by a woman (apparently) with a pinfire revolver which fired 7mm cartridges. Moreover, his client had no alibi for the time of the murder and had refused to tell the police where she had been. So there was still some considerable work for the defence team to do. Ironically, given the role of men in her story (and putting aside, for the moment, that the jury would ultimately decide her guilt or innocence) Marie's fate would rest very largely in the hands of one 62-year-old man – Sir Charles Montague Lush.

Appointed a judge of the King's Bench Division in September 1910, Mr Justice Lush was merely fulfilling his destiny. His father, the late Sir Robert Lush, had been a Lord Justice of Appeal and his older brother was a judge of the Exeter and Plymouth County Court. There could be little doubt that Charles himself, known as one of the cleverest junior barristers of his

Mr Justice Lush

time, would end up on the bench, although a profile of him in the *Sunday People*, in May 1915, commented: 'If you met him in the street, with his bowler hat and lounge suit, you would never take him for one of his Majesty's judges' and he was, according to the *Daily Express*, 'gentle in demeanour and quiet of voice'.[111] A keen golfer, proud of his handicap of eleven, Lush also enjoyed a spot of mountaineering when he had the time. Most of his time, however, was spent in the High Court, deciding relatively unexciting matters of civil litigation, but he made front page news in September 1911 when he controversially granted an injunction applied for by the freeholders of the Earl's Court Exhibition Building to prevent a much anticipated boxing match which had been planned between the American world heavyweight champion, Jack Johnson, and British challenger, William Wells.[112] He also made it into the papers in February 1913 when he enquired of counsel, in true, slightly out of touch, judicial fashion: 'What is a Joy Wheel?' despite this being a very popular funfair ride of the period.[113]

In addition to his civil law duties, and like all judges in the King's Bench Division, Justice Lush would put in a stint in the criminal courts every year. In doing so, he again came to national prominence in April 1913 when he sentenced Mrs Emmeline Pankhurst to three years penal servitude after she was found guilty at the Old Bailey of inciting her supporters to blow up a country house being built for the Chancellor of the Exchequer, David Lloyd George. Although, in sentencing, he told Mrs Pankhurst that her actions were 'wicked', he also said that it was his 'very painful duty' to send her to prison and showed a sympathetic side to his character by telling her: 'If you would only realise the wrong you are doing and the mistake you are making and see the error you have committed and undertake to amend matters by using your influence in the right direction, I would be the first to use my best endeavours to bring about a mitigation of the sentence I am about to pass'.[114] Following the sentence of three years imprisonment there was uproar from a large group of women in the public gallery, leading Mr Justice Lush to order the court to be cleared, shouting 'I will not have such behaviour!' Nevertheless forty or fifty women refused to leave and started singing Suffragist songs, forcing the judge to declare: 'If any of you repeat this conduct I shall consider the question of committing you to prison. I will not have this court turned into such an indecent exhibition'. His threat did the trick and, after everyone calmed down, Mrs Pankhurst was taken away to Holloway prison where, in June 1915, Marie now resided (but not Mrs Pankhurst who was released after only a year).

It was, of course, Justice Lush who would have the very last word in Marie's trial and it would be a crucial one. Whatever the prosecution and defence barristers had to say, the jury would inevitably look to the judge for guidance. Although, in theory, a judge was only supposed to sum up on the facts, in most cases it would be crystal clear what verdict he thought it was proper for the jury to bring and there would only rarely be a difference of opinion between a judge and his jury. In a capital case, jurors obviously knew that it was the judge's solemn duty to pass sentence of death on a convicted prisoner and few would wish to force a reluctant member of the judiciary to do so.

If Marie were to be convicted of murder, in a dramatic ritual the court usher would cry 'oyez! oyez!' and demand absolute silence in court. With a chaplain appearing as if from nowhere by his side, the judge would don a black cap - which was no more than a small, square folded, handkerchief - and say in a grave voice to Marie: 'The sentence of the law is that you be taken from this place to a lawful prison, and thence to a place of execution, that you be there hanged by the neck until you are dead, and that your body be buried within the precincts of the prison in which you shall be confined before your execution', concluding with the words: 'And may the lord have mercy on your soul', to which the chaplain would respond 'Amen'.[115] In the five years he had been judge, Lush had sent three murderers to the gallows while at the Old Bailey (and at least two more at the assizes), all of them men.[116]

Being a woman in post-Edwardian England was disadvantageous in many ways, not least of which was the inability to vote, but it had certain advantages when it came to being tried for murder. It was one thing to send an evil Crippen, a crafty Seddon or another similarly demonised man to the gallows but everyone from juror to judge, from prosecution to the press, seemed to balk at the judicial killing of a woman. Whereas Frederick Seddon had been unhesitatingly convicted of murder and condemned to death, his wife Margaret, against whom there was probably just as much evidence – not only did she admit to purchasing the arsenic fly papers which were alleged to have killed their lodger, Eliza Barrow, but she also cashed Ms Barrow's bank notes using a false name and address - was acquitted. During Seddon's appeal, his counsel, the legendary Edward Marshall Hall, complained that Mr Justice Bucknill's summing up at the trial 'was a most direct invitation to acquit the female prisoner and a strong invitation to condemn the man'. He was told bluntly by Mr Justice Darling, sitting as judge of the Criminal Court of Appeal, that: 'There is no getting over it that the present judges, and juries too, do judge a woman more leniently than a man. They may be wrong but they do it.'[117] This curious reverse prejudice reflected a general distaste amongst not only the judiciary and juries but the entire legal system regarding the execution of women. There was also more appreciation of how unfortunate circumstances could lead a female to kill than might be thought, considering the nature of the male dominated society at the time. One might even ask what a woman had to do to be sentenced to death for murder in England in the early 1900s. The examples of Daisy Williams and Florence Pettifer are cases in point.

Daisy Williams was just seventeen years old when she stabbed Dolly Steer in the neck with a knife, severing her windpipe, and then threw nitric acid into her face, at her lodgings in Florence Street, Islington.[118] A year earlier, she had left home with a female friend who had taken her to the West End and introduced her to a life of prostitution. Shortly after this, in September 1911, she happened to meet a professional violinist, Thomas Andrews, known as Theo, who had just broken up with his girlfriend, Dolly Steer.[119] He did not know of Daisy's line of work, thinking she worked in a confectionery shop, but they had sex on the first afternoon of their meeting. They started 'walking out' and got along so well that Theo took her to Sheffield to meet his father. However, a mutual acquaintance told Theo that Daisy was a prostitute and he, in turn, told her their relationship had to end because they could never marry. He explained that, if his elderly father ever found out she was a prostitute, it would kill him.[120] Daisy continued with her work, earning £15 or £20 a week, living in luxury accommodation, wearing expensive clothes and going out to dinner or the theatre every evening but she was alone, desperately unhappy and missing Theo.

In June 1912, Theo unexpectedly returned to her

and they started seeing each other again. Daisy gave him money and expensive presents such as a silver moulded walking stick, gold chain, cigarette case and silk shirts. Theo, while accepting her gifts, nevertheless asked Daisy to give up prostitution and go 'absolutely straight', holding out the prospect of marriage if she did so. Although she found it difficult, in the last week of June she packed up all her possessions and moved from a nice house in Claremont Square to a small, cheap, dingy room in Florence Street where she stayed on her own, not working, feeling lonely and only being happy when she saw Theo.

Theo, however, was an unpleasant drunk and bully who was particularly cruel to women. On one occasion, he brought the drummer from his orchestra back to Daisy's place and suggested she sleep with him, attempting to force her to do so when she refused. It was, supposedly, his way of attempting to cure her attachment for him because he felt their relationship was doomed. Earlier in the year, after transferring from the Shoreditch Olympia to the Islington Empire, a venue which Dolly Steer regularly frequented, he had become friendly again with his former sweetheart and had started seeing both women at the same time. Over time, his old feelings for Dolly emerged and, despite the brief rapprochement with Daisy, it was Dolly he preferred.

On 4 July, Theo mentioned to Daisy that he and Dolly had spoken of getting back together. Two days later, Daisy walked into a pawnbrokers in Goswell Street and purchased a revolver for three shillings. On 8 July, she bought some nitric acid from a chemist in Upper Street, saying she needed it 'for warts'. The very next day, Theo wrote to Daisy in order to put a final end to their relationship, telling her: 'I have been fortunate to win the affections of a True and loveable girl & I seriously intend considering her before anyone else'. Daisy took the phrase 'True and loveable' to mean pure and innocent, everything she felt was not as a result of her profession. It was a massive blow to her self-esteem. Furious, she immediately wrote back to Theo telling him that she felt 'nothing but hatred and loathing' for him and warned 'I can be just as bad an enemy as I was a good friend to you'. She then spitefully wrote to Theo's father and told him about her being a prostitute and the precise nature of her relationship with his son.

Daisy met Dolly briefly on Friday 12 July and then decided to write to Dolly's mother to tell her all about her own relationship with Theo and the type of man who wanted to marry her daughter. Unexpectedly, however, Dolly wrote Daisy a very nice letter on the morning of Saturday 13 July – before she would have had news from her mother of Daisy's character assassination of Theo – telling her she wanted to be friends. It was a desire that would cost the young girl her life.

Daisy would have been heartened to read in Dolly's letter that she felt sure her relationship with Theo was over. She immediately wrote back saying that Dolly's feelings of friendship towards her were 'returned a hundredfold by me' and suggested they meet up that very afternoon (the efficient postal service allowing same day communications of this sort). Dolly agreed and they met up for a few hours after lunch, spending an enjoyable time together. The next morning, Dolly wrote to Daisy saying, 'I have only known you a short time, yet I love you as much as it is possible for two girls' and suggested they should remain friends, even if Daisy got back together with Theo. The two women had arranged to meet for lunch on Sunday but Miss Steer pulled out, claiming she was too ill. Despite this, she met Theo in the afternoon and, as was her prerogative, changed her mind about their relationship, believing that she might now marry him after all. She probably signed her death warrant by writing to Daisy on the Monday: 'I have promised to give Theo another chance. He said he would never go back to you even if I gave him up, so you will see dear I might as well have him as any other girl'. Not surprisingly, although kindly meant, that undiplomatic comment did not go down well with Daisy who nevertheless wrote to Theo on the same day: 'You have told Dolly not to be friends with me, but I have had two very nice letters from her asking me for my friendship and I hope in the future we shall be firm friends'. News of Daisy's letter to Dolly's mother had still not apparently reached Dolly so there was nothing to prevent the friendship between the two young women continuing for the moment although it was only a matter of time before Dolly found out about it.

In the early hours of Tuesday 16 July, Daisy appeared outside Dolly's house, claiming to want to speak to her new friend. Theo, who had spent the evening with Dolly, emerged from the house and confronted Daisy in the street, asking her if she hadn't already done enough harm by writing to his father. 'I have only just started', she replied, causing Theo to lose his temper and hit her hard across the face, knocking her to the kerb. Daisy picked herself up and launched herself, screaming, at Theo but Dolly intervened and sent him back inside the house. Presumably believing that she could soothe over the dispute, one woman to another, Dolly then walked off with a tearful Daisy back to Daisy's room in Florence Street and, after a friendly discussion, no doubt complaining about men in general, the two women spent the night together.[121] In the morning, Daisy brutally murdered Dolly without any provocation or warning and immediately told her best friend, another prostitute called Norah, what she had done, commenting 'I don't know why I did it'. To Theo, however, she wrote, in a letter on the morning of 16 July, 'I killed her because I knew you loved her', adding, rather predictably and pathetically, 'although you have treated me cruelly I love you passionately'.

After Daisy gave herself up to the police, an inquest was held at Islington Coroner's Court before Walter Schröder. Just as with Marie, his jury returned a verdict of wilful murder and committed Daisy for trial at the Old Bailey - as did the Clerkenwell magistrate - the judge assigned to the case at trial being Mr Justice Lush. However, in a surprise move, the grand jury threw out the bill for murder and, with the agreement of Justice Lush, Daisy was only tried for manslaughter, to which she pleaded guilty. The judge, making allowances for Daisy's youth and taking the view that the crime was committed without premeditation in 'a moment of anguish', sentenced her to eighteen months hard labour. It was a compassionate decision which acknowledged that Daisy had been badly treated by Theo but, at the same time, the judge appears to have given little consideration to the fact that a totally innocent young woman had cruelly and painfully lost her life.[122] What Dolly's mother thought of the sentence is not recorded.

Another female killer to appear before Justice Lush was Florence Pettifer.[123] On 28 February 1913, she had walked into Peckham Police Station, placed a loaded revolver on the counter and said in a very excited way 'I've just shot my husband'. When the police went to her house at 40 Moncrief Street they found the dead body of her husband who had been shot in the back with a single bullet. Also in the house was a letter Mrs

Pettifer had written (but not sent) to the local coroner before the shooting in which she stated: 'I am prepared for trouble as my husband has threatened to do me in tonight so I am going to be first if I can'.

Investigations revealed that Frederick Pettifer had regularly beaten his wife and treated her with extraordinary cruelty. Indeed, five years before the killing, Florence had attempted suicide as a result of her husband's violence towards her. The couple had separated but Frederick, out of work and with no money, pleaded to be taken back and Florence accepted him. She paid for him to obtain a driver's licence which helped him get back into work with an omnibus company but, as soon as he did and was able to support himself, his personality transformed and he started ill treating her again, often giving her black eyes and bruises. She was so frightened of him that she used to sleep with her bed pulled across the door to prevent him coming into her room and kept a loaded revolver, for which she had a licence, under her bed. It wasn't just her husband; his brothers threatened to 'smash her face in' if she disobeyed her husband's instructions so she felt completely trapped.

For Florence, what was worse than the violence was that her husband was in a relationship with another woman he was financially supporting, paying her ten shillings a week. In her letter to the coroner, Florence wrote that this woman, Elizabeth Clayton, had been 'the curse of my life this last five years. May my bitterest curse rest on her now.' In mid-February 1913, she visited Miss Clayton's house and told her that she would get no more money from her husband because 'I have got something in my pocket to stop you and him doing it.' That was undoubtedly a reference to her revolver but it was unexpectedly taken away from her on 25 February by another resident of 40 Moncrief Street, Fred Thorpe, who picked it up off the floor after he was awakened by a late night fight between the couple. After Florence told him the weapon was hers, he took it to the police station but, as it was legally in Florence's possession, the officer he spoke to was unable to offer him any advice about what to do. Thorpe told Florence he would only return the revolver to her on condition that she pawned it and gave him the ticket. She did this and Thorpe immediately handed the ticket to the police. However, on the morning of 27 February, Florence boldly made a (false) declaration at Greenwich Police Court that she had lost her pawn ticket, obtaining an order from the magistrate which allowed her to retrieve the revolver from the pawnbroker. That evening she waited in an excited state for her husband to return from work. Fred Thorpe noticed Florence's strange manner and warned Mr Pettifer when he got back home that 'there was mischief about' but the warning was not taken seriously and, early the following morning, he was dead.

In this instance, the grand jury did find a bill of murder against the prisoner and, at the Old Bailey, on trial for her life, Florence told Justice Lush that her husband had been in a bad temper at the time and threatened to strike her. She had, she said, put the revolver up and it went off accidentally. Despite this very unlikely story, the jury took fifteen minutes to find her not guilty of murder. The clerk of the court asked the foreman: 'Do you find her guilty for anything else?' expecting a verdict of manslaughter, but the foreman replied 'No' and Justice Lush had no option but to discharge her.[124] It was a compassionate decision. The jury had been fully sympathetic to the prisoner's treatment at the hands of her violent and adulterous husband.[125]

The escape of Daisy and Florence from the noose may be contrasted with the case of Sargent Philp who, penniless and hungry, stabbed and killed his estranged wife, Rose, on 26 July 1912 in a house off the Old Kent Road in South London after she refused to go back to him because he had no money.[126] Like both Daisy and Florence, Philp confessed immediately, telling police: 'I did it. I don't know what made me do it I am sure... It's her own fault, she won't stay with me...I've had no food for three days...I did not know what I was doing. If she had come back to me this morning this would not have happened'. At the same time, showing no real remorse, he also said that he would happily have killed his wife's mother and sister too, blaming them for the problems he had with his wife. It emerged that Rose had left him due to his 'persistent cruelty' and drinking, having obtained a court order three weeks before the murder which ordered him to pay her ten shillings a week to help support their children. There were some mitigating circumstances in that, while working as a farrier for the London General Omnibus company, a piece of steel flew into his right eye causing him to lose the sight in that eye, yet he lost his claim for compensation against the company, leaving him broke.[127] However, he received no sympathy from the jury or the judge and, having been found guilty of his wife's murder, Justice Lush put on his black cap and sentenced him to death. He was duly hanged at Wandsworth prison on 1 October 1912.

Jon Albis, a young Romanian merchant seaman, only fared a little better after he was arrested for cutting the throat of a Russian boatswain, Bernard Balod, while he slept out on the High Seas off Las Palmas on board the steamship SS Bowes Castle in the early hours of 22 September 1913.[128] The evidence of other crew members was that Albis and Balod had been on good terms until the day before the murder when, probably both drunk, they quarrelled. Balod had made some provocative comments causing Albis to insult him which led to a fist fight. Albis told other members of the crew that he was going to take further action but they didn't believe him. During the night he found an axe in the engine room and used it three times on Balod's neck before throwing it overboard. In the morning he did not attempt to deny the murder, saying in broken English: 'I am sorry. I cannot help it. He laugh all the time at me'. Albis was brought back to Britain and arraigned before Mr Justice Lush on 9 October 1913. Without any legal representation he pleaded guilty to murder but subsequently withdrew his plea on the advice of the judge who also arranged for counsel to defend him. Nevertheless, he was found guilty of wilful murder and sentenced to death but he got lucky and won a reprieve at the end of the month when the Secretary of State commuted the sentence to penal servitude for life, probably for diplomatic reasons considering he was a Romanian citizen.

As a woman charged with murder, therefore, the odds could be said to be in Marie's favour. There were parallels of Marie's case in both the Daisy Williams and Florence Pettifer killings. Daisy had eliminated a love rival but had received the slightest of sentences while Florence had fired a single shot from a revolver yet had not even been found guilty of manslaughter, let alone murder. All three young women had been badly treated at the hands of men although, in Marie's case no-one had physically harmed her. If Marie had admitted to the shooting, and pleaded guilty to manslaughter, saying that she had intended to threaten Mrs Wootten but that the revolver went off by accident, there can be little doubt that she would have avoided a conviction for murder and would probably have received a sentence of only a few years penal servitude, if that, for manslaughter. But that was not the approach to be taken by Marie in this case and she was to plead not guilty to murder.

If she was found guilty and sentenced to be hanged there was still a reasonable chance of a recommendation by the jury for mercy, which would be forwarded by the judge to the Home Secretary who would probably commute the sentence, although he did not always do so. In January 1903, an Old Bailey jury found Annie Walters and Amelia Sach guilty of the murder of a baby in their care at a private nursing home they ran in East Finchley where unmarried pregnant women could pay for their newly born babies to be taken away and adopted.[129] When giving their verdict, the jury made a recommendation to mercy for the pair 'because they were women', although both the judge and the government ignored it, undoubtedly because Walters and Sach were suspected by the authorities of murdering many more babies than the single one they were convicted of, and the two women were hanged at Holloway prison a few weeks later. However, that was an exception; a recommendation for mercy by a jury usually ended in reprieve for a condemned prisoner as long as the trial judge agreed with it.

In February 1914, Justice Lush had found himself in such a situation after his jury at Staffordshire Assizes recommended mercy for chimney sweeper, Charles Longmore, when they found him guilty of murdering his wife of 33 years by stabbing her in the throat. Longmore had made a number of threats to kill his wife in the period leading up to the murder and it was clearly no accident but the jury accepted he had been provoked: his wife having treated him very badly. Home Office papers at the National Archives show that the judge's views were critical in this case as to whether Longmore was hanged or not and Justice Lush strongly supported the recommendation of the jury on the grounds of 'the provocation he had received from his wife's long continued drunken and irritating habits' and also because he believed Longmore had been affected by an accident in about 1912 when he had been knocked unconscious by a horse and trap.[130] As a result, Longmore was reprieved by the Home Secretary and his sentence was commuted to one of life imprisonment.[131]

In the case of a woman being convicted of murder in the circumstances Marie found herself in, with only one shot fired and the mitigating circumstances of Wootten's treatment of her, it is almost certain that a jury would have recommended mercy, that the judge would have agreed with the jury, and that the Home Secretary would have acted upon that recommendation. Very few women were hanged in Edwardian and Post-Edwardian England and, in fact, no woman had been executed in England since Walters and Sach over twelve years earlier (albeit that one woman, Rhoda Willis, had been hanged in Wales in 1907 for murdering a child she had been paid £6 to adopt). Only four women, including Walters and Sach, had been hanged in England during the previous fifteen years so the chances were extremely good that Marie would escape the rope even if she were found guilty of murder. Alternatively, an appeal of the verdict to the recently established Criminal Court of Appeal was possible, although it rarely overturned a jury's decision in such cases. Even if an appeal failed and there had been no recommendation for mercy, it was possible that a petition could be raised by the public, with noises in the press, and this would usually influence the Home Secretary to grant a last minute reprieve.[132] However, none of this could be absolutely relied upon and Marie's trial could still conceivably end with her own death.

Richard David Muir, Marie's prosecutor, in 1914

CHAPTER 10

TRIAL

*'Speak of me as I am; nothing extenuate. Nor set down aught in malice:
then must you speak of one that loved not too wisely but too well.'*

Othello, William Shakespeare, c. 1602

Number One court of the Old Bailey was the
largest court in the new building and the most famous
courtroom in the land. Panelled in Austrian oak,
with a huge glass dome fanlight in the ceiling, the
judge sat on a high backed oak chair with an olive
green leather cover upon which the City of London's
arms were stamped in gold while, above the chair,
hung an old, sixteenth century, sword, known as
the Sword of Justice. It was in this courtroom on
Monday, 21 June 1915, that Richard David Muir,
Senior Counsel to the Treasury, who, by coincidence,
had unsuccessfully prosecuted both Daisy Miller
and Florence Pettifer before Mr Justice Lush, opened
the Crown's case against Marie, again before Justice
Lush.[133] Although by no means a gifted orator - on
the contrary, he had a dour, rather ponderous, style
of delivery - Muir was nevertheless one of the leading
prosecuting barristers of his day. His success came
through hard work and meticulous preparation and
he has been described (by his biographer) as 'the most
thorough man at the Bar'.[134] He became a household
figure after tormenting Crippen in the witness box in
October 1910, successfully securing his conviction for
the murder of his wife, but had been a feared criminal
prosecutor in murder cases long before this, having
led the prosecution of the Stratton brothers, against
whom he deployed the groundbreaking fingerprint
evidence mentioned earlier, in May 1905. Crippen was

supposed to have said to his lawyer before his trial that he wished it had been anybody else but Richard Muir prosecuting him but this story, not having any reliable first hand source, is probably apocryphal.[135] Much would depend on how vigorously Mr Muir prosecuted the case against Marie. In the absence of a murder weapon, fingerprint evidence and any eye-witnesses to the shooting, was he sufficiently motivated, and did he have enough energy in his fifty-eighth year, to put in the hard work to convince the twelve men in the jury that she should be convicted and sentenced to death for her alleged crime?

According to his biographer, Muir generally did not like prosecuting women for murder at a time when prosecutions for child murder were frequent in respect of unwanted babies (abortion being illegal) and he much preferred it when a medical officer would inform the judge that the prisoner was unfit to plead so that she would be detained at His Majesty's Pleasure for a short while before being quietly released. Nevertheless, he had been involved in at least one prosecution of a female murderess who was found guilty and executed. This was in December 1899 when 36-year-old Louisa Masset was convicted of smashing her illegitimate three-year-old son over the head with a brick and then suffocating him in the ladies toilet at Dalston Junction train station, where his body was found a few hours later. At her trial she told a story that she had handed him over, alive, to two women who had agreed to take care of him for £12 a year but she was not believed by the jury.[136] Given the horrific nature of the crime, this was a rare example of a clamour by the press and public for a woman actually to be executed rather than reprieved and she was hanged at Holloway Prison in January 1900. Muir was only the junior barrister in this case, the prosecution of which had been led by Charles Mathews, but he had been sufficiently convinced of Masset's guilt to participate in an energetic prosecution. When he strongly believed in his brief, Muir was as tenacious and as dangerous an opponent as anyone the Crown could offer to lead a prosecution.

Perhaps the most important fact about the identity of the prosecuting counsel, however, was that it was not the Attorney General, Sir Edward Carson KC, nor the Solicitor General, Sir Frederick Smith KC. It was not so much that their appearance in court put pressure on juries to convict and on judges to impose strict sentences – although this was undoubtedly the case – nor were they especially feared prosecutors (although Sir Edward Carson was known as a brilliant barrister). Rather it was that they would have enjoyed a peculiar advantage in being able, if they so wished, to deliver their closing speech after Mr Pratt delivered his own speech at the end of the trial. This was a unique right enjoyed by law officers as a matter of public policy and, despite complaints about its unfairness from many defending barristers, there was nothing they could do about it. True, it was highly unlikely that the Attorney General would become involved in a murder case of this sort; he normally only prosecuted matters of national importance such as those involving breaches of the Official Secrets Act, espionage or action by suffragettes. However, assisted by Richard Muir, the then Attorney General, Sir Rufus Isaacs KC, had taken the lead in the prosecution of Frederick and Margaret Seddon in 1912, so it was by no means impossible for such a prosecution to occur, although the attraction of the Seddon case to the Attorney General was that it was a poisoning case, for which law officers traditionally exercised their right to prosecute (although they did not in the Crippen case), presumably because it was

such a dastardly form of murder that it threatened
the very fabric of civilised society. Mr Pratt knew
that being able to have the last word in a murder trial,
albeit before the judge summed up on the facts, was
absolutely essential so that he would be able to repair
any damage done by the prosecution's closing speech.
As long as he did not call any witnesses (apart from
Marie) in support of his case, or did not adduce any
additional evidence, both of which would have meant
he would have to make his closing speech before the
prosecution's – another strange quirk of the ancient
legal system then in force – he would be safe in having
the final say.

Marie was brought to the court from the basement
up stone steps which led directly into the dock. She
was, we are told, wearing a blue costume together with
her favourite black hat. The dock was directly opposite
the judge's bench and Marie's first sight of the judge
would have been through a bouquet of flowers that
Mr Justice Lush liked to keep in front of him to scent
the air of his courtroom. In opening the case for the
prosecution, Mr Muir told the jury that Marie took the
room at Ecclesbourne Road, 'with the object of getting
an opportunity to murder Mrs Wootten and kept the
fact of her having taken the room as great a secret as
she could from anyone connected with the Woottens'.
The bogus telegram, he said, although admitting it was
not in Marie's handwriting, was sent by Marie with
the object of getting the Dixons out of the house. He
pointed out that Marie 'has preserved an unbroken
silence as to her movements on the day of the crime'.
What he did not tell the jury, because he was not
allowed to, was that Mrs Wootten had informed her
girls that 'Mrs Higson's friend', otherwise known as
Marie Wheatley, had been at the door when she was
taking up a glass of water on the night of her murder.

Mr Justice Lush had ruled this evidence inadmissible. The prosecution's best point had been eliminated and, for all intents and purposes, did not now exist.

The remaining evidence against Marie was, of course, entirely circumstantial. She had a motive, a weapon and, in the absence of an alibi, an opportunity to kill Mrs Wootten but, now, no-one could place her at the scene of the crime. There was no admissible evidence that she had been in Islington, let alone Rotherfield Street, on the night of the murder and no evidence that she had pulled the trigger of the gun which shot Annie. This was not necessarily fatal to the prosecution's case; circumstantial evidence can be just as good as direct evidence if there is enough of it. Prosecutors like to compare circumstantial evidence to strands of a rope; individually each strand is weak but collectively those same strands are strong and unbreakable. The more circumstantial strands there are, the stronger the hypothetical rope. If they were admirers of William Shakespeare, prosecutors might quote from *Othello* that there are 'strong circumstances which lead directly to the door of truth'.

At the same time, conclusions drawn from circumstantial evidence can be badly mistaken if there are in existence other, unknown, circumstances which might lead to a completely different conclusion. For that reason, when relying on circumstantial evidence, a lot of faith is needed in the competence of the investigating authority - in this case the Metropolitan Police - to have ensured that the fullest possible enquiries have been made and that all the available, relevant, evidence has been uncovered. It is by no means ideal, especially if police methods of investigation are not terribly sophisticated, as they were not during the period, but, with only limited forensic science techniques and knowledge to hand, most convictions for murder in the early twentieth century were based on circumstantial evidence and that was certainly the type of evidence which condemned Crippen and Seddon (the latter complaining: 'I am surrounded by a set of circumstances from which there seems no way of extricating myself') and it was shortly to convict Smith in the 'Brides in the Bath' case.

Speak of the devil and he shall appear. On the second day of the trial, everyone involved in the case of Rex v. Wheatley was unceremoniously moved to court number two because number one court was taken over by the star attraction of the month.[137] The trial of George Joseph Smith commenced on Tuesday, 22 June 1915. This was the show everyone in town wanted to see. Indeed, the press and public had, to a large extent, lost interest in the case against Marie. The sensational parts of the evidence had been reported twice in great detail already in most of the national and local newspapers during the previous few months – once from the coroner's court and then from the police court – and no-one wanted to read or hear it all over again.[138] Although the Smith committal hearing had also been widely reported, there was still much of interest to anticipate at the trial, not least because Smith was always likely to interrupt proceedings from the dock. Moreover, he was an alleged multiple murderer. The nation was both fascinated and appalled in equal measure by the idea that a string of women could be murdered in their bath in seconds without any evidence of foul play and, to the disapproval of the male dominated press, ladies flocked to the Old Bailey to see the monster. The Wheatley trial was very much the substitute viewing for those who could not get into number one court and everyone involved in it knew they were being demoted in the move to the second court.

A consequence of all this was that the Wheatley trial was not fully reported in the newspapers and, in the absence of any surviving transcript, the press is our only source for what happened at the Old Bailey. Another consequence might have been a reduction in Mr Muir's morale. He was too professional and experienced to say anything, of course, but he was only human and it would hardly be surprising if he was not a little upset in having to make way for a bigger case. He was the man, after all, who had successfully prosecuted Crippen, yet when the Seddons were put on trial the Attorney General had stepped in and, to everyone's surprise, taken that prosecution away from him as if he was not capable of doing it himself; he remained involved in a supporting role only. Now it was Archibald Bodkin, in some ways Muir's rival, who was to take the spotlight and engage in a battle of wits not just with George Smith but with the renowned Edward Marshall Hall, acting for the prisoner, in the number one court.

As it happens, there was a strange sort of relationship between the Smith and Wheatley cases during 1915. The inquest verdict at the Islington Coroner's Court into the death of Smith's third dead wife, Margaret Lofty, had been reported in the *Islington Gazette* on the very same day in January 1915 that Wootten's promotion to Lieutenant had been reported in the same publication. Smith was eventually charged with murder on the very same day of Annie Wootten's murder and it transpired that, like Marie, he had briefly taken lodgings in Richmond Road. In fact, by pure chance, the two prisoners being tried in the two main courtrooms of the Old Bailey in June 1915 had lived in adjoining houses during the year, albeit not at the same time. George Smith had rented a room at 14 Richmond Road in January, only a few months before Marie had stayed at number 12. When Smith was arrested in February, he actually gave his address as 14 Richmond Road. It was an extraordinary coincidence. If Selina King, the landlady of number 14 ever had a chat over the garden fence with her neighbour, Margaret Connor, during the summer of 1915, they would no doubt have had a very interesting conversation.

Most of the evidence of the prosecution witnesses at the Old Bailey trial was the same as in the coroner's and police courts with only a few differences. Mrs Higson was too ill to attend so the jury never heard from her, although her deposition would have been read. Lily gave evidence but the judge prevented Ivy from doing so a few moments after she stepped into the witness box on account of her young age. Auntie Mabel, who Lily initially thought was the woman at the door on 23 March, had been tracked down. She was Mabel Tilbury, the wife of Annie's brother, William, and confirmed that she did not visit Rotherfield Street on the night of the tragedy.[139] Her voice, apparently, did not sound like Marie's.

Second Lieutenant Caldwell-Cook of the 10th Bedfordshire was called to confirm that he remembered seeing Lieutenant Wootten dine in the Mess at the White City on the evening of 23 March and rise from the table at 8pm. We only know about his evidence from the newspapers, which do not provide any further details about his identity, but he was almost certainly Reginald Caldwell-Cook, although it is a curious fact that there were two (and only two) officers in the whole army at the time with the surname Caldwell-Cook, both of whom were second lieutenants in the 10th Bedfordshire Battalion! These were Reginald and Edward Caldwell-Cook, albeit

that 'Caldwell-Cook' was not really their surname.
Their late father, William Cook, had married Jessie
Euphemia Caldwell and the couple gave their sons the
middle name of 'Caldwell' which, over time, became
abbreviated with their surname to the rather grander
sounding 'Caldwell-Cook'. Reginald was born on 21
September 1890 and joined the Bedfordshire Regiment
at the age of 24 as a temporary Second Lieutenant on
1 February 1915, having only returned to the country
from Argentina within the previous fortnight - he
arrived at Liverpool aboard the *Desna* on 20 January
1915. William Cook had worked in the meat import
trade for the Sansinena Frozen Meat Company,
for whom he was European General Manager, and
had lived in Buenos Aires which explains why his
son was in South America. Reginald's immediate
promotion to an officer was possibly because he had
been trained in the Highgate School Cadet Corps as
a youth like his older brother, Edward, who had also
been living in Argentina at the outbreak of the war
and had patriotically arrived back in England on 28
December 1914. Shortly afterwards, Edward enlisted
as a private in the 3/28th Battalion London Regiment
(Artists' Rifles).[140] Extremely tall for his day, standing
at six foot, two and half inches, he was an impressive
soldier, being appointed lance corporal after only two
weeks' service, on 30 January, and was promoted to
corporal on 4 March, with his commanding officer
noting at the end of the month that he had only
been in the army for eleven weeks, 'but he would
not have been promoted so quickly had he not been
exceptionally promising'. However, Edward could
not have been the Second Lieutenant Caldwell-Cook
who gave evidence at the trial because he did not join
the 10th Beds as a temporary second lieutenant until
13 April 1915, after the date of Mrs Wootten's death,

having specifically applied for a commission in the 10th Bedfordshire on 30 March 1915 - no doubt because his brother was already an officer in that battalion. In any event, Caldwell-Cook's evidence was accepted without question by the defence and he was not cross-examined by Mr Pratt. Wootten himself stated that he had been on an attack scheme all day in Richmond Park, marching out at about 9:45am and returning at about 4pm.

The prosecution also had a statement from Jane Hadden, another lodger at 12 Richmond Road, who said she might have made the noise which Mrs Connor had heard in the evening of 23 March and thought was Marie. The most important new evidence, however, came from Ernest Ashdown of Eley Brothers and it was elicited by the judge who asked him if there was anything in the bullet removed from Mrs Wootten's body to show whether it was fired from a central fire or a pinfire revolver. Ashdown admitted there was not. It was a crucial point for the defence; one which had evidently been missed by Mr Pratt up to this point. Although Ashdown said that the bullet was consistent with a pinfire cartridge manufactured by Eley Brothers, the fact that he could not rule out that it might have come from a central fire cartridge manufactured by another company meant that Mrs Wootten could have been shot by either type of revolver. The fact that Marie had been in possession of a pinfire revolver thus became a little less incriminating.

On the second day of the trial, Lieutenant Wootten came in for another hostile cross-examination from Mr Pratt:

> **Pratt:** At the time you met Miss Wheatley, were you posing as a single man?
> **Wootten:** I did not pose as anything, either as a single or a married man. Nothing was said on the subject.

Pratt: But she believed you to be a single man?

Wootten: I suppose so, at first.

Pratt: You were content for her to remain under that impression?

Wootten: It was neither one way or the other. It was only an ordinary acquaintance.

Pratt: The incidents were only those of an ordinary acquaintance?

Wootten: Yes, at first.

Pratt: Did the misconduct between you at Shoreham result in her leaving her situation at the George Hotel?

Wootten: No, not as far as I am aware.

Pratt: Did she give you the reason for being discharged?

Wootten: Yes, she told me it was because her employer said she was getting too familiar with soldiers.

Pratt: Why did you help her and promise to provide for her?

Wootten: Knowing she was out of employment and knowing of my relations with her, I felt I ought to do something for her, and I did.

Pratt: You led her parents to believe that she was married to you?

Wootten: No, I had led no-one to believe that.

Pratt: Was it out of a sense of duty to your wife and children, or because you did not care for her, that you said your relationship with her must cease?

Wootten: Both.

Pratt: During the time you and Miss Wheatley stayed at Gillingham Street in Pimlico did you live together as 'Mr and Mrs Wheatley'?

Wootten: Yes.

Pratt: Did you ever buy certain medicines for Miss Wheatley?

Wootten: No.

Pratt: Or give her money to buy medicines herself?

Wootten: No.

Pratt: Regarding the letters you obtained from Miss Wheatley at Mr Higson's house in February, I put it to you that you obtained the letters from Miss Wheatley by force?

Wootten: That is not true.

Pratt: Were those letters signed 'Your loving husband'?

Wootten: No, I would not write like that.

Pratt: What word do you object to?

Wootten: 'Husband'. I have never signed like that, even to my wife.

Pratt: After the breaking off of arrangements in February did you continue to receive letters from Miss Wheatley?

Wootten: Yes.

Pratt: Did you reply to them?

Wootten: No.

Pratt: Why not?

Wootten: Because she wanted me to address them to 'Mrs Wootten' at her parents' house.

Pratt: I put it to you that you did reply to her. You sent her a postal order for 7/6 and told her to come down to London?

Wootten: That is not true.

Pratt: Did you lead Miss Wheatley to believe that you would marry her if you were free to do so?

Wootten: No.

Pratt: Do you know a Mrs Rufus of Islington?

Wootten: Yes, I do.

Pratt: Are you the father of her child which was born last December?

Wootten: No.

Pratt: Was your married life a happy one?

Wootten: Yes, my wife never had occasion to complain of my conduct with any woman other than Miss Wheatley.

Pratt: When did you first learn that Miss Wheatley's attaché case contained a revolver?

Wootten: Not before Mrs Alland, her landlady, gave evidence at the coroner's inquest.

Pratt: You knew Miss Wheatley's father had a revolver?

Wootten: Yes.

Pratt: Did you suggest it would do for you on active service?

Wootten: No.

Pratt: I put it to you that she gave you the gun?

Wootten: No, she never gave me the gun. I never saw it.

Pratt: I suggest that you had the revolver repaired at Hove in December?

Wootten: That is not true.

Pratt: And that you bought cartridges for it?

Wootten: I did not. I can say definitely that I have never seen a revolver in Miss Wheatley's possession nor have I ever bought cartridges.

Pratt: I put it to you that you saw that revolver at Richmond Road on March 22?

Wootten: I did not.

Pratt: And that you knew then that she contemplated committing suicide with that revolver?

Wootten: No.

Pratt: And that you took that revolver away from Richmond Road that day?

Wootten: I say no. I never knew she was in possession of the revolver or the cartridges.

That is as much of the cross-examination of Lieutenant Wootten as can be established from newspaper reports but Mr Pratt must have pressed him about his motives for going over to Shepherd's Bush to question Marie. Too much so, in fact, because Mr Muir argued that this allowed him to ask Wootten about what Lily had said to him in the early hours of 24 March and the judge agreed. In re-examination, Mr Muir dealt with this but he first tackled the issue of the revolver:

Muir: You see what the suggestion is – when your wife was killed on March 23 you were the person in possession of the revolver and cartridges. Is there any foundation for that?

Wootten: There is no foundation whatsoever for that. I was cross-examined for hours at the police court and it has never before been suggested that Miss Wheatley handed me a revolver and cartridges.

Muir: What was the reason you gave to Miss Wheatley for believing that she had been at your house on the night of the murder?

Wootten: It was in consequence of a statement made to me by my daughter Lily. I told Miss Wheatley that my daughter had said her mother informed her that 'Mrs Higson's friend' had called. Miss Wheatley then denied having been near the house that evening.

So 'Mrs Higson's friend' *was* mentioned in evidence but, in the absence of any evidence from Lily or Ivy about her, or an explanation from the absent Cora Higson about who her 'friend' was, it would not have meant much to the jury unless they had read previous accounts in the newspapers which they were supposed to ignore. Nothing further was said about Mrs Rufus and her baby, who Mr Pratt had sensationally introduced into the proceedings, but records at the General Register Officer reveal that Florence Rufus,

a 35-year-old fur finisher, and widow, who lived
in Islington High Street, gave birth to a baby girl,
Winifred, on 9 December 1914. The name of the father
on the birth certificate is blank.[141] Where Mr Pratt
obtained his information about the baby or why he
believed Wootten was the father is not known. It could
have been local gossip or might have come from Marie
who had learnt something from Wootten himself.

After Wootten's evidence was concluded, Inspector
Davis received a judicial dressing down for his failure
to follow the Judge's Rules. 'Is it not the habit to
caution an accused person?' asked Justice Lush. 'Not
the habit,' replied the inspector 'but I think it would
have been advisable to have done so in this case.' A
little late for such reflection.

At the close of the prosecution case, Mr Pratt
immediately stood up and submitted that it was a
case that could not safely go to the jury in view of the
fact that the evidence was purely circumstantial. The
burden of proof was on the prosecution – it was not for
Marie to prove that she was innocent – and Mr Pratt
argued that guilt had certainly not been proved. He
requested that the judge direct the jury to acquit his
client. However, Marie's possession of the revolver
and her lack of an alibi weighed on the judge's mind
and he ruled that he could not withdraw the case from
the jury.

The next question was: would Marie enter the
witness box and give evidence in her own defence?
She did not have to and, indeed, it was only within the
previous twenty years, with the introduction of the
controversial Criminal Evidence Act of 1898, that she
was even allowed to. Before 12 October 1898 (when the
Act came into effect), any statement that prisoners had
made under caution to a magistrate could be read out
in most criminal trials and perhaps a judge might give

them permission to make a statement from the dock - not on oath and they could not be cross-examined on it – but even this would not normally be allowed in a murder case. The prevailing view had been that, because the burden of proof was on the prosecution alone, a prosecutor either proved his case or he did not and there was no need for criminal defendants to say anything at all. Lawmakers, and some members of the judiciary, thought defendants, especially at murder trials where the stakes were so high, would only end up incriminating themselves, so it was best, indeed in their own interests, that they did not speak. Even if the accused was innocent it was not believed that giving evidence would be of any help. As one Member of Parliament said in June 1898, during a House of Commons debate on the legislation (then known as the Evidence in Criminal Cases Bill): 'the notion that any innocent prisoner would gain in the smallest degree by putting themselves in the box ought not to be imposed on them'.[142] This reflected a widely held view and, even some years after the introduction of the Act, not everyone was convinced it had been a good idea. Mr Justice Bigham, a former Old Bailey judge, then President of the Probate, Divorce and Admiralty Division of the High Court, opined during a speech at a dinner of the Leeds Law Students' Society in 1909 that: 'A prisoner might do his best in the witness box but his best might do him harm' and he believed the 1898 Act 'was not really of great benefit'.[143]

The first person tried for murder to give evidence in his own defence at the Old Bailey was a man called John Ryan, accused of the stabbing of a police constable in a street fight, but it didn't help him because he was found guilty and sentenced to death by none other than Mr Justice Bigham on 27 October 1898.[144] Another police officer had witnessed the incident so there was

not much Ryan could say to make any difference to
the outcome, despite his denials that he was carrying
a knife. At it happens, Justice Bigham – apparently
unhappy with the lame questions put by counsel for
the prosecution – took on the task of cross-examining
Ryan himself from the Bench and seemed to enjoy the
experience.

Perhaps surprisingly, the popularity of the right
to silence for defendants in criminal trials was not
confined to anti-reformers like Justice Bigham.
Prisoners seemed to like it too. Not many accused
murderers chose to give evidence in their own defence
in the first ten years of the new Act. Of those who
did, only a few were acquitted: the most famous being
Robert Wood, accused of killing Emily Dimmock in
September 1907 in what was known as the Camden
Town Murder.[145] Ironically, he had no real need to
say anything. The evidence against him presented
by the prosecution was flimsy at best (regardless of
whether he committed the crime or not) and it was
probably unnecessary for him to step into the witness
box. His performance under cross-examination
certainly did him no favours. He professed to be
completely unable to recall or reconstruct one of his
own handwritten documents, fragments of which
had been found burnt in a fire in the victim's room,
and his insouciant manner when being questioned by
Sir Charles Mathews for the prosecution could easily
have cost him his life. The well-known dramatist, Hall
Caine, who observed the trial said: 'It is not for me
to say who was responsible for putting Wood in the
box, but sure I am that the case of the prisoner would
have been more convincing and immeasurably more
sympathetic if he had never gone there at all'.[146] In the
event, he was acquitted to somewhat baffling popular
acclaim. Both Crippen and Seddon had also taken

advantage of the new law in 1910 and 1912 respectively but, in these cases, Bigham J might have been right after all - their testimony may well have played a part in ensuring their own convictions and subsequent executions. They certainly did not do themselves any good. George Joseph Smith, on the other hand, would choose to remain silent in the 'Brides in the Bath' case over in court number one – although he would frequently interrupt proceedings from the dock – but this would not help him either. Nevertheless, Marie stepped confidently into the witness box in the second court at the Old Bailey on Thursday 24 June and took the oath in a loud, emphatic, tone. 'I swear by almighty God,' she would have said, with the New Testament in her uplifted hand, 'that the evidence I shall give to the court and jury touching the matters in question shall be the truth, the whole truth and nothing but the truth'.[147] She was then gently examined in chief by Mr Pratt and told a sensational story, quite the opposite in many ways of everything that had been said up until that point:

Pratt: How old are you?

Wheatley: I was 22 last February.

Pratt: Where did you meet Lieutenant Wootten?

Wheatley: At Shoreham. We became friendly and went for walks together.

Pratt: Did you know he was married?

Wheatley: I asked before I went out with him and he told me he was single. I had been told by one or two of his regiment that he was a married man. I asked him and he stoutly denied it and I put it down to jealousy on the part of others.

Pratt: Did misconduct take between you?

Wheatley: Yes, on two occasions. Once in Shoreham and once in Hove.

Pratt: Did you have a situation while you were in Shoreham?

Wheatley: Yes, I was working at the George Hotel but I was discharged when it was discovered that Lieutenant Wootten had been in my bedroom.

Pratt: Did you then move to Hove?

Wheatley: Yes.

Pratt: Why?

Wheatley: Because he wired me.

Pratt: Did you live there with him as his wife?

Wheatley: Yes.

Pratt: What happened next?

Wheatley: When he had leave from the army we went to Gillingham Street in London and stayed there for a week then we returned to Hove.

Pratt: Were you in a certain condition at the time?

Wheatley: Yes, I was pregnant.

Pratt: Did Lieutenant Wootten give you anything to assist you?

Wheatley: He gave me medicine.

Pratt: When he went to Dovercourt did you forward letters to him?

Wheatley: Yes.

Pratt: Were those letters couched in endearing terms?

Wheatley: Yes.

Justice Lush: Could I ask a couple of questions. Who wrote the letter to your parents in December 1914 signed 'Mawks'? Was it you or Lieutenant Wootten?

Wheatley: It was Lieutenant Wootten.

Justice Lush: Could you give the effect of a letter written to you in February 1915 by Lieutenant Wootten which was destroyed?

Wheatley: He said that the letters I had sent had been forwarded to Annie, his wife, and there had been an awful row about it, and he asked me to send no more for a time.

Pratt: What did you do then?

Wheatley: I had no money and I wanted to see him so I came to London.

Pratt: Why did you go to Mr Higson?

Wheatley: Because I did not know where to find Lieutenant Wootten.

Pratt: You spoke to Mrs Wootten?

Wheatley: Yes. There was a long discussion. The conclusion arrived at was that I should have nothing more to do with him, nor he with me. It was proposed that he should provide for me until I should find a situation, because it was through him that I had lost my situation at Shoreham and I could not apply there for a reference.

Pratt: What was the reason you stayed with the Higsons?

Wheatley: To see if I could get a situation in London.

Pratt: Did you obtain a situation?

Wheatley: No, sir.

Pratt: When you went to Sussex on February 22nd was that agreement for you to give up Lieutenant Wootten varied in any way?

Wheatley: He said I was not to take any notice of any arrangement made before the others, and that he would always stick to me.

Mr Pratt: When did he say that to you?

Wheatley: He said that on two or three occasions, and said it was providing that I should take the children. I said I could not take four children. It was impossible for me to do that.

Pratt: Had you decided to give him up?

Wheatley: Yes. I made up my mind not to have anything more to do with him.

Pratt: Did you write to Lieutenant Wootten after this?

Wheatley: Yes, I wrote to him asking for money but only received one postal order. He did not reply to my letters. On March 13th or 14th I wrote and said if he did not answer me or send me money I would commit suicide.

Pratt: Did you say how?

Wheatley: Yes. I said I would blow my brains out.

Pratt: Did you tell him you had a weapon?

Wheatley: He knew.

Pratt: What weapon?

Wheatley: He knew I had an old revolver belonging to my father.

Pratt: Where was it?

Wheatley: It was in the children's toy box, but when I went home in December I took it away with me. I showed it to Lieutenant Wootten at Hove in December.

Pratt: Why?

Wheatley: When he was obtaining a commission he spoke of things he had to get. He told me he would have to have a revolver and a sword and said to me: 'Your father has been in the police force. Didn't he carry a revolver?' I said there was an old one at home and he said. 'If you go home you might bring it down and show it to me.' I did so and he said, 'This is a fine thing; it won't work. I'll see if I can get it repaired.' He showed it to me two or three days later, and it was then repaired. He had one or two cartridges in his pocket and we went on the Downs. He loaded it, and he instructed me how to use it. He said, 'You had better carry this; you never know when the Germans will come.' He gave me a box of cartridges a day or two later and I put the revolver and the box in my trunk.

Pratt: When you told Lieutenant Wootten you would shoot yourself, what did he say?

Wheatley: Not to be so silly as to take my life.

Pratt: Did he mention the revolver to you again?

Wheatley: Yes, he told me bring the revolver and cartridges up to London.

Pratt: Did you do it?

Wheatley: Yes.

Pratt: When was that?

Wheatley: That was on 18th March and he sent me seven shillings and sixpence for my train fare.

Pratt: Why did you take a room in Ecclesbourne Road in Islington?

Wheatley: Because I wanted to see Lieutenant Wootten.

Pratt: Did you meet him on 19th March?

Wheatley: Yes, I saw him at the White City about luncheon time.

Pratt: What did he say to you?

Wheatley: He said 'Hello Marie, I expected to see you yesterday'.

Pratt: Anything else?

Wheatley: He asked me: 'Did you bring the revolver and cartridges with you?'

Pratt: What did you reply?

Wheatley: I gave him an evasive answer at first because I didn't want him to know that I had brought them.

Pratt: Why didn't you?

Wheatley: I thought he would take them from me and I did not wish him to.

Pratt: Why did you wish to keep them?

Wheatley: I had thoroughly made up my mind that if he did not provide for me as he had agreed to that I should commit suicide. Eventually he talked me round and I said I had brought them and they were in the attaché case at Ecclesbourne Road. He said 'You must go and get the case at once'. He gave me the money and I went on the Sunday. On March 22nd I again met the Lieutenant in Richmond Road. He opened the attaché case and took out the revolver and cartridges. He said: 'I think I had better take care of these. I will destroy them. You are not to be trusted with them if you are going to shoot yourself.' He put them in his pocket and I have not seen them since.

Pratt: What were your movements on March 23rd?

Wheatley: I went out in the morning and again at luncheon and then went to Surrey Square, Old Kent Road. I had been looking at the paper and situations and was going there to enquire about one. The visit was fixed for 4 o'clock in the afternoon.

Pratt: What did you do when you got to Surrey Square?

Wheatley: I didn't take the situation because I didn't like the look of the place.

Pratt: What then?

Wheatley: I looked at shop windows and walked back to the Elephant & Castle after looking at another public house. From the Elephant & Castle I took a bus back to Oxford Circus arriving there when the time was nearing six o'clock. I had some tea at a restaurant in Oxford Street.

Pratt: Do you know the name of the restaurant?

Wheatley: No, but it was on the right hand side going to the Marble Arch, and I think it was a Swiss café.

Pratt: What did you do after tea?

Wheatley: After tea I walked back to my room at Richmond Road and I glanced at the clock and saw it was about twelve minutes to eight. I arrived in my room a minute or two later.

Pratt: On the following day what happened?

Wheatley: Lieutenant Wootten and Mr Higson called and asked me if I'd been to Rotherfield Street the night before.

Pratt: What did you tell them?

Wheatley: I denied it.

Pratt: Did they show you anything?

Wheatley: Yes, a telegram.

Pratt: Did they say why they were showing it to you?

Wheatley: They told me I had sent it with the object of getting everyone out of the house.

Pratt: What did you say?

Wheatley: I said 'I did not send that telegram'. I did not know Mrs Higson's sister-in-law's name.

Pratt: Had you knowledge of that telegram before it was shown to you?

Wheatley: None, whatsoever.

Pratt: Did Mr Higson say anything else to you?

Wheatley: He said: 'Things look black against you Marie'.

Pratt: What did you reply to that?

Wheatley: I said 'Well surely you are not going to drag me into this'.

Pratt: Is there a shadow of truth in the suggestion that you went to 114 Rotherfield Street on the night of March 23rd?

Wheatley: None whatsoever, sir.

Pratt: Or that you pushed Mrs Wootten?

Wheatley: No, sir.

Pratt: Or that you shot Mrs Wootten?

Wheatley: No, sir.

Pratt: Did you have a revolver or cartridges on that day?

Wheatley: No, sir.

Pratt: Did you say to the police 'I have never had a revolver'?

Wheatley: No, what I said was 'I have not got a revolver.'

So it had taken Marie three months to reveal that she was having tea in Oxford Street during the evening of the murder. Given the passing of time, it was pointless for the police to check with the tea shops if they remembered her. And that in itself was not even an alibi for the murder. If her tea lasted, say, half an hour, which would have taken her to 6:30pm, she could still have got to Rotherfield Street by 7pm, enough time to engage Mrs Wootten in conversation and then commit the murder (although, admittedly, she would not have been able to send the telegram from the St John Street post office in Islington at just after 6pm if she was having tea in Oxford Street at the time). Her actual alibi for the murder, such as it was, was that she was walking home alone towards Shepherd's Bush at the time Mrs Wootten was shot. It begs the question as to why she did not tell the police when they asked her for her movements in March. One might also wonder why she told the matron at Islington Police Station that she could prove her whereabouts at the time of the murder when it must have been perfectly clear to her that she could do no such thing. It had, moreover, taken three months for Marie to claim that she had given the revolver and cartridges to Wootten. She had obviously not even told her solicitors about this because Wootten had not been cross-examined at the coroner's court, or at the police court, on the basis that he had possession of the revolver.

Yet it seems that Marie had made a favourable impression upon the jury with the way she answered Mr Pratt's questions. She would later say that she was initially met with harsh looks from the jury members when she stepped into the witness box but that their cold faces melted into warmth while she gave her

evidence. We might also note that Mr Pratt had used
one nice little trick while questioning her. There was
no need for him to ask Marie if there was any truth in
the suggestion that she had pushed Mrs Wootten down
the stairs because no-one at all was suggesting she had
done this. That allegation had been mistakenly made
by Wootten and Higson before they knew Annie had
been shot. Yet by asking his client if she had done so,
it enabled her to deny it (which must have been an
honest denial even if she had murdered Mrs Wootten)
and thus impress upon the jury that she was not only
the victim of a false allegation but that she was telling
the truth about everything else.

It was time for Mr Muir to begin his cross-
examination. This was his speciality and his
destructive cross-examination of Crippen five years
earlier was already regarded as a textbook example of
its kind. His success in this field was based on the most
thorough preparation beforehand at his Chambers. He
would first read through all the evidence while sitting
in his favourite armchair then he would write most of
it out in longhand in order to enable him to get it clear
in his head. His secret weapon was a unique colour
coded card system whereby he set out the points of
attack to be made in cross-examination on a set of what
he called his 'playing cards'. These points were listed
under alphabetical headings then further sub-divided
into numbered categories. He used different colour
pencils to indicate different sorts of points with the
most important noted in red pencil. According to his
biographer: 'He never went into court without being
fully being prepared with his system'.[148] The obvious
weakness of this system, which required hours of
preparation, was that he needed to know in advance
the defence to be adopted by the prisoner so he could
fully prepare to meet it. Crippen, for example, had told

Chief Inspector Dew the story of how his wife had left him and disappeared long before his trial and never departed from this, giving Mr Muir plenty of time to assess its weak points. In this case, however, Marie had sprung her defence on him at the last minute while he sat in the courtroom at the Old Bailey. Although he would have known that Marie was going to claim she had given the revolver to Wootten - because Mr Pratt had put this to the lieutenant in the witness box - he could not have known the precise details of her story. All his preparation would do him no good now. He just had to get on with it and think on his feet. There was plenty of cross-examination material there, it just depended on whether Mr Muir was sufficiently aware of it in the circumstances to be able to deploy it.

Unfortunately, none of the newspapers appear to have reported the cross-examination of Marie in full. The Smith case was attracting all the attention of the court reporters and taking up most of the column inches in the space devoted for home news, at a time when news of the war abroad was filling most of the available pages. We can get a decent flavour of Marie's cross-examination, though, from what does exist:

Muir: Miss Wheatley. What name were you going under when you met Lieutenant Wootten?
Wheatley: Marie Lanteri.
Muir: Lanteri? Whose name was that?
Wheatley: A gentleman I was engaged to, sir.
Muir: Did Wootten's letter to which you referred express the wish to end the relations between you?
Wheatley: No, sir.
Muir: Did you ever get a letter to that effect?
Wheatley: No, never.
Muir: Was your object in coming to London to persuade Lieutenant Wootten to leave his wife and come with you?

Wheatley: No, he had already said he would do so.

Muir: And your object in coming to London was to get him to do so?

Wheatley: No, because he had said he would not come with me until after the war.

Muir: What did Mrs Wootten say to you when you met her in February in the public house?

Wheatley: She said, 'Have you two people settled this matter yet, for I am sick of it all.'

Muir: Did she say to you, 'Do you think it is right to take a married man away from his wife and children?'?

Wheatley: Yes.

Muir: Why did you not tell Mrs Wootten that you had not known he was married when you met him?

Wheatley: I did. I said 'I never knew Bert was married'. I said that if I had known he was married I would have had nothing to do with him.

Muir: Did you tell Lieutenant Wootten that you wanted to go away with him and his children?

Wheatley: No. Lieutenant Wootten said he wanted 'Marie and the children'. I told him that I did not want four children.

Muir: I put it to you that you said to Lieutenant Wootten: 'Bert, bring the children with you.'

Wheatley: No, that is not true.

Muir: You have told us that Lieutenant Wootten wanted to use your father's revolver?

Wheatley: Yes.

Muir: Did Lieutenant Wootten ever have a revolver?

Wheatley: Yes, but it was not like mine.

Muir: How was it that the revolver you were carrying had one spent cartridge in the chamber?

Wheatley: I fired it.

Justice Lush: This is the first time we have heard of this.

Muir: When was it?
Wheatley: In March.
Muir: Where?
Wheatley: Near my home in a field in Sussex. I contemplated suicide and was frightened. The thing went off over my shoulder and I was too frightened to try again. I went into a field at the back of my father's house. I intended shooting it at my head.
Mr Justice Lush: And you were too frightened?
Wheatley: I was too frightened to try again.
Muir: What date was that?
Wheatley: March 15th to 17th.
Muir: Who loaded the revolver for you?
Wheatley: I loaded it myself.
Muir: How many chambers?
Wheatley: Three.
Mr Justice Lush: What did you do with the other chambers?
Wheatley: I left them there.

This sudden and unexpected revelation by Marie, which she had obviously not mentioned to her legal team beforehand (if she had, Mr Pratt would have asked about it in-chief), certainly explained why Mrs Alland and the Islington police had found a spent cartridge in the chamber of what had previously only been used as a toy but, at the same time, it negated her father's evidence that he did not think the revolver could be fired at all because of the flaw in the barrel. On the contrary, if her evidence were true, it proved that it could be fired and, thus, could have been the weapon which killed Mrs Wootten. Now that she was saying she had given the revolver to Wootten, however, this was not as damning a point against Marie as it might otherwise have been. Mr Muir continued with his cross-examanation:

Muir: Did you have a licence?

Wheatley: No.

Muir: What did you say to Mrs Alland when she asked you why you were carrying the revolver?

Wheatley: I said: 'You want a revolver in these troubled times'.

Muir: When did you tell your legal adviser that Wootten had repaired the revolver and got cartridges for you?

Wheatley: On Saturday last.

Muir: Why did you not tell him before?

Wheatley: I wanted to shield him.

Muir: Shield him from what? Be frank.

Wheatley: Well if Wootten had done anything wrong I did not want to do him any harm. I meant that if Wootten had shot his wife I did not say anything. At the interview on March 24th Wootten said to me 'Say nothing. Be quiet'.

Muir: If you did not want the lieutenant to take the revolver from you, why did you not leave it at home?

Wheatley: Because I meant to shoot myself if he did not treat me properly.

Muir: What did you tell your parents about all this?

Wheatley: My parents believed Lieutenant Wootten was my husband and that I was going to London to go straight to him.

Muir: Did you ask Sergeant Wesley when you were arrested at the Gun Tavern: 'What are you going to charge me with?'

Wheatley: No.

Muir: Did you say to the sergeant either that you never had 'the revolver' or 'a revolver'.

Wheatley: No. He said to me: 'Tell the truth, for if they once find you out in a lie they will not believe you again'.

Muir: You had an interview in Surrey Square at four o'clock on March 23rd. Is there any person you know who can prove where you were between that hour and 8.40?

Wheatley: No, I was alone.

Muir: Except for what you told us there is no evidence of what you were doing between those hours?

Wheatley: No, I was quite alone.

That is all we have and it is not very impressive. It may be that the newspapers omitted the most important questions asked by Mr Muir. Lines of enquiry that might not seem interesting to a reporter or a newspaper editor who is not intimately familiar with a case can sometimes be absolutely crucial ones. Certainly, one would have expected Mr Muir to ask Marie why she chose to stay at 36 Ecclesbourne Road in order to 'see Wootten' on 18 March when Wootten was based in the White City and it would be extraordinary if he failed to do so. Yet some of the questions which have been reported seem to lack punch and he does not appear to have pressed Marie on obvious weaknesses in her answers. His encouragement to Marie to 'Be frank' as to why she wanted to shield Wootten was a classic prosecutor's error which allowed the witness to give fresh, unheralded, evidence about her belief that someone else had committed the crime. He almost gives the impression that his heart wasn't in it. Marie had spent more than four hours in the witness box but at least half of that time must have been taken up with her examination-in-chief. This means that Mr Muir spent only about two hours cross-examining her. Yet, for Mrs Wootten's sake and the sake of her children, if not for the sake of justice, this was a case demanding an interrogation which lasted the best part of a court day. There were many questions Marie needed to answer and there was much cross-examination material for Mr Muir if he had managed to absorb Marie's new story and analyse its contradictions by comparing it to all the known evidence. Yet, before he would have had any chance to do that he was on his feet cross-examining her.

In many ways it was unfair to the prosecution. Marie had sprung a completely new version of events on them and they were supposed to react to it on the same day. Mr Muir was a very experienced barrister and perhaps he should have asked for an adjournment to assimilate what he had just heard. In fairness to him, though, such an application would probably not have gone down well with the judge. In the Old Bailey, proceedings moved briskly forward. Judges did not want to hold up trials in any way. The jury was being accommodated in the Holborn Viaduct Hotel every night at great cost to the taxpayer and there was no time to pause for thought.

The day after she stepped down from the witness box, Mr Muir applied to call evidence to rebut two of Marie's statements made for the first time during her own evidence. It is not known exactly what the rebuttal evidence was but one witness the prosecution wanted to call was Marie's landlady from Hove. Presumably she had seen the revolver at Hove sometime in February, contrary to Marie's claim, probably made during cross-examination and unreported, that the weapon had been placed in the trunk at her father's house in January and not been removed from it until March. The second part of Marie's evidence the Crown wished to rebut was a claim she had made, also presumably in an unreported part of her evidence, that the letter sent by Wootten to Wheatley on 9 February was not a letter breaking off his relations with her but, on the contrary, was an invitation for her to come to London from Hove and to bring her revolver and cartridges with her. It is likely that the rebuttal witness here was Joe Higson who had made clear in his evidence at the police court that he had read the letter when Marie handed it to him on the day she showed up at his office in February.

Surprisingly in the circumstances, the judge refused to allow the prosecution to call any further evidence, saying that it only went to Miss Wheatley's credibility, not to the central issue of whether she had committed the murder. One does wonder if his ruling would have been the same if it had been a man in the dock and, indeed, Mr Muir had been allowed to call rebuttal evidence in 1910 after Crippen merely offered a theory in the witness box that human remains found in his house might have been there before he moved in.[149] Over in court number one, the judge had controversially ruled that the prosecution could introduce 'similar fact' evidence relating to the deaths in the bath of two of George Smith's former wives, Alice Burnham and Margaret Lofty, despite the fact that he was only being tried for the murder of Annie Mundy. It seemed like the judge in Marie's trial was bending over backwards to help the prisoner rather than the prosecution.

Having been defeated on this important application, it was then time for Mr Muir to deliver his closing speech. Unfortunately, it was barely reported by any newspaper of the time and we do not have much more than Marie's later account that Mr Muir 'marshalled all the facts so clearly that I wondered, as I had so often done before, how my own story would stand against that of the forty-two [prosecution] witnesses' and, in an ironic choice of phrase, considering the persistent challenges Mr Pratt had made to Joe Higson's evidence that Marie had said on 24 March that things 'looked black' against her, she was to say 'it appeared very black' for her as Mr Muir made his final speech for the prosecution. From what the judge would say in his summing up, Mr Muir must have conceded that Wootten's testimony should not be accepted without corroboration but all that survives of his closing speech is the following short passage:

It is regrettable that the prisoner's movements on the day of the murder only came out yesterday. At one time it looked as if the intention of the defence was to fix upon Mr Wootten responsibility for the death of his wife by his own hand. In view of the cross-examination of Lieutenant Wootten, an officer from his regiment was called and that gentleman had proved that it was a physical impossibility for Lieutenant Wootten to have committed the offence. That line of defence had to be wholly abandoned. One fact appears plain – the murder was committed by a woman. There is not a shadow of a doubt about that. The prisoner has accused one witness, Joe Higson, a friend of Lieutenant Wootten, of giving false testimony, but what man with a human heart would go into the box to talk fiction while a woman was on trial for her life? When all the facts are carefully weighed, the evidence points to guilt in one direction only.

Rather more of Mr Pratt's closing has survived. As he had called no witnesses, other than Marie, he was entitled to deliver his speech after Mr Muir and was in good form, commencing with a touch of Shakespeare:

Miss Wheatley's only crime was loving not too wisely but too well. You have no doubt formed your own opinions respecting Lieutenant Wootten. He gave her money and from what you have seen of Wootten you can only conclude that he expected something in return, whether Miss Wheatley desired it or not. Owing to her relations with him, Miss Wheatley had lost her situation and had lost her references and was going to have the very greatest difficulty in getting another situation. When she came up to London to see Wootten, as she has told you, she wanted to know if he was going to carry out his promise to help her until she got a situation and she was going to try and get a situation. But her prospects were bad – very bad – and she made up her mind then that if she failed to get a situation she was going to make an end of it all and shoot herself. She brought up the revolver for that purpose. He talked her over ultimately and gave her money to get the attaché case and she went and got it. He denies that he gave her money for this purpose. But he knew she was taking it home through City Road on Sunday March 21st because she was seen there by Higson. You will judge which of them is telling the truth by what Wootten did afterwards. Did Miss Wheatley bring the revolver and cartridges to London because Lieutenant Wootten told her to? Lieutenant Wootten has denied it but she did receive a postal order for 7s, 6d at her home and if he did not send it who did? If he did send the money it goes a long way in proving that her story of his knowledge of the revolver was true.

After the way Miss Wheatley was treated by Lieutenant Wootten she meant to have nothing to do with him. She came to London to seek assistance until she could get a situation and if relations with Wootten were resumed you will have to judge as to whose fault it was. The prosecution has sought to establish that it was Miss Wheatley who called at Rotherfield Street on the night of the murder and in this I submit they have entirely failed. The only bit of evidence on which any jury in a case of this gravity can attach the slightest importance is the evidence as to the bullet and the revolver. It is not denied that Miss Wheatley was in possession of a revolver and cartridges on March 21st. From that, the prosecution ask you to infer that she was still in the possession of the revolver on 23rd March and that it was that weapon that caused Mrs Wootten's death. The question is: who was in possession of that revolver on 23rd March? Miss Wheatley has sworn that it was in Lieutenant's Wootten's possession the day before. It was only when Miss Wheatley found that Lieutenant Wootten was going to give evidence against her and that she was in peril of her life, largely as a result of that evidence, that she decided she would shield him no longer, and that she would tell the truth.

In my submission you can only draw one inference from what was known of the person who called on Mrs Wootten that fateful night and that was that it was a person whom Mrs Wootten was expecting and with whom she had an appointment. There was evidence to show the voice was not Miss Wheatley's. Recall the testimony of Mrs Wootten's children. One of them said that the voice she had heard talking to her mother on the night of the tragedy was like Auntie Mabel's voice. You have seen Auntie Mabel and it is for you to judge whether there is any similarity between Miss Wheatley's voice which you have heard in the box and that of Auntie Mabel.

It was a physical impossibility that Miss Wheatley could have been at Rotherfield Street when the crime was committed because while the crime occurred about 7:45pm the landlady said Miss Wheatley was back at her lodgings at Shepherd's

Bush just after eight. The murder was committed at twenty minutes or a quarter to eight: the time occupied in journeying from Rotherfield Street to Richmond Road, Shepherd's Bush was from 40 to 48 minutes. Miss Wheatley was seen by her landlady at 8.40 and the landlady thought she heard prisoner moving about half an hour previously. That brought the time to 8.10 and gave prisoner 25 minutes to make the journey – a physical impossibility.

Miss Wheatley had been in the house at least half an hour when Lieutenant Wootten called, and yet he had said she had wiped her brow as if she had been hurrying. Why should he go out of his way to make that statement? Because I suggest it was going to injure Miss Wheatley.

There are grave dangers of making a decision based on purely circumstantial evidence. If you make a mistake it would be a fatal mistake. It could never be rectified. There is a danger of drawing a wrong inference from many of the facts. I am sure you will not convict anybody charged with the gravest of all crimes on the evidence of somebody's recollection of a particular conversation on a particular occasion. This girl has told lies, but some were at the instigation of Lieutenant Wootten. It is a wicked thing to tell lies, but this girl has been terribly punished. She was tricked and betrayed by Lieutenant Wootten, cast aside by him, accused of murder by him, and cast into prison with all the anxiety of practically three trials. She has been more than punished for anything she did wrong.

Mr Pratt had taken full advantage of the fact that Marie was on trial for her life and the jury would have been well aware that mistakes could easily be made. The most famous miscarriage of justice in English legal history had come to light a little over ten years earlier when a Norwegian businessman, Adolph Beck, had been mistaken for a conman called Wilhelm Meyer and spent five years in prison after being wrongly convicted at the Old Bailey in 1896 and, almost unbelievably, before his innocence had been established, wrongly convicted again three years after his release from prison. The subsequent capture and conviction of the real conman in 1904 had given the entire judicial system pause for thought.

This was reinforced only shortly before Marie's trial, in April 1915, when it emerged that a perfectly innocent woman, Emily Morse, had been confused by witnesses with a similar looking lady named Mabel Powell who had illegally abandoned her two baby boys in 1906.[150] A bemused Mrs Morse had been convicted at Brentford Quarter Sessions in August 1913, spending three months in prison with hard labour, for a crime which had absolutely nothing to do with her. Apart from her uncanny resemblance to Mabel Powell, a series of unfortunate coincidences had been responsible for her arrest and conviction, including that her maiden name was Powell, that she had lived in the same small town of Ross in Hertfordshire as the real Mabel Powell, that she had been assisted by Dr Barnardo's during her childhood, as had the real Mabel Powell, and that she had worked as a maid for a Mr & Mrs Cook in London while the real Mabel Powell had lodged in London with a Mr & Mrs Cook. Being too poor to afford legal representation, and ill during her trial, Emily was not able to put up any kind of defence. Her innocence was only established by pure chance during a hearing regarding the future of the children when the Settlement Officer of the Lambeth Guardians, who happened to be in court about another matter, was struck by the resemblance of the two boys to a woman in the Lambeth Infirmary who he knew as Mabel Powell and who, indeed, turned out to be their real mother.

These two cases were shocking enough but at least they arose out of genuine mistakes and unusual coincidences although, in the case of Emily Morse, identification evidence in her favour was ignored and, even worse, the superintendent of the Herefordshire police, corroborated by an officer of the Brentford Guardians, had testified that Emily had confessed while in custody, a feature of the case which even the Home Office privately regarded as 'unsatisfactory'.[151] The case of Mary Johnson of Redhill was probably the most shocking proven miscarriage of justice of the period, however, because it involved her being deliberately framed for crimes she did not commit by the person who committed them. Going one better than Beck, Mrs Johnson was falsely convicted not twice, but three times: the first occasion on 15 October 1912 at Surrey Quarter Sessions of sending letters threatening to kill a railway porter's wife, Eliza Ellen Woodman, for which she was sentenced to six months imprisonment (serving five months) and then again at the same court, on a similar charge, on 20 May 1913 (quashed on appeal on a technicality in June) and finally on 1 July 1913, this time receiving a more severe sentence of twelve months hard labour. Mrs Woodman was a key witness for the prosecution on each occasion, giving evidence that she had seen Mary Johnson throw letters attached to stones into her garden. At her second trial she said that she saw her throwing a piece of paper out of the window in April 1913 on which was written 'I know you have your eyes on me'. Mary's ordeal was not over upon her early release from prison in 1914. No sooner was she out than she was arrested yet again – this time along with her husband, Albert, charged with sending 116 threatening letters in six weeks to a number of people including Eliza Woodman. The couple were remanded in custody on 24 June 1914 and committed for trial in July.

Events took a dramatically different turn on this occasion, however, as the Johnsons were acquitted by a jury at the Quarter Sessions on 11 August and the police began to suspect that Eliza Woodman was the real author of the threatening letters. Echoing an investigation into another deranged letter writer, Annie Tugwell, which had taken place in the same county of Surrey a few years earlier, the police used an ingenious device of marking postage stamps with invisible ink which, it was secretly arranged with postal officials, were sold to Mrs Woodman only. Notepaper and envelopes were also left at her house on the pretence of being commercial samples dropped off by a stationery salesman. When the next batch of threatening letters arrived it was discovered that the letters were written on marked notepaper and posted in envelopes with marked stamps, causing Mrs Woodman to be arrested. She was charged not only with sending threatening letters to a justice of the peace and a police constable – one read 'I will blow you and your lot to blazes' - but also with perjury for the false evidence which had helped to convict Mary Johnson.

Mrs Woodman came up with a creative explanation for the evidence against her while in custody. She said that a neighbour who lived a few houses away had followed her into her house one evening and told her she must post some letters for him or he would cut her throat with a table knife.[152] Lest this threat be not regarded as sufficiently terrifying, he also informed her that if she did not post the letters he would tell the police that he had seen her post them. To explain how the letters ended up being sent on stationery which had been marked by the police with invisible ink, she said that this man had been to her house a number of times and once demanded notepaper from her so that, for this reason, she gave him two of the sample packets left at her house. She claimed he also gave her fourpence to buy stamps for him. To further ensure her compliance, she said, he hit her on the head one day with his pocket knife.

The story was an obvious fabrication and even her own barrister at trial accepted she had written the letters. The only question for the court to decide was whether she was insane at the time. Dr Francis Forward, the medical officer at Holloway prison, where Mrs Woodman had been held on remand, stated his opinion that she was indeed insane and could not be held accountable for her actions but the jury disagreed and Mrs Woodman was convicted at the Surrey Assizes in Guildford in February 1915, following which she was sentenced to eighteen months imprisonment with hard labour. On 27 February 1915, the *Daily Express* ran a sympathetic story about Mary's plight, revealing that her husband's greengrocery business had been ruined by the scandal - he had to become a dustman to earn a living - and their furniture had been sold in order to get money for food while she was in prison. 'I couldn't stop thinking about my husband and my girls, and wondering what was happening to them,' she told the newspaper, 'all the time I tried to keep my spirits up by telling myself it would all come out some day, and now it has come out. But I've had two Christmas days in prison.' Of Mrs Woodman, she said: 'She must be mad'. In March 1915, Mrs Johnson was granted a free pardon by the King on the recommendation of the Home Secretary for all the offences she had been convicted of and was awarded £500 in compensation by the Treasury.[153] The *Daily Express* described it as 'one of the most remarkable cases in the criminal records.'[154]

The stakes were much higher, of course, in respect of a murder charge and there remained disquiet in some circles at the outcome of the Seddon trial. The radical *New Age* newspaper of 18 April 1912 referred, with some justification, to 'shadowy circumstantial evidence' which had convicted Seddon and, in a later issue, after a petition to save him from the gallows had failed – he was, in fact, executed on 18 April – remarked indignantly of the 'legal murder of Frederick Seddon.' Even the Crippen verdict was not universally accepted. A letter to the editor of *New Age* of 25 April 1912 by W. Gilbert Saunders reminded the paper's readers that Crippen, 'was hanged on the evidence of an analyst, who found hyoscine in the half-decomposed remains of a woman' and informed them that: 'A few months ago there appeared, in a technical journal, the interesting statement that the analytical tests for hyoscine are untrustworthy and even misleading'. Saunders concluded with the comment, 'How very reassuring!' with the clear implication that the hanged Crippen might have been innocent after all.

While, as we have seen, it was, on balance, unlikely that Marie would be hanged if she was convicted - so that a mistake could be rectified - it was only natural that Mr Pratt would rely on the dreadful possibility of an innocent woman being hanged in order to persuade the jury to acquit. It is very likely that some examples of miscarriages of justice, especially the very recent cases of Emily Morse and Mary Johnson, would have been in the minds of the jury members as they listened to the closing speeches. Not only would they need to be certain beyond any reasonable doubt that Marie had murdered Annie Wootten but they would also have to be unanimous. Majority verdicts were not allowed in 1915.

On Monday 28 June, it was the turn of Mr Justice Lush to have his say about the proceedings for the benefit of the jury. It did not make pleasant listening for Lieutenant Wootten who was sat expressionless in court:

> The case is one which presents many strange features. It is a case that to some extent has involved, in regard to certain portions of the evidence, quite a degree of mystery and to use a mild word it presents many disagreeable features.

> Mr Pratt has nothing to reproach himself with. He has carried out with great ability his responsible duty. There is one point which Mr Pratt did not feel called upon to labour which I feel I should deal. That is the conduct of Lieutenant Wootten. It is in relating only to its effect upon the credibility of his testimony that I speak of his part in the story. But the case against the accused rests in material points upon the testimony of the lieutenant. It is difficult to speak temperately of Lieutenant Wootten's conduct towards his wife and this woman. I most strongly agree with what Muir said when he spoke of the injustice or wrong that would be done if the evidence of Mr Wootten were relied upon unless it was corroborated.

> Lieutenant Wootten came before you as a discredited witness and had the case rested on his evidence alone I should have had no hesitation in advising you that you would do wrong if you were to act upon it. I will not speak of his infidelity to his wife, for which he has sufficient cause for reflection and shame all the days of his life. I cannot

help saying that the matter of the postcard which he admits writing to the father and mother of the accused shows that at times he has little regard for the truth. It seems to me, and no doubt you will think so too, to be shocking, when he was living with the accused as man and wife, that he should, whether it was dictated to him by her or not, to have written to the parents of this girl as 'Dear dad and mum' in order to deceive them into thinking that he was married to their daughter and to no-one else. It is for you to consider whether, when she came back to London in March, he did what he swears in the witness box he did, namely simply visit her, and have no improper relations with her. She swears that they resumed their old relations.

It was upon Wootten's testimony that the prosecution relied to prove that the accused was in possession of the revolver on the day of the murder. He said she had it but she said he had it. It was not suggested that Wootten committed the crime but it is for you to consider what value was to be attached to his statement that Wheatley had the revolver on that day. It is unfortunate that on that important question – her possession of the revolver – the only two persons who can enlighten us are Lieutenant Wootten and the prisoner. You will bear in mind what I have said about Wootten being a discredited witness. You must therefore decide between the testimony of the prisoner and the testimony of Wootten. If it becomes a conflict of evidence you have to consider how far you can rely on what Lieutenant Wootten has said.

As to the evidence identifying the accused with the woman who visited the house on the night of the murder (sic), the only veil the accused was proved to have in her possession was a white motor veil whereas the veil the woman wore was black. A bogus telegram had been sent to the other residents of the house in which the Woottens lived, calling them away that night. The sender of that telegram had not been traced and it had not been shown that Miss Wheatley's statement that she did not know the name of the people was untrue. As to the conversation which was overheard between the murdered woman and the visitor, in which the expression 'I do not know the bar' was used, that rests entirely upon the evidence of a child of eight years of age and the phrase, even if correctly heard, did not necessarily suggest it was the accused barmaid who used it. I remind you as to the light in which the evidence of Lieutenant's Wootten's children should be accepted. They were very young and whether their statements could be relied upon in respect of the conversation between their mother and the strange woman is a matter entirely for you, members of the jury.

I call your attention to an important piece of evidence which has not previously been emphasised. Lieutenant Wootten's usual hour for the two or three days for calling at Richmond Road was at eight o'clock or soon afterwards. On the night of the murder he rose from Mess, but called at a hairdresser's and did not reach Richmond Road until 9:10pm. I am not suggesting complicity on the part of Lieutenant Wootten but it is a matter for you to observe that, but for the fact that Lieutenant Wootten called at the hairdresser's, he would have reached Richmond Road and found no-one there if the prisoner committed the murder in Rotherfield Street. The accused's case was that she got home, as she always did, about eight o'clock. She said that as Lieutenant Wootten did not arrive at the usual time she called and asked the landlady what hour it was as she thought she had made a mistake.

If the prisoner was the person whom the landlady heard moving about, then there was no case against her. Unquestionably she could not have been in two places at once, or have got from one to the other in the time. Was she in the house half an hour before she was seen? The landlady was not definite and that was all you will get.

In describing the accused's attitude when he told her of his wife's death, Wootten said 'she looked flushed, not astonished'. I don't think you can pay much attention to how he thought someone looked. The girl was arrested at the Gun Tavern, Pimlico, where she had obtained a situation after the tragedy, having left information of her whereabouts.

The evidence is purely circumstantial. Motive is an important factor but motive cannot convert suspicion into proof. It would be wrong to say that the prisoner must be convicted because she had a motive. This case requires the utmost care. The facts must be such as to enable you to say that this thing charged against the prisoner must have happened. It is not enough to establish a case of suspicion, or even of great suspicion, against the accused. If you feel it rests upon suspicion and does not go further, however great the suspicion may be, it is your bounden duty to say the case is not proved. Even if you believe it did happen, that is not the thing upon which you are embarked. Are you able to say: 'It must have happened; there is no other reasonable possible theory'? Unless you are, however grave the suspicion, you ought not to convict. Unless the case has gone out of the region of suspicion into the region of reasonable certainty in your minds the verdict must be one of not guilty even if it leaves the matter inconclusive and uncertain. It is only after you are satisfied beyond all reasonable doubt that you are justified in returning a verdict of guilty.

The judge might as well have directed the jury to find Marie not guilty because that was the effect of his summing up. It was a shockingly biased summary and, in his evident desire for Marie to be acquitted, fundamentally flawed. It was not, as Justice Lush asserted, Wootten's testimony that the prosecution relied on to prove Marie was in possession of the revolver. Wootten said precisely nothing about that. It had been proved by Mrs Alland's evidence that Marie had been in possession of the revolver two days before the murder. The only reason Wootten's testimony was in any way relevant was because he denied having seen the revolver when the suggestion that Marie had given it to him was put to him for the very first time in the witness box of the Old Bailey. It was *Marie* who claimed Wootten had it, not the other way round. He said he had never seen it. Furthermore, Marie's story that Wootten gave her the revolver was tied in with her story that he gave her the cartridges at the same time, yet Marie had told Mrs Alland that she had bought the cartridges herself in London and there was no obvious reason for her to have volunteered such a lie. While the judge was correct to warn the jury not to accept Wootten's evidence without corroboration (although he does not seem to have taken into account Joe Higson's independent evidence which did corroborate Wootten), he should have been dealing with the issue of whether the jury could accept Marie's word that she had given the weapon to the lieutenant. His failure to do so shows that he had no interest in attempting to properly analyse the evidence.

He made other errors too. Leaving aside his

apparent claim that the veiled woman was seen in Rotherfield Street on the night of the murder, which might in fairness have been a mistake made by the reporter transcribing his words, it was wrong for the judge to say that the veil was black as a matter of fact. It certainly appeared black, or 'dark', to the witnesses who saw it but it was a dark night and he should have allowed the jury to consider that the darkness of the veil was a trick of the light, or rather a trick of the absence of light. The judge's 'important' evidence about Marie not being in Richmond Road to meet Wootten's possible arrival at 8pm if she had committed the murder was nothing of the sort. Had Wootten arrived and found her absent, all she would have had to do is say she had been out to the post or the cinema or for a walk or any other story she cared to invent. Certainly, if she committed the murder, she was lucky that Wootten did not turn up at 8pm sharp that evening but he did not leave Mess until then and he said his usual time of arrival at Richmond Road was about 8:30pm, thus giving Marie a sporting chance of returning before him.

On this timing issue, the judge was not the only person in the court to have become confused. Mr Pratt was wholly incorrect when he said it was a 'physical impossibility' that Marie could have been in Rotherfield Street on the evening of the murder. His claim that the murder was committed at 7:45pm was not supported by the evidence. The key witness here was James Jordan. He said that he looked at the clock of the Three Brewers pub on the corner of New North Road and Essex Road and saw that it was 7:42pm. He then walked down Ecclesbourne Road and into Rotherfield Street where he was accosted by Mrs Higson who told him of Mrs Wootten's death. It is about one minute at normal walking pace from the

corner of New North Road to 114 Rotherfield Street
but Mr Jordan said he was walking very slowly and
estimated that it took him three minutes to get to
Rotherfield Street. So that brings him outside 114 at
7:45pm but the murder had obviously been committed
before that. After running up the stairs, Lily and Ivy
had attempted to lift their mother up and, when they
realised she was dead, wondered what they were
going to do. Once they decided to fetch their Aunt
Lily they started to get dressed. Lily had not got far
in dressing herself when Mrs Higson called but we
are wholly dependent on those two young girls for an
estimate of the time between them finding their mother
dead and Mrs Higson's arrival. Lily guessed at two
minutes but, in their shock, it could easily have been
longer. Nevertheless, if we accept two minutes as the
correct length of time, that brings us down to 7:43pm
as the time of the murder. However, the prosecution
obtained evidence about the clock at the Three Brewers
which, although it was accurate and checked every
Thursday, nevertheless tended to add a minute or two
every week.[155] As the murder occurred on a Tuesday
evening it could well have been out by two minutes so
that the murder was committed at 7:41pm. If the two
girls had been more traumatized than they were aware
of immediately following the death, so that it took
them ten minutes or so to calm down and work out a
plan to get dressed and run to their grandparents, Mrs
Wootten could easily have been murdered as early as
7:30pm.

Nevertheless, if we follow Mr Pratt and take 7:45pm
as the time of death, Marie could still have committed
the murder because she could have been back at 12
Richmond Road forty minutes later – as shown by the
police's timing of that journey - at 8:25pm. She was
not seen by her landlady until some fifteen minutes

later at 8:40pm (and it is to be assumed that the police confirmed that Mrs Connor's clock was accurate). It is true that Mrs Connor said that she heard a noise earlier in the evening but not half an hour earlier as Mr Pratt claimed. Her exact words, as recorded in her official deposition at the coroner's court, were: 'She [Marie] had a key to let herself in and I fancied I heard her come in a little time before'. At the police court, again from the official record, she said 'I thought I heard someone come into the house, earlier in the evening of 23 March. I can't fix the time'. From that, it is self-evident that she might have heard Marie return at about 8:25pm which would fit with her having committed the murder in Islington and travelled back to Richmond Road via King's Cross.

Discreetly out of sight, the chaplain was ready to make an appearance and the black cap was at hand but, given the way the judge expressed himself, it would have been extraordinary if the jury had brought in a guilty verdict and, indeed, after just twelve minutes consideration they returned, at 3:25pm on 28 June, and announced their unanimous decision: 'Not Guilty'. Newspapers reported that there was some subdued applause in the courtroom. Marie called out 'Thank you my lord' to the judge and left the dock smiling, a free woman. Her mother, who had been following the trial anxiously, collapsed and had to be helped out of the building. The jury was excused by the judge from further service for ten years.

Shortly before this, during a break in the day's proceedings, an interesting incident had been witnessed by the reporter for *The Daily News & Leader* who recorded that Marie could not see Lieutenant Wootten from her position in the dock but, when he stood up during an interval to leave the courtroom, 'she sought his eye, and she gave him a long, searching, nervous look when they came face to face'. This was to be the last ever time the two former lovers would see each other. After the verdict, Lieutenant Wootten remained in the court to speak to police officers and other friends.

With an eye to the press photographers, Marie changed her outfit in the time between the judge's summing up and the verdict: from a plain white woollen jacket into a stylish blue dress with ruffled white lace at the front of the blouse. A heavy shower had recently drenched the surrounding area and it was still drizzling but she walked out of the court to find a large crowd waiting for her in Newgate Street. She had evidently won their sympathy because, after she posed for some press photographs, they followed her taxi cab for a short distance as it drove away, waving their hands and handkerchiefs in support.[156] In her moment of triumph, she gave the following statement to the press: 'I owe my discharge to the eloquent appeal made by my counsel, Mr Pratt, on my behalf. From the moment the judge began his summing up I knew the result would be in my favour. I shall not forget Mr Muir. He asked me many ticklish questions but I sometimes found it easier to answer him than Mr Pratt. I am now going on a long holiday'.[157]

Marie with her barrister John Lhind Pratt
outside the Old Bailey on 28 June 1915

CHAPTER 11

IN HER OWN WORDS

'She hath no faults, who hath the art to hide them.'

The White Devil by John Webster, 1612

Like many of her pronouncements, Marie's claim to be going on a 'long holiday' was not quite true. Not just yet anyway. There was work to be done. She managed to sell her 'exclusive' story to two Sunday newspapers in which she expressed her opinion about who committed the crime. This would almost certainly have been done to pay her legal fees: common practice at the time. On occasion, these types of articles would be ghost written by a journalist but Marie, who had apparently been privately educated, was quite capable of writing her own account – her grandson recalls that she could write a very good letter.[158] As both articles were signed by her (there is even a photograph in existence of her supposedly writing one of them), and because they are both fascinating insights into Marie's mind, it is worth reproducing them in full here.

The first, entitled 'On Trial For My Life', appeared in *Lloyds Weekly News* of 4 July 1915. It was advertised in the previous day's *Daily Mirror* as: 'Why I was found Not Guilty of the Murder of Mrs Wootten' with the blurb stating: 'In To-morrow's Lloyd's News the young barmaid who was this week, at the Old Bailey, acquitted of the murder of the wife of Lieut Wootten at Islington, tells her story of the trial, describes her hopes and fears as she sat in the dock with her life in the balance and puts forward Her Own Theory of the Crime. The signed story of a woman's fight for life has been specially written for Lloyd's News and will appear exclusively in that paper to-morrow'.

Marie wrote:

I am free!

Free after all the anxiety and suspense of the past months – after those three weeks when I lay in prison awaiting the Old Bailey trial, weeks that seemed the longest and loneliest of my life.

And now, how do I feel? Well it is so difficult to describe. I feel as I imagine a bird would feel suddenly released from a cage. None but those who have been robbed of their freedom, and regained it at last, can understand what I mean.

Now I think of it, I can hardly realise what I have gone through.

The hardest and blackest part of all was the three weeks I spent in Holloway Prison after the inquest and police court proceedings were over, waiting for the trial at the Old Bailey to come on.

I was all alone – alone with my thoughts and memories and fears. No one came to see [me]. My solicitor, to whom I owe so much, did not visit me till the Saturday before the trial. I thought even he had deserted me but I know now that all the time he was working hard for me.

My parents did not come to see me. I had begged them not to, for the meeting would have been too much for all of us. Do you wonder that in my loneliness I became depressed?

And the depression grew deeper and deeper as, with nothing else to occupy my mind, I brooded over the evidence I had heard brought against me at the inquest and in the police-court. For though I knew I was innocent of the dreadful charge brought against me, there had been forty-two witnesses for the prosecution and I realised how amazingly their stories seemed to fit together. It was just my own word and the story of how I had spent that day of the murder, against all those people.

One against forty-two!

Though I knew that my story was true, I wondered how it would fare. For I knew that juries sometimes make mistakes, and I had read of people being convicted of evidence that appeared less clear than all this evidence against me.

Besides those terrible three weeks, few other things stand out in my memory. They are the opening speech for the prosecution and the hours when I passed from the dock to the witness box to tell my life story.

When Mr Muir made the speech for the Crown, telling the jury and judge why the prosecution said I was a murderer my spirits fell. It seemed such a clear and concise story. Little facts and incidents as I have already said, seemed to fit together so strangely that I wondered how I could convince the jury of the truth of my statement. Could the truth prevail against this masterly array of evidence that seemed to point to me as the person who shot Mrs Wootten?

Mr Muir spoke for two hours and as I heard him I began to shiver. I realised that my only chance was to tell the whole truth and to conceal nothing.

And later on, came my ordeal, the greatest ordeal of my life. My four and a half hours in the witness box.

It was easy to answer the questions of my own counsel, for to do that I had only to tell the true story of all that had happened. When Mr Muir began to cross-examine me I knew it was his duty to try and show that my statements were false and to make me "give myself away". But I did not feel anxious. I knew that if I kept on telling the truth and nerved myself to give my evidence well and clearly, I should be safe. That gave me confidence.

And now let me jot down what I believe to be the chief points that told in my favour, and set me free from that dreadful dock and the terrible anxieties and fears of the past weeks.

First, I believe it was the clear and truthful way I gave my evidence. All the time I had been sitting in the dock I had been watching the faces of the jurymen. Some of them seemed hard, and from the way they looked at me I felt that I could expect little mercy from them – even if it were a case for mercy.

But as I gave my evidence I kept turning, perhaps unconsciously, to see what effect it was having on the jury. And after a time their faces seemed to soften towards me, and I felt that the impression made on them by counsel for the prosecution was being changed in my favour.

Another point that cheered me concerned the letter-card which Lieut. Wootten had received after the murder warning him that a similar fate awaited him and his children. It was mentioned when I was in the police-court and the suggestion was that I had written it. Of course, if that had been so it would have been a terrible piece of evidence against me.

But at the Old Bailey it was never mentioned. The judge asked the counsel for the Crown if they were not going to produce the document as evidence against me but they said no and I believe the police established to their own satisfaction that I was not the writer.

One of the points made by the prosecution was the sending of a mysterious telegram to the people in whose house Mrs Wootten was sharing. This read as follows:

```
Dickson, 114, Rotherfield-street - Come
at once - FATHER
```

This telegram was handed in at St John's post office

271

(which I have learned since was a quarter of a mile from the Wootten residence) shortly before the murder. It was suggested by the prosecution that the telegram was sent by the murderer in order to lure Mr & Mrs Dixon (for that was their real name, not "Dickson") away from the house at the time the murderer intended to call.

Now there are two important points about the telegram which must be remembered.

It was not in my handwriting. It was never suggested it was.

At the time it was sent I did not know that the people in the house where Mrs Wootten was living were named Dixon. I had only heard Mrs Dixon spoken of as 'Lil'. So to insist that the murder was committed by the person who sent that telegram could only help to establish my innocence.

The prosecution, too, had made me out to be a clever woman who had ingeniously planned the crime. But my counsel drew a different picture when he asked if it was the work of a clever woman to take lodgings near Rotherfield Street (as I did before I went to live at Shepherd's Bush), live there in my own name with a revolver and a piece of writing which showed that I was acquainted with the husband of the dead woman.

Again I fancy that the jury was influenced by the fact that on the same day as I was informed of Mrs Wootten's death (the day after the murder) I had applied for and secured a situation, in which I was actually employed when the police arrested me on a charge of murder.

It was a situation which opened to me the prospect of starting life afresh, away from the temptations which had cost me so dearly. And I was only there a few hours when I was told that I was wanted in the private room by two gentlemen.

They were detectives and it was then that I heard for

the first time that Mrs Wootten had been shot and not, as I had thought, had fatally injured herself by falling downstairs.

I think the jury considered that my action was not that of a guilty woman, and further, I was able to state in detail where I was on the day of March 23, the day of the murder.

Let me tell once more how I spent that day – a day that was to figure so prominently in the tragic story told in court, and a day of which I had to recall my own doings and movements so clearly and exactly if I was to save myself from the terrible charge that hung over me.

First of all, people may ask why I did not call witnesses who saw me elsewhere at the time when, according to the prosecution, I was at Islington shooting Mrs Wootten.

Well, remember that I was practically a stranger to London. I had only been there once or twice in my life and there was hardly a soul in the vast place who knew me even by sight.

Suppose tomorrow you go to a strange town and having nothing to do you walk about the streets to pass the time. That is a very natural thing to do. But if your life depended on it, whom could you bring forward, later on, to say that you had walked along certain streets at a certain hour on that day?

I was then lodging in Richmond-road, Shepherd's Bush.

I awoke that day at 9.30 in the morning and had breakfast in bed. Afterwards I went out, bought a paper, and returned to my room, where I sat reading till about 1.30.

Then I went out with the idea of looking for two situations that were then vacant in public houses in the Old Kent-road district. I walked from Shepherd's Bush *straight up the main road to Marble Arch. On the way I posted a letter at Notting Hill. It was an application for a situation. I have since seen the envelope and it bears on the postmark the time – 3:30pm – so it must have been posted sometime before that.*

At the Marble Arch I took a motor bus to the Old Kent Road. The names of the public houses I was looking for do not matter. I did not like the look of them so did not try for a situation at either of them.

I then walked to the Elephant and Castle and there took a motor bus to Oxford Circus, arriving there about six o'clock. From there I began to walk to Shepherd's Bush, stopping to have tea at a shop near Marble Arch.

After tea, I continued my walk to Shepherd's Bush, arriving at my lodgings a few minutes before eight.

It may be asked why I did so much walking that day. Well, remember that I am a country girl, used to walking and fond of it. I had the whole day before me until eight in the evening when I was expecting Lieut. Wootten to see me, and in a strange city, with no friends to go and see, I had to pass the time somehow.

It was stated by the prosecution that the murder was committed between 7.30 and 7.45 that night. So it was clear to the jury who probably all knew London far better than I do, that if, as I insist, I got to my lodgings about eight, I could not have committed the murder.

It was not till the following afternoon that I knew anything had happened to Mrs Wootten.

Lieut. Wootten came to see me then, and told me that his wife had been found dead on the stairs and had broken her neck, for it was not known then that she had been shot. I knew she had a defective knee and I thought she had fallen down the stairs.

I exclaimed, "What, dead Bert? What are you going to do with the children?"

I did not know she was shot until I was arrested the following day, when I was told this. Had I known it when Lieut. Wootten told me she was dead, and had I had the slightest notion that I would be suspected, I should have said to him, "How could I shoot her when I have already given you the revolver?"

I certainly never dreamed when I first heard of Mrs Wootten's death that I should be suspected. There was no bitterness between us, and as it had already been arranged that Lieut. Wootten and I should part, and I should get a new situation, there was no reason why I should kill her.

I first met Mrs Wootten when I came to London on Feb 11. I saw her twice that week. She seemed a quiet, retiring woman. We had no quarrel. She said I had been led away and ought to be provided for.

I saw her again and for the last time, on Feb 21. She came to see me at the lodgings I was then in at Islington. No angry words passed between us and she shook hands with me.

So much has been said of the revolver that was in my possession for a time that I must mention it here.

It was given to my father twenty-seven years ago by a soldier friend [an officer in the 5th Lancers according to her father's evidence at the police court]. *All through my young days it lay about the house, or in our toy boxes and we children often played with it. How little I dreamed in those happy childhood days that it would ever be mentioned in a court of law where I was on trial for my life.*

Last December, when Lieut. Wootten and I were at Hove, and he had just got his commission, he wanted a revolver. I remembered this old one at home, and said I would get it for him. I did so, but he laughed when he saw it, saying it was a useless old thing.

However, he said he would get it repaired. A day or two later he produced it. It was repaired then and he said he would show me how to use it. This he did on the Downs and afterwards I put it in my box with some cartridges.

There it remained till the day before the murder, except for one rather silly incident.

This was early in March, when I was at my old home in Sussex. I was very depressed and disappointed, and went out into a field behind my house, intending to commit suicide. I pointed the revolver at my head, shut my eyes, and pulled the trigger. In doing this I must have moved my head, for although there was a terrific bang, so loud that it made a horse bolt, the bullet missed me, and I ran indoors terribly frightened.

I last saw the revolver on March 22, the day before the murder when Lieut. Wootten called to see me at Shepherd's Bush and, taking it away, said "I think I had better take care of these. You are not to be trusted with them if you are going to shoot yourself". He put the revolver and cartridges in his pocket, and they have not been seen since.

Among all the anxieties of the trial many little points stand out in my memory.

I have never been in a big court like the Old Bailey before, and to be perched up there all alone in that big high dock was so different from the small railed enclosure at the police-court where I seemed to be among the people.

In spite of my terrible position, I was interested in such trivial things as the fact that the judge carried a bunch of flowers in his hand and that men in gowns – whom I now know to be the City dignitaries – kept coming in sitting on the bench with the judge for a little while, and then going out.

I was told that one of these personages was the sheriff and I shuddered when I remembered that it was his duty to superintend the hanging of people who had been condemned to death.

As I sat in the dock I felt that all eyes were upon me. I used to look up in the public gallery and study the faces of the people sitting there. Many of them were women. It came as a shock to me to see these well-dressed women taking such a close and morbid interest in my ordeal. There seemed to be fresh faces each morning and afternoon, new audiences arriving as if my trial were a 'two-houses-a-night' show.

Several of the women, I could detect, seemed convinced of my guilt and as I looked at them I could fancy that they almost bared their teeth at me.

I have already told how my hopes rose and fell as the case was presented to the jury. It appeared very black as Mr Muir made his final speech for the prosecution. He marshalled all the facts so clearly that I wondered, as I had often done before, how my own story would stand against that of the forty-two witnesses.

Then my counsel made his speech for the defence, and pleaded my case so eloquently that I felt cheered up. While he was speaking to me quite in my favour, I watched the jury's faces softening, and felt more confident.

Indeed, I felt so confident that now when I had to wait whilst the jury considered their verdict, and my fate was being decided I was by no means so anxious and depressed as I had been at some stages.

As the jury left the court, and I was about to be taken below, my kind solicitor stood on tiptoe to reach up to the dock and said to me "Cheer up, you're all right".

For twelve minutes I waited in a tiny room beneath the dock in the charge of the wardresses. Naturally, it was a very anxious period but I had constantly before my eyes the change in the jury's faces which I believe meant so much in the urgent matter of life or death to me.

Then suddenly I was taken back to the dock. Everything was very quiet indeed and the voices of the clerk of the court and of the foreman of the jury seemed to come from a great distance.

I heard the words "Not guilty". Then the judge was speaking to me and in a rush of joyous emotion I gathered that I was free.

Friends pressed about me with congratulations – many of them strangers – and it was oh! so different from those awful times at the police and coroner's courts, when a hostile crowd had shouted their enunciations of me, and I had had to be protected on my way to the conveyance.

I have pondered often upon the problem of who fired the fatal shot at Mrs Wootten for I have no doubt that she was murdered.

I feel certain it was a woman – a woman who had nourished a deadly hatred against her. As a barmaid, I have some experience of the world, and I know that no enmity can be more deadly than that of a woman who is torn with jealousy, for instance.

I think it must have been somebody who knew her and whom Mrs Wootten knew, and it is important to remember that on the night when she was shot dead her movements seemed to show that she was expecting a visitor. And that visitor unquestionably arrived.

Who was this mysterious, sinister visitor? One of the children told their father that on the night of the murder their mother went into the bedroom, pulled the blind aside and looked out of the window. From this I gather that she was watching for a visitor. Then, according to the same child, a lady called and asked for water. She said she was thin and hungry and asked for money.

The child was asked if she knew who the lady was and replied, "Mummy said it was Mrs Higson's friend. I saw mummy take a glass of water to the lady in the passage. I heard her give her some coppers and then I heard mummy slam the sitting-room door. Then I heard her say, "Oh, Oh!" and the lady went."

It seems clear to me that this description of the mysterious visitor does not in any way fit me. But it does bear out my theory that the murderer was a woman.

Will her identity ever be known, and will this crime be added to the long list of unsolved murders? Time alone will show, and time alone can produce the evidence which will prove to any people who still doubt the innocence which I have maintained from the beginning.

Marie Wheatley

Before moving to the second article, there are a number of features of the first which are worth mentioning. Marie's conclusion that the description of the mysterious visitor on the night of the murder did not 'in any way' fit her is baffling. If the visitor was 'Mrs Higson's friend' then not only had Mrs Wootten described her but she had as good as named her. She might as well have told Lily that it was Marie Wheatley at the door. What is so remarkable about Marie's account is she does not even explain to her reader that she was known by Mrs Wootten and others as 'Mrs Higson's friend'. It is not the only omission and, indeed, Marie's story is more interesting for what is not included. For example, she did not pose, let alone answer, the obvious question as to why she had not told the police of her movements on the day of the murder at the time she was arrested. If she really had hoped the police would realise they had made a terrible mistake and free her, why not let them know she had an alibi and assist them in coming to this conclusion even faster? She could have taken them to the Swiss café in Oxford Street and enquiries could have been made to see if anyone working in the café remembered her.

Marie also avoids the issue of why she had not mentioned, even to her legal advisers, that she had given her revolver to Wootten. Perhaps she felt that the explanation she had provided during the trial would not bear scrutiny. If so, it was with good reason because it was nonsense. It might have been possible to claim that she wanted to protect Wootten in the days immediately following her arrest, when she could have thought Wootten was on her side, despite the way he treated her on 24 March when he kicked her out of 12 Richmond Road without a penny, but once the lieutenant had explained to the coroner why he thought Marie had murdered his wife and then repeated this explanation to the magistrate at the police court, giving his evidence on both occasions about Marie having been breathless on the night of the murder, there was no possible reason for her to remain silent any longer. Yet she only told her legal advisers that she had given away the revolver to the lieutenant in the week before she entered the witness box at the Old Bailey. Perhaps this accounts for the inclusion of the sentence 'My solicitor, to whom I owe so much, did not visit me till the Saturday before the trial'. Even if this was true, she frequently spoke to her legal advisers during the coroner's court and police court proceedings and it would have been a simple matter to have whispered, or passed a note, to them that Wootten had taken the gun.

In any case, her claim that her solicitor did not visit her until just before the trial is as dubious as her claim that her father did not visit her at all. During the police court proceedings, on Saturday 3 April, Mr Pratt made an application for Marie's father to be allowed to visit her in prison and the magistrate did not object. As the application must have been made by Mr Pratt on his client's instructions, it is to be assumed that the visit went ahead. The sense of isolation Marie wanted to convey to the readers of *Lloyds News* was part of her central message that *she* was the victim. For, in her self-serving account, there is no expression of sadness at the death of Mrs Wootten nor of the terrible ordeal her two daughters had gone through that evening. The emphasis on Marie being alone against forty-two witnesses does not quite match the reality. Most of those witnesses, one of whom was her own father, had little or nothing to say about Marie being the murderer but were there to provide uncontroversial evidence relating to the discovery of Mrs Wootten's body or similar factual matters. This is not to downplay the difficulties faced by a defendant in a serious criminal trial but her failure to mention the importance of the judge's rulings on the admissibility of evidence does make her story a rather unconvincing explanation of why she was acquitted.

A final point to note, for the moment, is Marie's claim that Mrs Wootten was a 'quiet, retiring woman'. This is no doubt true but it will be recalled that Mr Pratt had put to Wootten that, during the evening of 11 February, his wife had said: 'What are you two going to do about it? I'm sick of it all' or words to that effect. This can only have been on instructions from Marie. That was when it was in Marie's interests to show that Mrs Wootten was upset by the whole situation and thus paint her husband in a bad light for having upset her. Now, it was in Marie's interests to show that there had been no quarrel between herself and Mrs Wootten and thus eliminate a motive for the murder. However, Wootten's evidence, corroborated by Higson, had been that Mrs Wootten had asked Marie if she had not done wrong by trying to take a married man from his wife and children which does not quite bear out Marie's claim that there was no quarrel at all between them (even if Marie was trying to say that the quarrel had been resolved by the time of the murder).

There is more to be said about Marie's account but let us now consider the second version of her story. Published in the *Weekly Dispatch* of Sunday 4 July 1915 it was entitled 'My Trial For My Life':

> *It all seems like an adventure to me now – my Trial for my Life – an experience through which I was fated to pass, and it is a terrible thing for a young woman of twenty-two to be tried for her life on a charge of committing murder of which I knew nothing whatever until the moment the police came to arrest me.*
>
> *I feel like a bird that has been released from a cage to the freedom which it once enjoyed. When the jury returned a verdict of 'Not guilty' and the judge – that great-hearted, kindly judge, shall I ever forget? – told me to leave the dock, I felt as though I could have embraced everyone within reach of me. I clasped my hands and said 'Thank God!' I then looked to the bench and called out to Mr Justice Lush, 'Thank you, my lord'.*
>
> *It is not easy to put down in words my feelings at this moment or to describe my impressions of the long ordeal which commenced with my arrest in March and ended with my release at the end of June.*
>
> *But for the knowledge of my innocence and the confidence that my innocence would be proved I am sure I should have broken down at some stage or other in the case.*
>
> *As I looked at the court in the Old Bailey and listened to the forty-two witnesses that testified against me, I was filled with wonder that so much law should be set in*

motion to prove the guilt of a guiltless woman.

Surely, I thought, it could never be possible for the prosecution to convince the jury that the shot which killed Lieutenant Wootten's wife was fired by me, when I knew that it was not fired by me but by someone else whose identity may yet be discovered or may never be discovered.

I suppose you could not find in England to-day another woman who has been in such a position as I occupied a week ago. How strange it appears to me that I should have been singled out by an evil fortune to endure this terrible ordeal which threatens to cast a shadow over my future life. It is sweet to know that my innocence has been proved, but it is still a heavy thought with me that my name should have figured in connection with such a tragedy.

My friends tell me that I have youth on my side; that it will only be a nine days' wonder; that people's minds at the present day are too much occupied with the horrors of the war to give much thought to me. But somehow I am not yet able quite to shake off the effect of it all upon my mind, though with each returning morning's light and sunshine I grow stronger and more cheerful.

Let me take you back to the twenty-fifth of March; when my tragic story really begins. If there are errors in the previous part of my life, in my relations with Lieutenant Wootten, these have been the subject of repentance in the presence of my God. The law laid its hand upon me in another connection which unhappily arose out of my relations with Wootten.

I had taken a situation as a barmaid in Pimlico. I had been at my work not more than one hour and a half when two detectives entered the place and summoned me into a room. I could form no idea in the world why they should *want me when one of the officers addressed me:*

'I have come to arrest you for causing the death of Mrs Wootten, the wife of Lieutenant Wootten, on the 23rd March, at 114, Rotherfield-street, by shooting her with a revolver or pistol. I shall now take you to Islington Police Station, where you will be charged with murder.'

Farewell to my freedom for three months! I was now 'in the hands of the police' as they call it, or as they say among the poorer classes 'in trouble'. I could not collect myself to speak a word. I merely remained where I was, dazed and dumb, while the police officers went upstairs and possessed themselves of all my belongings. Why they should do this struck me as strange as time but I know all about it now.

Perhaps they thought that I should have done something violent to myself if they had sent me upstairs to get on my hat and coat. But they need have had no fear on that score. I knew that for whatever reason they suspected me, the officers had got hold of erroneous information: I knew – I really knew, so positive was I then – that I should be liberated within a few hours, or within a few days, because, you see, I could not possibly doubt that they would immediately find out that I was not the person they wanted, and that they were really doing an unwitting injury to this discharge of their duty.

Weeks afterwards I would sit in my room at Holloway and ask myself such a question as this: Why does the prosecution make a dead set at a woman for doing a thing she never did? Of course I became wiser later on and began to understand that in no other way could guilt be proved or disproved and innocence confirmed.

They took me in a taxicab to Scotland Yard, where they left me for about an hour with my own jumbled thoughts. I did not let my father and mother know what

*had happened to me because I argued that as it would
soon all be over there was no occasion to disturb them. I
had not realised the gravity of my position for the simple
reason that I expected the police officers every moment to
say they were exceedingly sorry for what they had done
and that a mistake had been made.*

*I do not blame them. They were never unkind to me.
They were only doing their duty and they did it as gently
as men could in the circumstances. Only once did an
officer in uniform at one of the police court investigations
make a rather hurtful remark to me. This is what he said
as he saw me smiling slightly (I have a habit of smiling
for no reason that I know of): 'Miss, your conscience
does not seem to prick you much!'*

*I felt like asking him why my conscience should
prick me at all but I excused him as being a tactless
young policeman. Still I must not say anything against
policemen as my father is a retired sergeant of the
Brighton police and you could not find a better man than
my dad.*

*They brought me some sandwiches at Islington
Police Station and looked surprised when I ate them all.
Perhaps it may seem strange but I never went off my
food or off my sleep during the whole three months of my
trial, for it was a 'trial' at the time. Perhaps I ought to
make an exception of the night before I was taken from
Holloway at the Old Bailey. I think my sleep was a little
broken that night because I could not keep from picturing
to myself the scene in that awful place where all eyes
would be turned upon me in the historic dock.*

*But it was not fear or anxiety for my fate that
disturbed my sleep. I suppose it was really curiosity.
Just fancy that! A woman on the eve of being tried for
her life feeling curious about the scene at her trial.*

Would you believe it? I almost began to see the

humorous side of things as they took me about from
court to court, going all over the same ground like a
steamroller over stones in the road till it fairly bored me
and I yawned in my seat and more than once fell asleep.
What I was waiting for was the time when I should be
allowed to go into the witness-box to give my story. I
knew that I should be able to prove my innocence when
they brought me into the presence of the jury and the
great judge who could balance the scales of justice
without trying to prove either my guilt or my innocence.

During my stay at Holloway I spent great part of
my leisure studying French, so as to keep my mind off
my trouble. The chaplain at Holloway used to speak a
little simple French to me and we were able to hold easy
conversations.

It was a great relief to me when the time came for
my appearance in the dock at the Old Bailey. I never
for one moment pictured the judge putting on the black
cap. That was something I was not to see. I have never
seen the impressive ceremony and I never shall, for the
criminal courts could never offer any attraction to me as
a spectator. I marvelled very much that so many women
should come day after day to see me tried, and I am
quite sure that if any one of them had been in my place I
should not have taken her place.

I was rather nervous as I entered the court the
first morning, but that passed away and before the
proceedings began I busied myself admiring the beautiful
carved oak and the bouquet on the judge's bench. I had
heard that the Old Bailey had been renewed some years
ago, and was anxious to see what it looked like. Then
I scanned the crowd and wondered what they were all
thinking about me.

I am sure I must have smiled, because I was amused
to see all the idle people sitting there waiting to have their
queer tastes gratified by seeing what they very likely

supposed to be a murderess. Yet I must say that the public cheered very heartily when I got off, so I suppose there was some good in them after all. They had watched me while my life was in jeopardy and they cheered me when my life was saved.

The witnesses for the prosecution did not interest me. I had heard most of them tell the same story over and over again. Sometimes the fear took possession of me that the judge might catch me yawning and sternly rebuke me, but I really could not help it as the monotonous story was reeled off to me for about the twentieth time.

My interest was quickened when Lieutenant Wootten got into the box – the man in whom I had put so much trust. Never once did he turn his glances in my direction, though I sought his face with my eyes all the time. I could see that he purposely turned his head away from me. Both when he was giving evidence and afterwards when I gave evidence I looked hard at him, but we never exchanged glances or in any way betrayed recognition.

At times Mr Muir, the prosecution counsel, frightened me, because he made so much of points against me that I feared the jury might see eye to eye with him. He did not like my habit of smiling, and I should like to say now that I was not smiling deliberately but only smiling because I could not help it. Perhaps I seemed to take things too lightly or too coolly, but we cannot help our natures, and it is my nature to smile at people who are trying to do what I know to be impossible. It seemed to me that Mr Muir was trying to prove my guilt but not all the King's Counsels in the world could have done that, because I had no guilt to prove.

I knew that Mr Muir was doing the right thing, the thing he was there to do but I also knew, as I have been saying, that he could not do it and nobody else could do *it.*

For four and a half hours I occupied the witness-box. I could hear my heart beating while I was taking the oath, but I had no sooner done so than there came to me a great thrill of courage and confidence. I had longed to tell the truth, and now I had solemnly pledged myself before God to tell it. This strengthened me, and I felt that I did not care what they asked me: it seemed so easy just to tell the straight, plain, simple truth, making no attempts whatever at producing any effect.

It was very funny that I should feel more confident when answering Mr Muir than I felt when answering my own counsel, brilliant, young, Mr Pratt, because I somehow thought I ought to do all I could to assist Mr Pratt which, of course, was a silly thing for me to think. Mr Pratt only wanted me to tell the truth.

In his address Mr Muir chilled my heart with a doubt. He clinched things in such an emphatic way and I found myself wishing that I had his skill at speaking. I looked at the jury, especially the strongly featured foreman, and I tried to gather the extent to which Mr Muir's arguments were taking effect. But I couldn't gather anything, and so I just fell back upon the thought that had kept me up all the time and must keep me up til the end – namely that the truth would prevail.

The summing up of the judge came to me like sunshine, as I realised that Mr Justice Lush was going to see justice done. His calm manner and mellow, musical tones fascinated me where I sat. I forgot the oak carving, the bouquet on the bench beside him, the curious crowd, the lawyers with their wigs and the solicitors with their black bags. I forgot my father and mother were waiting in the court and listening as anxiously as I was. I do not think I was smiling then. I realised that my life was very largely in the hands of that great, good man, who would not be swayed by any passion or by any prejudice as he helped the jury to make up their minds by indicating to them the manner in which his own was made up.

But if I realised the crucial position in which I stood, I did not see the gallows at the end of it. The thought of the death sentence never possessed me. I had only a vague sense of danger, though what that danger exactly was took no definite form. I just thought that I was being tried for murder, and that the penalty for that crime was death.

The jury only kept me waiting twelve anxious moments. My mother fainted when she heard the good news of my acquittal: my solicitor, Mr Lewis, who had worked so hard for me, jumped up and congratulated me, and all the jurymen, whom I met on the stairs, shook hands with me one by one. The strong featured foreman, whom I had so feared, was the heartiest of them all.

At London Bridge station that night, when going to my home in Sussex I overheard two porters discussing my case, and, drawing near, I caught the words of one of them: 'I think she was a lucky girl'. So listening ears never hear any good of themselves. I smiled again.

I am naturally asked the question: 'Who killed Mrs Wootten, since you have been acquitted of the charge?' Of course, I cannot say, and I cannot even go so far as to help the police to find the murderer or murderers by pointing to any one person on whom my suspicions fasten. But still I have my own ideas, though they do not take definite shape.

It is always possible that the dead woman may have had some secret enemy, unknown to me or even to her husband, Lieutenant Wootten; and I have all along puzzled my mind to understand how the first theory was that she met her death by falling down stairs.

The disappearance of the revolver is a great mystery

– my revolver, I mean. It was, I suppose, the fact of my having a revolver that made the case look black against me. But how I came to have that revolver is quite easily explained.

It was an old thing that lay for years in the children's toy-box at home.

Only the night before the murder, I think it was, something upset me, and in my pique I threatened to commit suicide with that same revolver. It was then that Wootten took it from me, as I told the judge, saying 'Oh! If that's the way of it, then it is not safe to leave you with it'.

I hope and pray that some day soon the mystery of Mrs Wootten's death will be cleared up, when people who now write to me saying I have had a 'miraculous escape' will understand the agony of mind and heart that this tragedy has caused me, notwithstanding the solace derived from my sense of innocence.

It is lovely to be back again in my father's cottage home among the Sussex hills, where all the neighbours seek to cheer and encourage me by every show of sympathy and kindness. I am happy, if not perfectly happy.

That will come, as I believe it will come, in due time, with the full and final solution of Mrs Wootten's death.

It cannot be though that the police are done with the case because they are done with me.

Marie Wheatley

Perhaps the most curious part of this version of Marie's story is her claim that she had 'all along puzzled my mind to understand how the first theory was that she met her death by falling down stairs'. In the absence of any evidence that she had been shot, especially following the examination by the doctor, it was perfectly natural for everyone to assume she had fallen down the stairs and Marie herself had written in the *Lloyds News* account: 'I knew she had a defective knee and I thought she had fallen down the stairs'. It is suggestive of a person saying whatever suits the point she wants to make at any particular time.

Also worthy of note is Marie's statement: 'It was, I suppose, the fact of my having a revolver that made the case look black against me'. Although there can be no doubt that Marie's possession of a revolver was an important part of the prosecution case against her at trial, it was her own case that Higson had suggested that the case looked black against her at a time when no-one was aware that Mrs Wootten had been shot. What initially made the case look black against her was, of course, Lily's information that the woman who had almost certainly killed their mother was 'Mrs Higson's friend' yet, once again, Marie has precisely nothing to say about this crucial but inconvenient part of the story.

Marie might at least have been right about one thing. The full and final solution of Mrs Wootten's death could now finally emerge. It needs to be borne in mind that the fact that she was found not guilty of the murder by a jury does not necessarily mean Marie was innocent of the crime. According to no less an authority than the Criminal Court of Appeal, at the appeal of Frederick Seddon in 1912 (responding to a point by Marshall Hall that Mrs Seddon's acquittal must mean Seddon was innocent too), Mr Justice Darling said: 'In this country a verdict of "not guilty" does not necessarily mean "did not do it". It may mean "not proven".' He repeated the point in his judgment, saying: 'It was a mistake to suppose that "not guilty" meant "nothing to do with the affair"', adding that: 'In this country there are no means of expressing in a verdict the difference between innocence and not proven.'[159] If we are to get to the truth of the matter, therefore, we cannot rule out Marie as a suspect, despite the jury's verdict.

Nor are we compelled by the jury's verdict to accept Marie's evidence and reject Wootten's. However, we cannot accept them both. It is evident that Marie's account of what happened in the five days between 19 and 23 March is virtually the complete opposite of what Wootten described when he gave evidence at the Old Bailey. One of them was obviously lying. And the only conceivable reason for those lies is that the person telling them was either the murderer or involved in the murder of Mrs Wootten. So, if we can work out which story must be untrue we will surely discover the identity of the murderer.

CHAPTER 12

BLACKWHITE

'....the ability to believe that black is white, and more, to know that black is white, and to forget that one has ever believed the contrary.'

Definition of 'blackwhite' in *Nineteen Eighty Four* by George Orwell, 1949

It really is quite extraordinary, considering the relatively brief glimpse we get into her life, how many lies Marie managed to tell to so many different people in such a short space of time. The most breathtaking was, of course, the lie to her parents that she was married to Albert Wootten. It was a lie which trapped her in an alternative reality of her own making from which she was unable to escape until after her arrest. But the lie to her parents was by no means the only one she told; for Marie was quite evidently a compulsive and accomplished liar.

No better example can be found than her conversation with Mrs Alland on 19 March when she pretended she was walking to the post office to withdraw her rent money, only to suddenly announce that she had lost her purse and bank book. Her earlier claim to be on her way to Tooting to get the money was equally untruthful as was her statement, later the same day, that she possessed a licence for the revolver she carried and that she needed her revolver for chicken farming. She also lied by assuring Mrs Alland that her revolver was unloaded and that all the cartridges remained in the box. On the Sunday she lied again to Mrs Alland by telling her she was going to Haywards Heath. When she met Joe Higson in City Road shortly afterwards, she lied that she had been window shopping at Dawson's when, of course, she had been collecting her revolver from Mrs Alland. She also lied to Higson that she had been staying at Gillingham Street and was on her way to Tooting. After the news of Annie's death, when Mrs Connor asked her what was wrong, without batting an eyelid, she came up with the fairy tale that the woman who had been shot was a woman her husband had been living with. To her mother, she lied in writing that Wootten had joined the Flying Corps and was off to the front. When arrested, she could not stop herself telling the police she was a widow who had been married to Lanteri and it was no doubt only when she realised the lie could be exposed, after Inspector Davis asked her where the marriage took place, that she admitted the truth. Although Marie denied it during the trial, Detective Sergeant Wesley was adamant she had told him that she had 'never' had a revolver while, to the matron at Islington Police Station, she certainly said she had come down to London 'last Friday' when in reality, as she well knew, it was the previous Thursday.

Mr Pratt attempted to downplay the string of lies told by his client by saying that she had been punished for them in being arrested. Yet Marie's propensity to lie with ease at the drop of a hat needs to be borne in mind when assessing the conflict of evidence between her and Wootten. There is no doubt that the judge was correct to warn the jury that Wootten's evidence should not be accepted without corroboration but exactly the same should have been true of Marie's evidence. While there was no corroboration on either side as to who had the revolver on 23 March, the entirety of the evidence given by both Wootten and Marie about the events leading up to the murder should have been assessed against the independent evidence which existed and the evidence relating to the revolver should have been viewed in that context. In this respect, the judge seems to have signally failed to take Joe Higson's evidence into account. Mr Pratt dismissed it by telling the jury that they should not convict Marie on the basis of 'somebody's recollection of a particular conversation on a particular occasion' but, considering that a witness' memory of what someone has said is usually the essence of most evidence in a criminal case, that simply will not do. Although Mr Muir tells us that Marie accused Higson of giving 'false testimony', virtually all of his evidence was unchallenged by Mr Pratt and no allegation was ever put to him that he was a liar. Certainly, the judge did not say anything adverse about Higson's character and we can safely take his evidence as being an accurate account of what happened and what was said.

Higson is the primary source for what happened during Marie's visit to London in February. He described her persistent, obsessive and somewhat extraordinary demands to be allowed to take Wootten's children away with her, which clearly revealed her unbalanced psychological state of mind. She was absolutely besotted with Wootten to the point of threatening suicide if she could not have him. Her statement to the Higsons that they should look out for her name in the newspapers suggests that something extreme was brewing in her mind. After her performance at the Higsons' house, including her collapse to the floor, the idea that she tamely decided to accept that her relationship was over once she returned to Horsted Keynes strains credulity. Indeed, she later admitted to Higson that she had been writing to Wootten without reply when she spoke to him in the City Road on Sunday 21 March. The fact that she was still carrying Wootten's photograph around with her at this time – as seen by Mrs Alland – strongly suggests that she did not regard her relationship with him as over. Furthermore, by her own dubious account, she attempted to commit suicide in a field, only to be scared by the loudness of the revolver which she had been unable to fire into her head. Such an attempt (if it ever happened) does not fit easily with a state of mind being untroubled by Wootten's ending of the relationship. Yet her evidence was: 'I made up my mind not to have anything more to do with him.'

A suicide attempt also does not square with Marie's claim that Wootten had secretly told her to ignore everything that had been said about the agreement for her to leave him alone. If such a thing had really been said then either she did not care because she had made up her mind not to have anything more to do with Wootten (and she would thus not have been suicidal due to the break-up of the relationship) or she must have believed that her relationship with him would continue so that she still had a chance to fulfil what, despite her denials in the witness box, seemed to be her ultimate goal of taking possession of the children (and she would thus not have been suicidal). Yet, her evidence was that she only wrote to Wootten to ask for money. Did she attempt to kill herself simply because he had not sent her money for a few weeks? That, ultimately, appears to be the effect of her evidence but it does not seem likely or credible.

If Wootten had told Marie that he did not want her to leave him alone, as she suggests, then he certainly managed to deceive Higson who portrayed Wootten as firm in his determination to stick with his wife and children. But if Marie's story were true, or, in fact, even if it were not, and she was still in love with Wootten, her supposed receipt of a letter from Wootten on 18 March enclosing a postal order for 7/6 and instructing her to come to London must have been extremely welcome. If she was still in love with him then this was, finally, the resumption of the relationship and she must have been delighted. If her ardour had cooled and she was only interested in the money then, again, he had provided some and, in summoning her to London, was presumably going to provide more. On either version of her story, the letter from Wootten should have cheered her up and suicide should have been the furthest thing from her mind. Yet, according to Mr Pratt:

> she made up her mind then that if she failed to get a situation she was going to make an end of it all and shoot herself. She brought up the revolver for that purpose.

Oddly enough, this was not what Marie told Mr Pratt in the witness box. During her evidence-in-chief she said that she brought the revolver to London because Wootten had told her to in his letter. Mr Pratt appears to have been basing his closing speech on what Marie told Mr Muir during cross-examination when she said that she did not leave the revolver at home because she intended to shoot herself, not if she failed to get a situation (as Mr Pratt claimed) but if Wootten failed to treat her properly. The different versions, which even Mr Pratt does not appear to have been able to keep up with, rather suggest Marie was making her story up as she went along. Despite the importance of the point, her two long newspaper articles contain no mention of her reason for bringing the revolver to London with her.

Yet one possible reason for Marie coming to London with a revolver, and indeed the most obvious, is that she intended to shoot and kill Annie Wootten. Her motive for doing so was also obvious. With Annie out of the way, Wootten would need someone to look after the children and Marie would have (at least in her own mind) been the obvious choice for this job. Looking after the children would, naturally, mean that she would live with Wootten as his wife. If that were so, she could present Wootten to her parents as her real husband and they need never know that Marie had not been married to him in 1914. The children could be presented as children from a former marriage. It was everything Marie had wanted in February and there can be little doubt that she wanted this in March too.

On that basis a lot of things fall into place. We do not know what time of day Marie left for London but her father said in evidence that she was holding a letter in her hand, which she claimed had come from Wootten, 'on the morning she went to London'. There does not seem to be any reason why Marie would have delayed her departure – she only carried a few items in her attaché case – and one would think that she would have left for London as soon as possible. But she did not arrive at Ecclesbourne Road until 6:45pm. So what was she doing all day? The most likely explanation is that she was purchasing cartridges for her revolver. One cannot believe anything Marie says but it is noteworthy that this is precisely what she told Mrs Alland she had been doing, informing her how difficult it had been to find the correct size pinfire cartridges and that she had needed to visit a number of ammunition shops in London in order to locate them.

It will be recalled that when the revolver was examined at the police station there was one spent cartridge in the chamber. This suggests that, having purchased the box of cartridges, Marie carried out a test firing, probably in a secluded area of one of London's parks where a single gunshot would probably not attract any attention. Only two months earlier in Richmond Park, a couple walking in the park found the dead body of a young man with a revolver lying by his side.[160] He was later identified as Albert John Dobbé, a 25-year-old clerk employed by the Anglo-South American Bank in Old Broad Street who had only returned to England a fortnight earlier from Chile. He had shot himself in the head on 19 January but no-one in the park had heard the sound of gunfire, or if they did, they had simply ignored it. Almost exactly a month later, on 18 February 1915, in an echo of the 'Jack the Ripper' murders, a forty-year-old prostitute called Alice Elizabeth Jarman was murdered – her throat cut – and mutilated, without anyone noticing, in broad daylight in Hyde Park, apparently by a soldier belonging to the Argyll and Sutherland Regiment who had been seen talking to her but who was never identified, despite an identity parade of 900 soldiers at the White City in March.[161]

So there would have been no real danger for Marie in test firing the weapon in a public park. It would certainly have been a sensible action bearing in mind that the revolver was very old and, according to Mr Wheatley, there was a flaw or crack along the barrel. He did not think it could be fired but he could not have been certain because it had never been tested. It is true the revolver was kept in the toy box but this was only because Mr Wheatley had no bullets for it. To state the obvious: a gun without bullets is useless and can be played with by children as a toy without the possibility of anyone being harmed but, as soon as ammunition is acquired and inserted, it becomes a deadly weapon.

The police conducted inquiries and a shopkeeper's wife in Fulham told them that a woman had attempted to purchase some 7mm pinfire cartridges from her shop on an unknown day but she failed to identify Marie in a line-up. This might be a point in Marie's favour, and the failure of the police to prove Marie purchased the cartridges was certainly a major weakness in the prosecution, but, at the same time, it does not prove she was not the woman. It is worth bearing in mind that, if the shopkeeper's wife had identified Marie, it would simply have meant that Marie (if guilty) could have adapted her story so that she bought cartridges herself on the Thursday with the intention of committing suicide in London but still gave them to Wootten on the following Monday along with the revolver.

One thing is for sure; when Marie arrived in London on Thursday 18 March she did not go straight to Wootten in the White City, as she would surely have done if she had been summoned by him and was carrying a revolver for him which he had requested. Instead, she went straight to Islington, the very place she knew Wootten would not be but where his wife lived. Her explanation for choosing lodgings in Ecclesbourne Road, so close to 114 Rotherfield Street, is not recorded other than her saying she wanted to see Wootten which does not make much sense because he was not living in Rotherfield Street at the time.[162] We do not know if she was ever challenged about this in court but perhaps she said that, having lived in Islington, she was comfortable with the area and knew that relatively cheap accommodation was available in Ecclesbourne Road. Had she wanted to, she could have said that Wootten suggested she stay there and no-one could have proved otherwise. One assumes that she did not say this otherwise it would have been mentioned by either Mr Pratt or the judge and reported. Of course, had Marie wanted to murder Mrs Wootten then 36 Ecclesbourne Road was an ideal staging post.

We have seen that, according to Marie, Mr Pratt made the point in his closing speech that it would have been stupid for Marie, if she intended to murder Mrs

Wootten, to take lodgings so close to Rotherfield Street in her own name with a revolver and a letter addressed to Lieutenant Wootten in her possession. This was no more than an advocate's equivalent of a conjuring trick. When she arrived at Ecclesbourne Road, Marie's revolver was safely concealed in her locked attaché case. The letter to Wootten was hidden away in her handbag. She could never have anticipated that either item would be discovered by the occupants of 36 Ecclesbourne Road or anyone else for that matter. As for identifying herself as 'Miss Wheatley', this meant nothing. There were hundreds, if not thousands, of Miss Wheatleys in England in 1915. The 1911 Census for England and Wales includes over 400 females called 'Mary Wheatley' (or variants of that name) alone and a further 200 called 'Alice Wheatley'.

It will be recalled that Marie gave Mrs Alland the impression that she was from Haywards Heath but this was only after the confiscation of her attaché case on 19 March and even this concealed the truth that she was actually living (with her parents) in Horsted Keynes, about five miles from Haywards Heath. As at 18 March, the bare fact that Mrs Alland and the others at 36 Ecclesbourne Road knew their guest was called Miss Wheatley would in no way have implicated her in the shooting of a local woman, even one just up the road. To Wootten, although he was aware of her supposed maiden name and wrote out her reference in this name, she was known as Marie Lanteri. In her own mind, during the evening of 18 March, if she was planning to shoot Mrs Wootten, Marie would have had no reason to think anyone would suspect her. If she was lying about having been summoned to London by Wootten, then everyone who knew her, apart from her parents, believed her to be in Sussex and no-one at all knew she was in Islington. Even if Wootten had asked her to come to London he would not have known she was in Islington.

From Marie's perspective, therefore, on the basis she intended to kill Mrs Wootten when she arrived in Islington, there was little risk in identifying herself to Mrs Alland and the other occupants of 36 Ecclesbourne Road as Miss Wheatley. They certainly had no idea she was connected to Mrs Wootten and there would have been absolutely no reason for them to link Marie to the murder if they had not known about her revolver. Even after she confessed to carrying a revolver, Marie could still reasonably have hoped that the connection between the woman who turned up at Ecclesbourne Road and herself would never be made. This no doubt explains why she told the matron of Islington Prison that she arrived in London on Friday the 19th March instead of the correct date of Thursday the 18th. Mrs Alland and the maid only had to keep quiet and the police would never have known about her lodging so close to Mrs Wootten or her being in possession of the revolver. She was not aware that Mrs Alland had shown the revolver to the police and, while she might have suspected it, she could not even have been certain that the landlady had seen the revolver.

In the absence of being identified by a shopkeeper, there was no way of proving that Marie purchased cartridges on 18 March but there is one part of her story which could, potentially, have caused her downfall if Mr Muir had been alert enough to spot it. According to Marie, she had received a postal order from Wootten for seven shillings and sixpence on 18 March. An ordinary single journey to London from Horsted Keynes, via East Grinstead, cost two shillings and eleven and a half pence in March 1915 although the same journey via Haywards Heath, was slightly more expensive at three shillings and four pence.[163] If

she came via Haywards Heath, this would have left her
with at least four shillings and two pence in her purse.
On her account, by which she went straight to Islington
after arriving in London, she would, presumably, have
caught the 4pm train from Horsted Keynes, arriving
at Haywards Heath at 4:12pm and then changed onto
the London bound train departing Haywards Heath
at 4:13pm, arriving at London Victoria at 5:48pm
before making her way to Ecclesbourne Road where
she arrived at 6:45pm. Had she taken the more direct,
and cheaper, route via East Grinstead she would, on
her account, presumably have caught the 2:11pm train
from Horsted Keynes, arriving at East Grinstead at
2:29pm and then catching the 2:52pm train from East
Grinstead arriving in London at 4:30pm. The next
train to London from Horsted via East Grinstead did
not arrive in London until after 8pm, which Marie
obviously could not have caught.

After arriving in Islington, Marie claimed to have
visited the cinema between 7:00pm and 9:45pm but this
need only have cost a few pence. There were a large
number of cinemas in Islington at the time, such as the
Electric Cinema in Upper Street, the Coronet in Essex
Street, the Angel Picture Theatre in the High Street
and, closest of all to Ecclesbourne Road, the Victoria
in the New North Road. Like most cinemas outside of
the west end, they charged from as little as three pence
up to a usual maximum of one shilling for an entrance
ticket, depending on the quality of seat. It is also
possible that Marie could have stopped for some food
during the evening. If so, she should have been able to
find something nourishing to eat, perhaps a sandwich
or a salad, for no more than sixpence. The cheapest
cooked meals in London at the time could famously
be purchased, not too far from the Angel, at a small
restaurant run by George Jacob at 47 Rosoman Street,

Clerkenwell, known as 'The Threepenny Ritz', where you could buy roast mutton, stewed beef or a steak pudding, plus two vegetables, for threepence. Dessert of a jam roll or a pudding would cost an extra penny. If you wanted to start with soup and finish with a cup of tea or coffee, the entire meal would cost six and a half pence.[164] While this kind of low price was unique and newsworthy in 1915, especially with food prices having risen steeply because of the war, it was perfectly possible for Marie to have been able to both visit the cinema and get at least some food for under a shilling. This would have been entirely sensible given her limited funds. Unless she foolishly treated herself to the top priced cinema ticket of one shilling and a slap up meal costing about three shillings (the starting price of a three course dinner at central London hotels in March 1915), Marie should, therefore, have had most of the four shillings remaining from the money sent to her by Wootten on 19 March. Yet, when she opened her purse to Mrs Alland during the morning of 19 March she supposedly only had one shilling and fivepence in her possession. While, on its own, this means nothing, Mr Muir should have asked her what she spent her money on during 18 March. If he did, there is no record of it.

Although it is not now possible to state the exact retail price of Eley pinfire cartridges in March 1915, had Marie bought a box of fifty such cartridges it can be estimated from the known trade price for Eley 7mm pinfire cartridges in 1914 (which was 27.5 shillings per thousand, probably equating to a retail price of somewhere in the region of 40 shillings per thousand) that she would have needed to have spent about two shillings. After deducting her train fare from a starting point of 7/6, this would be broadly consistent with the amount of money she apparently had left on 18 March.

In fact, if the train journey to London was 3 shillings and the ammunition was 2 shillings (and her supposed visit to the cinema never happened), Marie would have had 2/6 left from the postal order, allowing her a shilling or so for minor expenses, such as tube or tram fares (costing no more than a few pence) in order to travel around London to locate the cartridges during the day. Alternatively, or in addition, she might have stopped off for some cheap food or light refreshments at some point during the day.

Of course, we only have Marie's word for it that she received a postal order of 7/6 in the morning of 18 March. The evidence of Marie's father was that she told him she had received a postal order for about seven shillings from Wootten, which appears to provide corroboration, but we have seen that Marie told lies at almost any opportunity, especially to her parents and especially where Wootten was concerned. She was still trying to maintain the fiction that Wootten was her husband - Wootten's evidence was that he refused to continue the correspondence with her because she insisted he address his letters to her as 'Mrs Wootten' when he wrote to her at her parents' house - but even by Marie's own account Wootten had not been writing to her, a fact which would not have gone unnoticed by her parents. Pretending to have received a letter, and money, from Wootten would support the story of her marriage but, more importantly, would provide an explanation to her parents as to why she was going to London. Obviously, if the story of the postal order was a fabrication, it begs the question as to where Marie obtained her money to get her to London. On this issue, Wootten might have inadvertently provided us with the answer. His evidence at the police court was that he asked Marie on 19 March what had happened to her 'rings'. She replied that she had left them at home but Wootten's question shows that Marie must normally have worn a number of rings and raises the possibility that she had pawned all of them, other than the one she gave to Mrs Alland as security for her rent, in return for the transport money to London.[165]

What of the veiled lady who appeared in Rotherfield Street during the evening of 18 March? Marie left 36 Ecclesbourne Road at about 7pm and, at about 7:30pm, the veiled lady was first seen in Rotherfield Street. It is a very close fit. Admittedly there is a gap in time between the woman knocking at the door of 114, which was said by both Mr and Mrs Dixon, as well as Mrs Higson, to have been somewhere between 8:30 and 8:45pm, and Marie's return to 36 Ecclesbourne Road about an hour later when it should have taken her no more than a minute to walk there from Rotherfield Street. Violet Thorn, who was cross-examined closely by Mr Pratt about timings, was adamant that Marie returned between 9:45 and 10pm – she said she was expecting her sister to arrive at that time which is why she remembered it. That being so, it is certainly strange that Marie should have stayed out for an hour longer than necessary on a cold night in March (it had actually been snowing earlier during the day in London). Perhaps, having claimed to want to speak to Mrs Wilson at number 14, she felt the need to maintain the charade and walked off in the direction of 14 Rotherfield Street, which would have taken her in the opposite direction to Ecclesbourne Road. She might have continued walking in a wide circle back to her lodgings, plotting her next move, possibly stopping for a cup of tea and a snack. Or perhaps the Dixons and Mrs Higson were all mistaken about the time.

But that is a relatively minor discrepancy. An extreme irony of any attempt to make a case against

Marie is that one literally has to argue that black
is white. She walked out of 36 Ecclesbourne Road
wearing a white veil yet the mysterious veiled lady
was, by all accounts, wearing a veil that appeared to
be black or at least 'dark'. The answer has to be that it
was very dark in Rotherfield Street that night – with no
street lighting - and, wearing a dark coat, the illusion
was given to those who saw her that the veil was also
dark. More important than the recollection of the
Dixons and Mrs Higson about the colour of the veil
was Mrs Wootten's (inadmissible as evidence) belief,
shared by Mrs Higson, on the basis of the sound of her
voice that the veiled lady was Marie. The ridiculous
and transparent lie told by the veiled lady that she
wanted to complain about the behaviour of Mrs
Wilson's children at number 14, and had knocked at
the wrong door, is reminiscent of the type of ridiculous
lies we know Marie told.

Whether she was staking out the premises to
observe the comings and goings of the occupants of
114 or simply stalking Mrs Wootten will never be
known. She wasn't in the process of carrying out the
murder because her revolver was back at Ecclesbourne
Road – Violet Thorn picked up her attaché case while
she was out that evening and found it was heavy,
so the revolver was presumably in it.[166] It is true
that she could easily have returned to her room and
collected the weapon if Mrs Wootten had been on her
own, although such comings and goings on her first
night might have aroused suspicion, but there may
be a reason why Marie wanted to wait until the next
day before taking any action. It will be recalled that
Wootten had told Marie that his unlucky day was the
nineteenth of the month. There is no evidence that
Marie had planned to murder Mrs Wootten on the
nineteenth of March but it must at least be possible that

this thought crossed her mind. From Wootten's point of view it would have been one more tragedy in his life that took place on the nineteenth and Marie could have offered him the comfort he needed as she had no doubt comforted him when he told her about the death of his son having occurred on the nineteenth of November 1904.

On the basis that Marie did intend to kill Mrs Wootten on 19 March, there is no reason why she needed to wait until the evening before acting. If she planned to kill Mrs Wootten inside her house, the murder could have been carried out during daylight hours. When she left Ecclesbourne Road she had her revolver and was heading in the direction of a post office. Was she planning to send her 'Dickson' telegram in order to lure Lily Dixon out of the house? Although Annie's sister might have been able to get to her father's house and back within half an hour, as Mr Pratt established, this would have given any murderer of Mrs Wootten enough time to carry out their dreadful deed. During the day, Fred Dixon would have been at work so, if Lily could be drawn out of the house, Annie would be on her own with only her youngest children as Lily and Ivy would have been at school.

Marie's main problem, if she was the killer, was that she could not go back to Ecclesbourne Road after the murder. Not, at least, without seven shillings for the rent. If she only had 1s/5d on her, as she claimed, she was about one and a half shillings short of the minimum train fare back to Horsted Keynes. While it is not impossible that she had some emergency pennies hidden amongst her garments it can be safely assumed that if she had any more shillings in her possession she would have offered them to Mrs Alland because, regardless of whether she was planning to murder Mrs Wootten, the one thing she would surely not have wanted to give up was her attaché case containing the revolver. As we only have her word that she started with 7s/6d, it is not impossible that she had already purchased a return ticket to Horsted Keynes (which would have cost 5s/11d if she travelled via East Grinstead) although in that event one would have expected the police to have found it in her handbag after she was arrested, but it was not listed in the exhibits at the police court of items in her possession.

Assuming she had neither return ticket nor a hidden shilling or two amongst her garments and she was planning to murder Mrs Wootten, she would have had nowhere to stay that evening. To that extent, the idea that she was in the process of carrying out preparations for the murder when she was stopped near the Angel by Mrs Alland is open to question. At the same time, it would appear that Marie had arrived at Ecclesbourne Road at 6:45pm on 18 March with nowhere to stay and only 1s/5d on her (assuming her story about going to the cinema is bogus and she spent no money during the evening of 18 March) so she seems to have had no problem in believing she could secure lodgings for herself without having to pay any rent in advance. Even if she had really been to the cinema and spent money during the evening of 18 March, after deducting three shillings train fare from her starting total of 7s/6d, she must have arrived at 36 Ecclesbourne Road with less than the 5 shillings she was told by Violet Thorn would be needed for the rent and would, thus, not have been able to pay her rent in advance. We know that the woman who called at 114 on 23 March asked for money and it is not impossible that Marie planned to get her train fare back to Horsted Keynes from Mrs Wootten before killing her.

One reason for pondering at length on this question is that it would have been an impressive, if evil and dastardly, plan for Marie to have murdered Mrs Wootten and then ended the day back in Sussex with hardly anyone knowing she had been in London. At this stage, on the morning of 19 March, Mrs Alland had no idea Marie had a revolver so, if she had simply returned to Sussex, she would just have been a woman who had failed to pay her rent and disappeared. It is unlikely that Mrs Alland, upon reading in the newspaper of Mrs Wootten's murder would have had any reason to suspect Marie of being involved and nor for that matter, in the absence of any reference to 'Mrs Higson's friend', would Albert Wootten.

Considering her references to Tooting in many of her fabrications, there is good reason to believe Wootten's evidence that Marie told him on 19 March, when she turned up unannounced at the White City asking for help, that, following an argument with her father, she had intended to go to Tooting to stay with her aunt who turned out to be on holiday. Although the 'discredited' Wootten is our only source for this, it is a story that is perfectly consistent with what Marie had told both Mrs Alland and Joe Higson. Perhaps the most important evidence in the whole case is Wootten's recollection that he gave Marie 'two shillings or so' for lunch. When he said this at the coroner's court, he was attempting to provide an example of his generosity in the face of an allegation that he had reneged on the agreement to provide financial support for Marie. He could not have known that Mrs Alland's evidence would be that, when Marie accosted her during the afternoon of 19 March, she had offered her half a crown, i.e. two shillings and sixpence, for the rent. Considering that Marie only had 1s 5d in the morning, the obvious question is: where did she get the extra cash from to be able to make such an offer to Mrs Alland? It can only have come from

Wootten and is perfectly consistent with Wootten's account of events. For if Marie had been summoned down to London by Wootten with instructions to bring down the revolver, why did Marie not simply ask him for seven shillings and sixpence so that she could immediately reclaim her attaché case from Mrs Alland?

We know that Marie did turn up at Mrs Alland's doorstep on the Sunday afternoon with the five shillings she needed to reclaim her possessions (having already given the landlady half a crown on the Thursday). If Wootten gave her four shillings on Sunday morning, as he claimed, she could have made up the additional shilling from what she had left of the 1s/5d we know she had on the Thursday. Marie's supposed explanation as to why she needed the four shillings, namely that she had lent money to her sister is, again, the type of lie we know she told (and the police do not appear to have made enquiries with her sister to prove or disprove it). If Wootten was lying about the events of Sunday morning during his testimony he was certainly a good liar, being able to weave into the story the fact that it was Sunday so Marie would not be able to transmit the money that day. Marie's response that she would do so first thing on Monday morning when the post offices would re-open seems too realistic to be a fabrication by Wootten. But the fact that lends most support to Wootten's story is that when Higson met Marie on the Sunday afternoon (after she had just collected her attaché case from Mrs Alland) she told him not to tell Wootten that he had seen her. In the witness box, Marie was to say that she had told Wootten that her attaché case had been taken from her by Mrs Alland and he had given her the money to redeem it. If that was true, there does not seem to have been any obvious reason for Marie to swear Higson to secrecy with respect to Wootten.

It could be argued that, for some reason (perhaps because she was planning to use it to commit suicide) Marie did not want Wootten to know that she had collected the revolver on Sunday afternoon. Yet, on her account, she obviously told him on the Monday (because that is when he supposedly took it from her) and it is hard to see what could possibly have changed in twenty four hours. If Marie's story was true, Wootten knew she was going to get the revolver at some point - he had supposedly given her the money for precisely that purpose - so what benefit was there in keeping from him the fact of her possession of it for one extra day?

It may actually be that Wootten did not see Marie on the Sunday evening. To the coroner on 25 March, he said: 'Last time I was with her [Annie] was from 2.30pm till just before 11:30pm on Sunday 21 March'. If this was correct it would have given him no chance to see Marie that evening and it would certainly explain why Marie did not show him the revolver until the Monday. It would also have been a point in Wootten's favour to explain why he never saw the revolver in Marie's room, because he would only have visited her on one occasion before the murder when he could conceivably have spotted it (i.e. Monday 22 March). However, at the police court on 4 May, Wootten said: 'On the 21st she [Marie] hadn't got a situation and *we spoke of it on the evening of the 21st'*. I went home and saw my wife and returned to the White City' (emphasis added). Likewise, Mrs Connor's evidence was that Wootten 'called every evening from the 19th to the 22nd'. Although the sequence of events would have been fresh in Wootten's mind on 25 March, it may be that he did not want to mention Marie at that point – she was certainly not referred to in his evidence – and he edited out his quick trip to Shepherd's Bush. Marie did not say one way or the other whether she had a visit from Wootten on the Sunday evening but her evidence was that Wootten did not take the revolver from her until Monday 22 March and then only after she had threatened to commit suicide. If Wootten visited Richmond Road on Sunday evening, and on balance it rather seems that he did, his apparent failure to even ask about the revolver, let alone take it, does not fit with Marie's story that he had specifically requested that she bring the weapon to London nor that he had given her the money to reclaim it from Mrs Alland.

Whoever committed the murder evidently put a lot of thought and preparation into it. There can be little doubt that it was the murderer who sent the 'come at once' telegram to 'Dickson' at 114 Rotherfield Street with the aim of removing one or both of the Dixons from the scene. The sending of a bogus telegram to lure someone out of their house was not an entirely original concept. In January 1915, the *Richmond and Twickenham Times* reported the arrest in Mortlake of a burglar who had sent a telegram to a woman at Stoke Newington telling her that her father had been taken to a hospital and who then broke into her house and stole her jewellery after she departed.[167] A year earlier, William Le Queux's novel, *The Four Faces: A Mystery*, published in January 1914, featured a beautiful female member of a criminal gang who sent a telegram from a post office in Regent Street in the name of the book's central character, Michael Berrington, to Berrington's fiancée, for the purposes of luring her to a house in London for some rather convoluted plot purposes. Like Wootten, Berrington conducted his own investigation into the telegram's origin (although, unlike Wootten, he did so with a police officer by his side), questioning the postmaster and the young lady who transmitted the message. Like Gertrude Taylor, this lady remarked: 'we see so many people, and most of them only for a few minutes' but she did eventually recall that it was a woman who handed it in. Interestingly, Berrington received two more telegrams during the course of the novel (one of which was dubious in origin) but the one completely genuine telegram he did receive, from his friend Jack Osborne, read: 'Come at once. Urgent:-- Jack.'

Le Queux might have been inspired by a real life incident which had occurred in Islington, two years before the publication of his book, and three years before the murder of Mrs Wootten. A former soldier turned hairdresser, William Whelen, sent a telegram to his girlfriend, Florence Howard, who had broken his heart by refusing to marry him, which read: 'Come at once, Upper-street police station. Have been arrested'.[168] An actual arrest would not have been surprising because Whelen, who was clearly unbalanced, had already threatened to murder Florence for not following his instructions to attend the local registry office for a wedding ceremony he had independently arranged and paid for. In turn, she had, not surprisingly, reported him to the police. When she left her house, as instructed, in order to travel to Upper Street Police Station, Whelen was lying in wait with a revolver. He wrestled her to the floor and was about the pull the trigger when she put up her arm and knocked it away. The weapon discharged and Florence was able to run for safety into a nearby barber's shop. Whelen attempted to flee the scene but was captured by a constable and quickly found himself in the North London Police Court followed by a swift visit to the Old Bailey where Mr Justice Ridley sentenced him to three years penal servitude for shooting with intent to do grievous bodily harm. While the fact that this happened in Islington might suggest that the writer of the 'Dickson' telegram was a longstanding resident of the borough, the incident was reported in the national papers in January 1912 so Marie could have read about Whelan's 'Come at once' telegram while living in Sussex. The similarity of the wording in the Whelan telegram compared to the 'Dickson' telegram certainly does create a suspicion that the latter was inspired by the former, if not by the Le Queux novel or the Stoke Newington robbery.

There can be no doubt at all that the murderer of Mrs Wootten sent the 'L. Davey' letter card to Wootten. This is clear from the fact that it was postmarked 8:30pm on the evening of 23 March and must have been posted a little earlier than this, at a time when Mrs Wootten had only just been pronounced dead by Dr Madden and the only people who knew of the death were those inside 114 Rotherfield Street. No-one at all (apart from the murderer) even suspected anything other than an accidental death, yet the letter card addressed to Wootten said 'Your kids come next' showing that the writer was aware that his wife had been murdered. It is also clear that the author of the letter knew Wootten very well but was clumsily attempting to disguise this fact. Apart from being addressed to Lieutenant 'Wootton', it also described him as being in the '9th Bedfords' yet, at the same time, the letter was addressed to White City, where very few people could possibly have known Wootten's regiment was based. The errors of 'Wootton' instead of 'Wootten' and '9th Bedfords' instead of '10th Bedfords' are too contrived for someone so familiar with Wootten's actual whereabouts. The mention of 'B. Wootton' in the text also shows the writer knew that Albert, who would always sign himself as 'A. Wootten', was often referred to as Bert. In her newspaper article, Marie said the police had established to their own satisfaction that she did not write the letter card, which is why it was not produced in evidence against her, but it is highly unlikely that the police would have communicated such a belief to her or her legal representatives. It was probably dropped from the list of exhibits by Mr Muir after he reviewed all the evidence and decided it would do more harm than good to the prosecution case. The errors in the letter card might have been contrived but they were enough to make it appear that Marie, who knew what regiment Wootten was in and could spell his name correctly, was not the author. There was certainly no way of proving she was.

Neither the handwriting of the telegram nor the letter card matched Marie's. The telegram was said by the *Evening News* to have been in a 'boy's handwriting' – although in reality there is no such thing – and we have no information about the handwriting of the letter card. Graphology, or the study of handwriting, had been regarded as a scientific discipline since the first half of the nineteenth century but it was still, to a large extent, in its infancy and it would not have been too hard for anyone to disguise their handwriting, perhaps by using their weaker hand, without detection.

There were no recognised experts of sufficient stature who the prosecution could call upon to assist them. Thomas Henry Gurrin, the leading handwriting expert of the period, frequently used by the crown as an expert witness in criminal cases and adored by the judiciary in an almost Spilsbury-like fashion, had died two years earlier and his reputation and credibility, as well as the credibility of handwriting experts in general, had, in any case, been seriously tarnished by his critical misidentification of handwriting in the Beck case. If that was not bad enough, he had then gone on to identify George Edalji as the author of a number of anonymous letters posted in South Staffordshire but Edalji, who was convicted of mutilating a horse in 1903, received a free pardon in May 1907 as a result of a powerful campaign by Sir Arthur Conan Doyle and it followed that he was almost certainly innocent of having written the letters as well. During committal proceedings at Croydon Police Court in March 1909, Gurrin identified Annie Dewey, a middle aged housekeeper to a Roman Catholic priest, as the author of a number of anonymous and libellous letters to various individuals, including Mrs Annie Tugwell, the wife of the registrar of Sutton, but then changed his mind before her trial in June causing the (private) prosecution to collapse. After Miss Dewey's acquittal on a second charge of criminal libel at Guildford in March 1910, it was discovered by means of chemically marked stamps and police observations of post boxes that Mrs Tugwell had a secret habit of writing bizarre accusatory letters to various people, including herself, in disguised handwriting: a crime for which she was twice convicted and imprisoned, for quite separate offences, in August 1910 and then again, following her release from prison, in October 1913.[169] Gurrin's string of embarrassing public failures continued two years after he provided his expert opinion to the Admiralty that a young Royal Navy cadet, George Archer-Shee, had forged a signature on a stolen postal order for five shillings which he then cashed, causing the cadet to be expelled from the Royal Naval College in November 1908. However, following the institution of legal proceedings by Archer-Shee's father, the Solicitor-General, on behalf of the Admiralty, accepted in court in July 1910 that Archer-Shee was entirely innocent of the charge. His client's reputation restored, Archer-Shee's barrister, Sir Edward Carson (the Attorney-

General at the time of Marie's trial), wrote a caustic letter to *The Times* in August 1910, saying: 'I certainly had hoped that the result of this case would help to put an end to the idea that any reliance whatsoever can be placed on the opinion of so-called experts in handwriting,' adding that: 'My own experience is that, however honest the so-called expert may be, no class of evidence is more likely to lead to a miscarriage of justice.'[170]

Gurrin's son, Gerald, succeeded him, and eventually became an authority on the subject, but in 1915 was relatively inexperienced and had only given evidence in a few major criminal cases. The remaining experts were not held in terribly high esteem by the courts. In December 1915, for example, Dr Walter de Gray Birch, formerly of the Manuscripts Department of the British Museum, who put himself forward as an 'ad hoc' handwriting expert with forty or fifty years experience, gave evidence as an expert witness on behalf of the defendants in a civil action in the High Court in front of Mr Justice Scrutton. Before he could state his opinion that certain signatures on various important documents in the case were forgeries, he was, quite remarkably, cross-examined by the judge who recognized him from an earlier case in which he had given evidence before him in York, regarding a dispute over a will. 'Did you give evidence to the effect that the will was genuine?' enquired Mr Justice Scrutton. 'I may have done so,' replied an unsettled Dr Birch. 'And did the daughter afterwards admit that it was a forgery?' asked the judge. 'I believe so,' said Birch, causing the defendants' barrister to request his own expert stand down immediately from the witness box! Another handwriting expert for the defence in the same case, Francis Compton Price, who said he had been in practice as a handwriting expert for 45 years, fared little better. He was asked by the judge, to laughter in the court, if he had kept a record of how many times juries had thought him wrong (or right) and was then told sarcastically by Justice Scrutton: 'You ought to be a judge' when he said in evidence he had 'no doubt' that signatures on some share certificates and a legal agreement were forgeries.

In the absence of any heavyweight experts, and with the Director of Public Prosecutions unlikely to want to pay the going rate of five guineas for an analysis which would be of no real evidential value, Mr Muir, who fancied himself as a bit of an amateur graphologist, would have had to form his own view, using his naked eye and a magnifying glass, about whether there was any similarity between Marie's handwriting and the handwriting on the 'Davey' letter card.[171] Unfortunately, the originals of both communications do not appear to have survived so there is no way proper tests can be carried out today.

What we can say is that the motive for the murderer in sending the letter card must have been to throw the police off the scent. By introducing the 'L Davey' character, who apparently bore a grudge against Wootten, the author created a clever smokescreen which, on the face of it, had nothing to do with Marie (or any other known suspect). Yet, if she was the murderer, Wootten's theory that 'L Davey' was supposed to be the publican, William Davy, with whom he had had a violent (and then legal) dispute is probably correct.

As for the 'Dickson' telegram, it is true that the prosecution was unable to call any witnesses to prove that Marie knew Lily's surname was Dixon (although one of those potential witnesses, Mrs Wootten, was dead) but she had stayed with the Higsons for ten days and it would only have needed one passing mention of the surname in conversation by the Higsons or Wootten in her hearing, which would never have stuck in their memory, for her to have acquired that information. The misspelling of the name on this occasion was almost certainly a genuine mistake based on the identical phonetic properties between Dickson and Dixon. Marie did not make many slips in her interview with Wootten and Higson after the murder but, in telling Higson that she did not know Lily's surname, after he had simply shown her the telegram addressed to Dickson at 114 Rotherfield Street, she gave the game away. Mr Pratt cleverly manipulated Higson to concede that Marie could have guessed that the telegram must have been meant for Annie's sister but that is only true in the sense that, if she had been asked who she thought the intended recipient might have been, it would have been perfectly possible for her to guess at Lily. However, that was not the situation which actually occurred. She was shown a telegram addressed to a 'Dickson', who she had supposedly never heard of, at 114 Rotherfield Street and she automatically replied on the basis that it was a reference to Annie's sister without even asking. That behaviour is only consistent with her knowing Lily's surname. Someone who did not know it would surely have asked 'Who is Dickson?'

We have been the long way round the case against Marie because the strongest evidence of her guilt was the information Mrs Wootten provided before she was killed and was available from the very start of the police enquiry. The woman who called at 114 Rotherfield Street on the night of the murder was 'Mrs Higson's friend' and Mrs Higson's friend was Marie. There can really be no reasonable doubt about it. True, it is not absolute, incontrovertible, proof that Marie was at 114 Rotherfield Street that night; Annie might have been lying to her children about the identity of the visitor or she might have attributed the label of 'Mrs Higson's friend' to more than one woman or the children might have been mistaken or lying or had the name suggested to them by their father but these are all theoretical possibilities only. There is absolutely nothing to suggest that Mrs Wootten was doing anything other than genuinely informing her daughter of the identity of the lady who was at the door at the time and that Lily and Ivy genuinely repeated this information in the coroner's court, the police court and, to the extent they were allowed the opportunity, at the Central Criminal Court. Certainly, as mentioned earlier, the idea that Wootten could have instructed his two girls, aged six and seven, to lie for him is ridiculous – it is doubtful if it is even possible to coach children to lie in such a fashion about the traumatic death of their mother – especially with Lily and Ivy being so well mannered as they showed at the various courts they were compelled to give evidence at. It would certainly have been madness for Wootten to have relied on his children giving false evidence about this for him without slipping up during cross-examination. It is true that with one question - regarding the time Wootten had returned home - Mr Pratt might have caught Lily saying in evidence something which she had, unknowingly, learnt subsequently (with no clock in her room it is difficult to see how she could have known that her father had returned home at midnight) but, otherwise, everything she said in the various witness boxes had the strong ring of truth about it.

None of this proves Marie killed Mrs Wootten, although the evidence about 'Mrs Higson's friend' comes very close. That evidence was, of course, inadmissible in the Old Bailey but there was still a rich body of cross-examination material for a determined and skilled prosecutor. If Marie was lying, her lies were complicated enough to make herself confused when she tried to put together a consistent story. A skilful cross-examiner could have first established which of Marie's contemporaneous statements she was now claiming were true and thus, for example, whether she really only had 1/5 in cash on her in the afternoon of 19 March, as she told Mrs Alland. Then, turning to her alibi for the previous evening she could have been asked if she genuinely did visit the cinema, what film she saw and whether she spoke to anyone. With that focus on establishing whether she could prove she visited the cinema acting as a distraction, Marie should then have been asked if she went anywhere else that evening. If she was lying, she would have wanted to minimise the number of people she had spoken to and is likely to have said she only went to the cinema. That would have then led to a question which could have been decisive, namely: what did she spend her money on during the day? The point being that, if she could not account for her spending, it would support the notion that she purchased pinfire cartridges that afternoon. If Mr Muir did attempt this line of questioning there is no surviving record of it and his rather poorly designed questions that are recorded in the press do not suggest he attempted anything quite so calculated.

Another potentially fruitful line of questioning, which Mr Muir should certainly have attempted, was in respect of Marie's letter to her mother, written after the interview with Higson and Wootten on 24 March in which she instructed her mother not to answer any of Wootten's questions. Such an instruction is all but impossible to understand if Marie's version of events is true. She claimed during cross-examination that

Wootten said to her during the interview 'say nothing, be quiet' (even though Higson who was present the entire time heard nothing of the sort) which should have led her to believe she had nothing to fear from him. Yet, immediately following the interview, she was evidently worried that Wootten would be making inquiries about her. If she was truly innocent of the murder of Annie Wootten such a fear is unfathomable. Why would she even begin to think that Wootten would ask her mother any questions? And why would she feel the need to tell her mother not to answer those questions?[172] It is true that we don't know what incriminating information, if any, her mother could have provided and Marie does not explicitly state that she anticipated Wootten asking questions *about the murder* but it was imperative that Marie was asked about this during cross-examination. As far as we know, no such effort was made by Mr Muir.

Perhaps one of the best points for the prosecution was in respect of Marie's claim to Mrs Alland that she needed a revolver for chicken farming. If her story about Wootten giving her the revolver was true then she only needed to tell Mrs Alland that she carried it for her own protection in case of a German invasion which, according to her account in the Old Bailey, was the reason Wootten repaired it on her behalf and provided her with bullets. The fear of invasion by German forces was admittedly a real one. Lord Crewe, the Lord Lieutenant of the County of London, for example, commented in March 1915 that: 'The possibility of an actual invasion of these shores has for long past been present in the minds of most thoughtful people'.[173] However, the fact that Marie resorted to such nonsense as chicken farming to justify carrying a weapon when she did not need to lie at all strongly suggests that her story about needing protection from

German soldiers was an invention dreamed up in Holloway prison for the purpose of her evidence in court. At the very least, she should have been asked by Mr Muir why she lied to Mrs Alland but there is no indication that the point was raised.

So much for the case against Marie. What can be said about Wootten? If we can eliminate him from having any involvement in the crime then it is almost certain that Marie was the killer. But can we? A close examination of Wootten and his life throws up a few unexpected surprises.

CHAPTER 13

BERT

'His honour rooted in dishonour stood,
And faith unfaithful kept him falsely true.'

Idylls of the King 'Lancelot and Elaine' by Alfred Lord Tennyson, 1859

The life of Albert Wootten was shrouded in mystery and deceit from the very start. His birth certificate states that his father was a watch pallet maker called William Wootten but this was a lie. No such person existed. On the same certificate, his mother is stated to be 'Elizabeth Wootten, late Wootten, formerly Stacy'. Elizabeth Jane Stacy was a real person, born on 14 April 1843, the daughter of a tailor, Stephen Stacy, and his wife Mary Ann. On 11 May 1861, at the age of 18, Elizabeth married a 21-year-old French Polisher known as Charles Edward Wootten, although the only Christian name on his birth certificate was Edward.[174] The couple, who lived in Islington, had four sons and three daughters over the next 14 years until Charles Edward died at the age of 35 of a contracted kidney on 30 April 1875. Elizabeth was left with three children below the age of ten years old including a baby boy, Stephen, who had been born in October 1874. She was forced to take up dressmaking, presumably learnt from her father, to survive.

Five years after her husband's death, in November 1880, at the age of 37, Elizabeth surprisingly gave birth to a boy, William Browning, whose father according to his birth certificate was a 'Butcher's Salesman' called William Wootten. However, this birth was either out of wedlock or 'William Wootten' died almost immediately afterwards because, in the 1881 census, Elizabeth, then living at 47 Camden Passage, Islington, with her seven children, is described as a 'widow'. Two years later, in August 1883, with Elizabeth now aged 40, Albert was born and the father is again a 'William Wootten' but his occupation has changed quite dramatically to 'Watch Pallet Maker'. With Elizabeth describing herself on the birth certificate as 'Elizabeth Wootten, late Wootten' it might appear that she had married another man with the surname of Wootten, perhaps a relative of Edward's, but there is no record of any such marriage at the General Register Office. Credulity is stretched to breaking point by the knowledge that, in August 1888, at the age of 45, Elizabeth registered the birth of a girl, Maud Louise, whose father was another Wootten, this time: Charles Wootten a 'confectioner'. So Elizabeth would have us believe that William has presumably died and she has married a third (or perhaps fourth) man with the surname of Wootten. Yet, once again, there is no marriage certificate for such a wedding at the General Register Office. Maud died in 1894 when she was stated to be the daughter of 'Charles Wootten, Confectioner (journeyman) (deceased)' so Charles clearly did not live very long after supposedly marrying Elizabeth and, indeed, must have been dead by 1891 when that year's census again records Elizabeth, now living at 95 Liverpool Road in Islington, as a widow. On Maud's death certificate, the informant is said to be one 'E. Wootten' who is described as the dead child's grandmother. While it is not impossible that this was the mother of Charles Wootten, who just happened to have the same first initial as his new wife, the likelihood is that this was indeed Elizabeth who had magically changed her status from mother to grandmother over the course of six years.

Albert himself was evidently unimpressed by the information on his birth certificate, if he was even aware of it. When he married Annie Tilbury in 1901 he declared that his father was 'Charles Wootten (deceased)', a french polisher, which was the name and occupation of Elizabeth's husband who had died eight years before Albert was born. So what was going on here? How does a widow in her late thirties and early forties manage to give birth to three children?

There are two obvious possibilities. The first is that Elizabeth was in a relationship, or more than one relationship, with a man, or number of men, between 1880 and 1888 and that the three children born within those years were illegitimate. It was not a particularly difficult matter to provide false information to the registrar at a birth, although it was illegal. Marriage certificates were not required to be produced at the time of registration and the system relied on the honesty of the informant. A woman could register a birth on her own at the local registry office, without the father present, and could easily claim to be married in order to avoid the shame of recording illegitimate offspring. It might have been difficult for someone living in the same district all their life, who was thus known personally to the registrar, to make false registrations of this nature but Elizabeth frequently moved around the Islington area. William Browning's birth had been registered in the sub-district of St James, Clerkenwell, when Elizabeth was living at 34 Perceval Street, Albert's birth was registered in Old Street, St Luke, when she was living at 54 Rahere Street, and Maud's in Islington South West while residing at 16 Denmark Street, so the registrar was different each time.

The second obvious possibility is that Elizabeth had resorted to prostitution and the three children were conceived as a result. Yet, while by no means impossible, it seems a little unlikely that a woman in her late thirties, with her best years behind her, would suddenly turn to prostitution. Similarly, it is unlikely that, after a period of five years following the death of her husband, and having given birth to so many children previously, a woman of 37 years old would suddenly become not just promiscuous but careless in this way so that she now has three additional children to raise on her own.

We cannot say for certain what was happening here but another possibility which must be considered is that Elizabeth adopted children for money and registered them as her own. This might sound incredible today but, at a time when abortion was illegal and there was no legal way of adopting children, it was by no means unheard of for women to falsely register births in this way. In August 1884, for example, Ann Fisher from Hull adopted an illegitimate child born to Tryphena Ann Kendrick and registered it in her own name, receiving a money payment from Kendrick for doing so. After the child died, the false registration was discovered and both women were arrested and eventually fined forty shillings each in April 1885.[175]

It seems that Ann Fisher simply wanted a child of her own but sometimes there were other, baser, motives for registering another baby as one's own. In February 1900, Amelia and Walter Guilford, using the fake surname of Wallace, responded to an advertisement placed by a Miss Wyatt in a Tunbridge Wells newspaper asking for a kind couple to adopt her newly born but unwanted illegitimate daughter, Hazel. The Guilfords took the baby and Amelia registered it as hers and Walter's, under the name of Violet Alice Muriel Guilford. This would have ensured that a portion of an inheritance of annual interest on £30,000 from the estate of Walter's father, who had died in 1899, would not be lost because, on Walter's

death, under the terms of his father's will, his share
of the money would go to his brothers' children if
he died without issue. The truth of the matter was
discovered when some of Walter's relations became
suspicious and started to make enquiries. Amelia was
44 years old after all, having last given birth under
a former marriage some eighteen years earlier, so it
was inevitable that questions would be asked, and
she was convicted and sentenced to eight months
imprisonment at Kent Assizes in July 1900 for making
a false statement to the registrar.[176] Walter, who must
have known what was going on, appears to have got
away scot free.

Another example of a false registration occurred
a few years later, in July 1904, when Mrs Sarah
Sophia Russell of Lansdowne Road in East London
advertised in a newspaper that she and her husband
were prepared to adopt a child. Shortly afterwards, she
received a visit from Henry Thomas Meade and his
wife who brought their newly born baby girl, Clara,
with them, offering £15 if she would take her off their
hands. Mrs Russell agreed and registered the baby as
her own daughter named May Russell, slyly telling
her husband that she had only been given £8 so she
could keep the difference for herself. The baby died in
August of epidemic diarrhoea which is how the false
registration came to light. At the inquest held in East
Ham, Mr Meade explained that he had no option but
to give away his daughter because his salary was too
low and, perhaps more importantly, he wished to keep
his marriage secret. He claimed that, if he had kept the
child, his 'prospects' would have been injured.[177] The
coroner's jury, in reaching its verdict on the death,
expressed the hope 'that something would be done to
prevent false registrations'. This was, of course, eleven
years after Albert had been born and it took a long time
for any action to be taken.[178]

The sum of £15 to adopt a child was very much on the low side - Mrs Russell claimed to be adopting for love as much as money - and it was quite possible to be offered hundreds of pounds if the child was from a wealthy family. The reasons for this are not hard to discern. The scandal of giving birth to an illegitimate baby could ruin a young woman's entire life and, if there was a way for her parents to avoid this, they would be prepared to pay a high financial price. We do not need to look far for an example of the terrible consequences for a young, unmarried, mother in Victorian England. Seventeen-year-old Elizabeth Lydia Brown was living with her parents at 74 Rotherfield Street in March 1863 when she was seen by a young child depositing a small bundle wrapped up in a shawl in the girl's playground at the Wesleyan School in nearby Mintern Street.[179] The child told the police and, when the bundle was opened, the body of a dead baby boy was found with one corner of the shawl tied around its neck. After blood stained nightdresses were found in her room, Elizabeth was arrested and, when being searched, told her searcher that she had delivered the baby herself and 'put it down a closet'. Things looked bad for her at the coroner's inquiry at the Black Horse Tavern in Kingsland Road when the medical evidence revealed that there was a pressure mark of a ligature around the baby's neck which would have been sufficient to produce death by strangulation. A mark of a finger and thumb was also found around the throat. The press described Elizabeth as a 'respectable looking lady' who appeared 'overwhelmed with grief'. Her father was said to hold a respectable position in a City House while her mother said that she and her husband had had no knowledge of their daughter's condition until she was arrested by the police. The jury returned a verdict of

wilful murder against the teenager but things looked a
bit brighter for her a few days later at the magistrate's
court in Worship Street when the police surgeon
admitted that, while strangulation appeared to be the
cause of death, it might have happened before the
birth had been completed and bruises found on the
windpipe could have been caused by self-delivery.
However, despite this helpful evidence, the description
of Elizabeth in the *Standard* of 16 March 1863 shows
that she was close to a complete nervous breakdown.
The reporter stated that: 'the wretched girl sat during
the entire hearing with her face concealed by her
hands and rested on the dock rail. She was manifestly
in extreme protestation, mentally and bodily, and by
desire of the magistrate was remanded to the waiting
room of Bendall, the Gaoler, until a cab could be
procured in which he then conveyed her to Newgate'.

Not surprisingly, there was no desire by anyone to
send the young lady to prison, let alone the gallows,
and the grand jury at the Old Bailey ignored the bill
for murder although it allowed a charge of concealing
the birth. At her trial on 6 April 1863, Elizabeth's
Counsel stated that 'this was one of that unfortunate
class of cases in which young girls become victim of
seduction and, when delivered of a child, concealed
the birth with the view of avoiding shame and
degradation'. Counsel for the prosecution announced
that the Crown did not wish to proceed against the
prisoner with the probability being that the baby had
been born dead and that Elizabeth: 'deeply sensible
of her shame and disgrace, had sought to conceal the
birth'. Mr Justice Mellor respited the sentence and
Elizabeth was free to go without any punishment.
However, we can see from the language used by both
prosecuting and defending Counsel that the mere fact
of giving birth outside of marriage was believed to

cause shame, disgrace and degradation. The stigma of illegitimacy was why people were prepared to take extreme measures in paying for unwanted children to be taken away. Equally there were couples, unable to have children, who were prepared to pay for them. In short, there was a black market in babies who could be bought and sold.

Such a market inevitably attracted criminal elements. One scam was for unscrupulous individuals to take an advance fee, supposedly to cover expenses, for arranging the adoption of a child and then disappear with the money.[180] However, there were even more sinister elements at large. A huge scandal erupted in 1870 after the arrest, conviction and execution of 35-year-old Margaret Waters from Brixton who, with her sister Mary Ellis, had been taking payments to 'adopt' illegitimate and unwanted babies before killing them by starvation or drugging with laudanum.[181] This type of activity was known as 'baby farming' and often involved advertisements being placed in the newspapers by what appeared to be a respectable couple or a nursing institution offering to adopt a child (in return for money) but which, in reality, were criminal enterprises that took the money and then neglected or murdered the babies. Dead babies were frequently found in the streets, usually wrapped up in paper, but there were relatively few convictions.

In an attempt to regulate baby farming establishments, which were not in themselves illegal, the government introduced the Infant Life Protection Act of 1872 which required any person receiving 'for hire or reward' two or more infants under the age of one year to be officially registered with the authorities. This still allowed people to legally nurse one child without any kind of licensing and one

unfortunate example of such activity was revealed at
the Islington Coroner's Court in January 1884 when
Dr Danford Thomas held an inquest into the death
of William Goosey, a child aged four months, whose
16-year-old mother had given him to a widow and
unemployed charwoman called Mary Baker who
was paid seven shillings and sixpence weekly by the
child's grandmother. Nevertheless, a doctor found
the baby in an 'awful state of filth and emaciation'.
The Baker residence was 'in an abominable condition
of filth…a disgrace to humanity' and her house
needed to fumigated by the parochial sanitary
authority. Poor baby Goosey was found to have died
due to consumption of the bowels and brain disease
'accelerated by foul air and improper feeding'.[182]

While illegitimate babies might be unwanted,
most parents certainly did not want them dead.
Although the criminal courts regularly dealt with
women charged with murdering their children - who
were usually found guilty of the lesser charge of
concealment of birth - infanticide was an extreme
measure. If a reliable, discreet and trustworthy
woman could be found who would not only look
after an illegitimate baby for a fee but was also willing
to register the birth as her own, thus avoiding any
chance of a scandal, it is obvious that she would be in
great demand. However, for this to work, secrecy was
essential and in a secretive world of this nature nothing
can be proved; we can only draw inferences from the
facts available. We have seen that there were some
distinctly odd features regarding the births of William,
Albert and Maud Wootten and we can add the fact
that Maud was born on 22 August 1888 but her birth
was not registered until 8 October, some forty-eight
days later. The significance of this is that, under the
1836 Births, Deaths and Marriages Registration Act, a

birth needed to be registered within forty-two days of its occurrence otherwise the parents could be fined 40 shillings. There might be a number of genuine reasons why Maud's birth was registered late but Elizabeth would certainly not have wanted to pay a fine of such magnitude if she could have avoided it and, having registered many births before Maud's, she would have known the rules perfectly well. If the delay was caused by the time taken to arrange an adoption and the real parents (or parents of the parents) were willing to pay the fine on Elizabeth's behalf to ensure that the correct date of birth was recorded on the certificate, this would provide an explanation for the unlawful registration.

Interestingly, at some point after 1891, Elizabeth Wootten changed her occupation from dressmaker to monthly nurse. The latter is recorded as her occupation on the 1901 and 1911 censuses. A monthly nurse occupied a similar role at a birth as a midwife but, not being allowed to deliver births themselves and requiring a doctor present, monthly nurses would usually attend wealthier women (who could afford a doctor) than midwives. As a result, despite being less qualified, they would often command a higher fee. In addition to assisting at the delivery, a monthly nurse would also reside with the mother full time for a period of about a month after the birth, hence the name. Consequently, it was not a job for women with young children of their own to look after and Elizabeth would only have been able to do it after Maud died in 1894.

Having said this, it was not unknown for monthly nurses to earn extra money by adopting or caring for other people's children while continuing to work. In February 1905, for example, a monthly nurse called Elizabeth Latham of Camden Town was summoned at Clerkenwell for contravention of the Infant Life

Protection Act for having taken care of two children below the age of three years old.[183] She had been given them by their father, a postman and widower, in return for 10 shillings a week. Both children subsequently died from bronchitis and it was complained that, during the two months the children were under her care, Latham went out nursing, leaving them to be looked after by her husband, a labourer, possibly assisted by another woman who lived in their house, and she was fined 3 shillings with 7 shillings costs. In 1908 a Parliamentary Committee on infant life protection referred to 'a practice on the part of some unprincipled women, who had qualified for a certificate on midwifery, of taking premiums from mothers of illegitimate children for securing the adoption of the children and then handing the children over for a smaller sum, or for nothing, to foster parents'.[184] Whether there was any connection between Elizabeth Wootten's possible adoption of three children during the 1880s and her subsequently becoming a monthly nurse cannot be known but her profession would certainly have put her in a position to know when babies were being born and, while she did not register any further births herself, she might have arranged adoptions for others.

There is one final mystery surrounding the life of Elizabeth Wootten which arose at her death at the age of 83 – in St Pancras Hospital of a heart attack while suffering from chronic bronchitis - on 26 May 1926. The informant named on her death certificate is 'L. Scott' who is stated to have been her niece, living with her at 19 Liverpool Street before her admission to hospital on 15 May.[185] However, this can only have been Louisa Scott who was, in fact, Elizabeth's *daughter*. Louisa Wootten had been born to Elizabeth and Charles Edward on 21 March 1868 and married

James Robert Scott on Christmas Day in 1887. In 1900, they had a daughter, who they called Louisa, but she married Sydney Isaac in 1921 to become Louisa Isaac and could not, therefore, have been the 'L. Scott' on the death certificate. By May 1926, when Louisa Scott was 58, her husband had died and the two widows, Elizabeth and Louisa, mother and daughter, were obviously living together in the same house.[186] Why Louisa described herself as Elizabeth's niece rather than her daughter is unknown and it is hard to think of a good reason for it unless Elizabeth was in debt and Louisa wanted to distance herself from her mother for that reason.[187]

Given the uncertainty regarding the true identity of his parents, Albert can perhaps be forgiven for having declared that his father was Charles Wootten (deceased) on his marriage certificate. One would, however, expect him to know his correct age but his marriage certificate states that he was 21 at the time he married Annie Tilbury on 12 October 1903 when he was, in fact, just 20 years old. This lie suggests that he did not have a good relationship with his mother, or that his mother did not approve of his marriage to Annie, because a man under the age of 21 needed the permission of his parent or guardian before he could marry (the same applying to women). It would appear that such permission was not forthcoming, hence the need for an illegal false declaration of his age. Perhaps by November 1913 there had been a rapprochement because Albert's baby girl Doris was given the middle name 'Elizabeth', presumably in honour of his mother. We also know from evidence at the police court that Albert tracked down his mother on the day after Annie's murder when she was nursing so they were clearly on speaking terms.

For Albert, the issues relating to his parentage

were best left alone. When the *Islington Daily Gazette*
published the news of his promotion to Lieutenant on
4 January 1915, the following story appeared in the
paper:

> *Councillor P. Reed informs us that Mr A. Wooten
> (sic), an old resident of Rotherfield-street, Essex-road,
> a member of the National Reserve, left the 4th Fusiliers
> as a private, after completing nine years, some few
> years ago, re-engaged on the outbreak of war, and was
> promoted Sergeant on September 5th. On September
> 12th he was again promoted to Company Quartermaster-
> Sergeant. On December 17th he was gazetted Second-
> Lieutenant 10th Batt. Bedfordshire Regiment.*

> *He is 31 years of age; his parents still reside in
> Rotherfield-street.*

> *He worked for Hope Bros., in Essex-road for some
> years.*

> *Good luck to Lieutenant Wooten: may he rise still
> higher.*

It seems a harmless enough story but Wootten was
so annoyed by the mis-spelling of his name, the fact
that he was described as a second lieutenant and by the
mention of his humble work at Hope Brothers that he
contacted the newspaper to complain. Four days later
it published the following correction:

> *The other day we called attention to the rapid
> promotion of an Islingtonian. As our information was
> incorrect in some particulars, we now give the exact
> facts. Mr A. Wootten, an old resident of Rotherfield-
> street, Essex-road, a member of the National Reserve,
> left the 4th Fusiliers as a private, after completing nine
> years, some few years ago, re-engaged on the outbreak of
> the war as a private in the Middlesex regiment and was
> promoted to Sergeant on September 5th. On September
> 12th he was again promoted to Company Quartermaster*

Sergeant. On December 17th he was granted a commission as Lieutenant (not Second Lieutenant) 10th Battalion, Bedfordshire Regiment.

He is 31 years of age; his parents still reside in Rotherfield-street.

It is true that as a boy he worked at a shop in Essex-road, but since then he has been engaged in various capacities – at the time of his enlistment acting as District Correspondent for Central London, and Special Sick Visitor, for the National Union for Insurance, of Colebrooke-row.

So, despite correcting a number of errors and providing some detailed new information, including the name of his former regiment, Wootten evidently had nothing at all to say about the statement that his parents 'still reside in Rotherfield-street' which, considering that he had claimed his father was dead on his 1903 marriage certificate, must have been untrue. As for how the newspaper obtained such inaccurate information in the first place, perhaps Wootten had initially been confused with his brother-in-law, Fred Dixon, whose parents were indeed living in Rotherfield Street at the time.

That Albert Wootten did not have a terribly close relationship with the truth in respect of the details of his life hardly comes as a surprise considering what we know of his adulterous relationship with Marie and his provision of a false reference for her. But is there any reason to believe he murdered his wife? There are certainly some suspicious elements in the story he told the jury at Marie's trial, especially the claim that his relationship with Marie while she was staying in Richmond Road was platonic. It is hard to believe that his hour long visits to Marie were not for sex. His supposed trip to the barber's shop for a haircut, a shampoo and a shave, immediately before visiting Marie on the night of the murder, seems like the preparation of man getting spruced up to see his sweetheart. It is true that there is no evidence other than Marie's word that any sexual intercourse actually took place but the probability is that, on this occasion, she was telling the truth. The landlady's evidence that Wootten introduced Marie as his wife is also likely to be true, although on this issue there is the point that Mrs Connor felt it necessary to ask Marie her name when she should already have believed she was called Mrs Wootten. The chances are, however, that Wootten did introduce Marie as his wife but he had probably told that lie to so many people before that he may well have genuinely forgotten he had said it on this occasion.

If he lied to the jury about introducing Marie as his wife or about having sex with her, does it mean that he killed his wife? The answer has to be that such a conclusion does not follow. Wootten may well have wanted to protect what little there was left of his reputation by pretending not to have succumbed to temptation and he would certainly not have wished the world to know that he was having sex with his mistress at the same time as his wife was lying dead in his home.

Of more importance in considering the issue of Wootten's guilt or otherwise is the curious issue of Marie's attaché case. During the interview at Richmond Road on 24 March, Wootten accused Marie of having lied to him about not having her attaché case with her. This was on the basis of Higson having seen her with it on the Sunday. Yet Higson denied ever having expressly told Wootten that he had seen Marie with the attaché case. It will be recalled that when Mr Pratt asked him about the importance of the attaché case, Wootten replied: 'To anyone connected with the matter, the circumstances of the attaché case seemed important' which is a very odd answer on any view. It is a crucial point because Wootten's entire story at trial rested on his not knowing that Marie had reclaimed the attaché case (containing the revolver) from Mrs Alland on the Sunday.

Higson recalled that he had told Wootten on the Sunday evening that Marie was carrying 'the usual luggage' when he saw her (a rather strange comment in itself) and it is surprising that, on the basis of this comment, without any further clarification, Wootten felt able to accuse Marie of lying. Yet, Mr Pratt did not press the point with Wootten during cross-examination which suggests that he did not feel it would go anywhere. Moreover, if Marie's story was true, why did she not respond to Wootten's accusation on 24 March that she was lying by saying that he knew full well that she had collected the attaché case? The fact that she said no such thing seems to be wholly inconsistent with the story she told in the witness box about Wootten giving her the money to reclaim the case from Ecclesbourne Road.

Support for Wootten's version of events comes from the fact that Marie asked Higson not to tell Wootten that he had seen her in the Islington area on Sunday. Why would she have done that if Wootten already knew she was collecting the attaché case? As discussed earlier, there may be an answer if Marie had told Wootten she would not collect the attaché case until Monday but there does not appear to be any sensible reason for her to have done this. On balance, therefore, while undoubtedly confusing, the evidence relating to the attaché case supports Wootten's version of events.

It is, furthermore, difficult to construct a coherent narrative in which Wootten is involved in the murder of his wife. If Wootten did plan the murder, and Marie's account of events is broadly true, then everything would appear to hinge on the revolver. When Wootten instructed Marie to bring the revolver with her to London, he must have had in mind that he, or an accomplice of his, would use it to kill his wife because there does not appear to be any other conceivable reason for the instruction. We can allow that he got lucky when Marie told him that she wanted to kill herself because it gave him the perfect pretext to confiscate the weapon from her. Perhaps, if she had not said this, he would have come up with another reason to take it, although it does seem rather odd that Wootten needed to use a revolver belonging to a third party to murder his wife, thus opening himself to the risk of exposure - blackmail even - when there were plenty of other methods available to him or an accomplice to achieve the same end.

Wootten's behaviour after the murder in accusing Marie of being involved only makes any sense at all if his plan was to frame her and ensure that she was suspected of the crime. Yet, in accusing Marie, it would have been patently obvious to him that she would tell the police that she had given him the revolver as soon as she was arrested and informed that Annie had been shot. As Marie herself wrote in one of her newspaper articles: 'Had I known it when Lieut. Wootten told me she was dead, and had I had the slightest notion that I would be suspected, I should have said to him, 'How could I shoot her when I have already given you the revolver?'. That Marie was not told Mrs Wootten had been shot when she spoke to Wootten and Higson on the day after the murder was only due to the fact that the doctor who examined the dead body had missed the bullet wound, something which could never have been anticipated by the murderer. Wootten the killer, and framer of Marie, would have been baffled when he returned home to find that everyone believed his wife had fallen down the stairs. Considering that his entire cunning plan rested on Marie being connected with the crime because of her ownership of a revolver, it must have taken enormous restraint for him not to point out the bullet wound, which he must have known was there, when he looked at the body in the parlour. If he reckoned that his discovery of the wound would be suspicious and kept quiet for that reason, such sensible thinking is completely at odds with his foolish use of Marie's revolver to shoot his wife, followed by his accusation against Marie and subsequent denouncement of her to the police.

Furthermore, a plan to frame Marie makes no sense because, had it not been for the completely unpredictable discovery of the revolver by Mrs Alland when she opened Marie's locked case after confiscating it for the rent, no-one would ever have known that Marie had a revolver with her in London. It might be that the idea to frame Marie only occurred to Wootten after she told him that she had admitted to Mrs Alland that she was carrying a revolver and Wootten thought he could use this information to his advantage by shooting his wife (or recruiting a female accomplice to shoot his wife) and ensuring that the police discovered Marie was armed. The problem with this theory is that we then have to go back and ask why Wootten instructed Marie to bring the revolver with her to London in the first place if he wasn't already planning to implicate her in the murder of his wife. But, if he was already planning to implicate her, it was not a very good plan because taking the revolver from Marie and shooting Annie would not have implicated Marie at all, considering that no-one would have known that she had a revolver. It was essential that someone like Mrs Alland discovered it by chance but this could not possibly have been planned by Wootten.

If all this wasn't enough, the case against Wootten meets its nemesis in the remark made by Annie to her daughter that the woman she was speaking to in the moments before she was killed was 'Mrs Higson's friend'. The only person known as 'Mrs Higson's friend' was Marie. For that we have the evidence of Mrs Higson herself. It would not have made any sense for Annie to have used that phrase to describe any other person. The reason Marie was called 'Mrs Higson's friend' was because she had been living at the Higson household so that the name applied to her and to her only. Whichever way one looks at it, there is no convincing way to argue that Wootten could have somehow manipulated his wife to inform his daughters that her visitor was 'Mrs Higson's friend' when it was actually someone else. It might be slightly easier to argue that Wootten could have coached Lily and Ivy to invent this piece of evidence but, as has already been discussed, it is all but impossible for such a conspiracy to have been implemented and there is nothing about the girls' evidence, tested in cross-examination, to suggest it was anything other than genuine and honest.

The telegram addressed to 'Dickson' also counts in favour of Wootten. The only possible reason for sending that telegram could have been to lure Mrs Dixon out of the house on the day of the murder. Spelling the surname wrongly undermined the entire purpose of the telegram which was supposed to have come from Mrs Dixon's father. Wootten knew how to spell 'Dixon' so that in itself eliminates him, at least, from having had any involvement in sending the telegram. Similarly, he knew how to spell his own name and, while he might have deliberately misspelt his surname on the 'L. Davey' letter, his confusion on the issue during cross-examination by Mr Pratt seemed genuine and, if the point of sending the letter was somehow to implicate Marie, he would have spelt his surname correctly because Marie knew how to spell it.

A further objection to Wootten being the murderer, or having been involved with a third party in committing the murder, is the fact that the murder of his wife with Marie's revolver would inevitably have exposed his relationship with Marie to the public gaze. While Wootten could not necessarily be expected to have anticipated the hostility of the multiple cross-examinations he was to face from Mr Pratt, nor the criticism of the judge at Marie's trial, it would surely have been obvious to him that his relationship with Marie would be discussed in a public forum and that he could not possibly emerge from the situation with any honour. It was not as if there were no consequences to Wootten from the evidence which emerged during the legal proceedings because, as a direct result, he was stripped of his rank as lieutenant and kicked out of the army.

Questions started to be raised in the upper echelons of the army about Wootten's future just over a month after the murder of his wife.[188] On 26 April 1915, Lieutenant-Colonel William Piers, the commanding officer of the 10th Bedfordshire Battalion, wrote to headquarters at the White City to ask whether 'any steps are to be taken in this case'. The reply from the brigade commander, Brigadier-General Ernest Rodwell, was that: 'I am of the opinion that Lieutenant Wootten's conduct and its indirect result are of a nature that affects unfavourably the reputation of the Battalion. I recommend that he be called upon to resign his commission'.[189] He was overruled for the moment by Major-General Sir Francis Lloyd, the commanding officer of the London District, who considered that the case, being before the courts, was *sub judice* and that no action need be taken at that stage. However, the evidence which emerged from the hearing at the North London Police Court brought about a change of mind within the military. Following Marie's committal to trial on 19 May 1915, events moved swiftly. On 25 May 1915, Brigadier-General James Dalrymple-Hay, commanding the 6th Reserve Infantry Brigade, which, following an army reorganization and a move of the battalion to Colchester, the 10th Bedfordshire now formed part of, recommended that Wootten be called upon to resign his commission. Three days later, a memo from Major-General Henry Jeffreys, the commanding officer of the Colchester Training Centre, where the 10th Bedfordshire battalion was now based, recorded that the case was no longer *sub judice* as far as Wootten was concerned and continued:

> *The facts of this officer's double life have come out and whether the barmaid murdered his wife or not makes no difference. I recommend the application [for Wootten to be called upon to resign] on the ground that Lieutenant Wootten cannot now have the position among his fellows and command the respect of his inferiors as he should if he is to be of any value to the Battalion. Moreover, apart from the unsavoury case in which he is concerned he is not, in the opinion of his commanding officer as proficient in his duties as he should be.*

Having transferred from London to Colchester, the 10th Bedfordshire came back under the jurisdiction of Eastern Command and Major-General Jeffrey's viewpoint was approved on 31 May by the commander-in-chief of Eastern Command, Lieutenant-General Sir Charles Woollcombe, who wrote: 'I recommend that the officer be called upon to resign his commission.' Brigadier Dalrymple-Hay offered his opinion on 7 June that: 'It will be to the benefit of the service to get this officer's resignation.' The matter was referred up to the Army Council in Whitehall whose decision, inevitably, was that Wootten should be called on to resign. This was confirmed by the Assistant Secretary at the War Office, Bertram Cubitt, in a memo dated 16 June 1915 and, when nothing happened, questions were asked by Eastern Command as to what was going on. Major-General Jeffreys in Colchester recorded on 26 June that the delay was caused by the fact that 'Lieutenant Wootten is absent from his unit being summoned to give evidence at a murder trial now taking place'. He stated that the officer commanding the 10th Bedfordshire Regiment had been requested to wire him to expedite the sending of his resignation. A formal instruction for Wootten to resign his commission had, in fact, been issued to him on 25 June, the very day Marie was giving her evidence in the witness box of the Old Bailey. Wootten prevaricated, replying from Colchester on 28 June (presumably in the evening because he was in court in London during the day to hear Mr Justice Lush's summing up, with its heavy criticism of him). He wrote:

> I have the honour to make an appeal against the request to me in a letter, dated 25th June 1915, on the following grounds; that I have been the victim of severe criticism '<u>unjustly</u>' and apart from the fact that misconduct took place, I have always acted as a gentleman...I claim I am proficient and under these circumstances respectfully beg to be allowed further consideration: thus being allowed to proceed overseas or to take up duty in East, or West office, as per Eastern Command Orders.

The decision having been made at high levels of the military, and confirmed by the Army Council, Wootten had no chance with his unconvincing appeal.[190] The fact that 'misconduct' had taken place was, of course, the problem - despite Wootten's attempt to brazen it out. Finally seeing that there was no escape, he wrote on 30 June, again from Colchester, to his commanding officer:

Acting on instructions I respectfully tender my resignation, regretting having been called on to do this.

However, Wootten persisted with his fruitless attempt to overturn the decision adding:

I have the honour to request that my appeal dated 28th June 1915 be forward to The Military Secretary and beg most respectfully to call for further consideration.

His call was declined. Major-General Jeffreys, in recommending his resignation be accepted, noted that:

'...at the trial the judge made some scathing remarks re. Lt Wootten & his conduct. He should not I suggest be allowed to remain an officer after these remarks & the notoriety the case has brought him into.'

Wootten's resignation was published in the *London Gazette* on 14 July 1915 although no reason was given and there was no indication that he had been forced to resign. Three days later, Wootten applied for a new commission, writing to the War Office:

I beg most respectfully to offer myself for a temporary commission in His Majesty's Army, for the duration of the war. I have relinquished a commission as Lieutenant but I feel I ought to offer myself again at this time of trouble when every man is so wanted.

His offer was dismissed in a one sentence letter from Bertram Cubitt on 22 July telling him: 'your application to be appointed to a temporary commission in the army cannot be granted'. Not to be deterred, a few months later Wootten made a written application for another temporary commission, dated 29 October 1915, suggesting that he be allowed to serve as an officer in the Service Corps, the Engineers or the Royal Flying Corps. It was turned down.

So Wootten was back to being a civilian and, although he could not have forseen the single mindedness with which the army would pursue his removal, he would have had to have been a supreme optimist to have assumed that the publication of his affair with Marie in every single newspaper of the day would not have any consequences for his army career. This strongly supports Wootten's innocence and, in addition, murdering his wife while he was in the army would have made no sense. Annie was performing a vital role in looking after his four children, something which he could not do while being in the army. Her death created the obvious problem of what to do with them and, as we have seen, Higson mentioned the fact that enquiries were made at an orphanage with a view to removing them there. (As it happens, in the short term, they were looked after by Annie's parents in Exmouth Street). While he was serving in the forces, Wootten could obviously not live with another woman and, if he wanted to pursue an affair, he was free to do so within the constraints of being in the army. So there was no obvious motive for Wootten in getting Annie out of the way.

This is not to say that there was no conceivable motive at all. If Wootten was having an affair with another woman, in addition to Marie, he could have been under pressure to take care of her. In this respect, his wife might have been proving a financial burden upon him which he wanted to remove. We have seen that Mrs Rufus, with her illegitimate daughter, was mentioned as someone who might have been in a position to apply pressure on Wootten to look after her but there was certainly another woman in Wootten's life in 1915. In a sensational development, Lieutenant Wootten married a 21-year-old woman on 9 July 1915, only ten days following the conclusion of Marie's trial and less than four months after the death of his wife. As his resignation from the army was not yet official, he could describe himself as an 'army officer' on the marriage certificate (and his father was again said to be 'Charles Wootten (deceased)' a french polisher). No newspaper of the day was aware of the marriage so it was not reported anywhere.

The woman he married was Leah Cable, another barmaid who by an incredible coincidence was, like Marie, also the daughter of a retired police officer from a seaside coastal resort. Charles Cable had been a constable with the Yarmouth Borough Police and, by further coincidence, joined the force in 1878, the same year Harry Wheatley joined the Brighton Police.[191] Charles, who resigned from the police in 1901 (having become too ill to continue), never rose above the rank of constable but was one of a small group of officers in the force who doubled as detective and carried out undercover plain clothes work. Some local newspapers referred to him as 'Detective Cable'.[192] In 1890, while continuing as a police constable and detective, he was appointed Inspector of Hackney Carriages, an important position because the state and proper regulation of the borough's taxi cabs was an issue of great concern to the Town Council, there having been many complaints about the behaviour of the operators.[193]

The appointment was a controversial one because Constable Cable replaced a more senior police officer, Sergeant William Drake, who, it was felt by the Town Council, was 'not quite competent' to fulfil the demanding task and was given a clerical job at the police station instead.[194] In addition to being called 'Detective Cable', Charles was now also referred to as 'Inspector Cable' due his new role.[195] It will be recalled that Harry Wheatley took a second role, as Chief Engineer in the Fire Brigade, while also a detective and, in another strange coincidence, he had initially been appointed as engineer in 1890, the same year Charles became the hackney carriage inspector. Unlike Harry, Charles Cable was never demoted but in 1895 he was reduced to Assistant Inspector of Hackney Carriages when a new Chief Constable of the Yarmouth Police Force, William Parker, took on the role of Inspector for himself.[196]

Charles' only daughter, Leah, was born in Gorleston, Great Yarmouth, in April 1894 at which time she had two brothers, Arthur and Claud, aged 10 and 8 years respectively but, in January 1895, Claud was tragically killed when he slipped from a shed roof covered in snow and fell into a greenhouse while attempting to watch his brother catch sparrows in the garden of a hotel next to the Cable residence. A shard of glass punctured the main artery of his right leg and tore through the main vein, causing death through loss of blood. It was probably of little consolation to Charles that, a few days later, he was praised by a jury at the Yarmouth Quarter Sessions, and highly commended by the Watch Committee, for his detective work, alongside a Detective Sergeant Lingwood, in apprehending three men involved in the 'Middlegate Jewel Robbery', as it was known, in December 1894.[197]

During his retirement, Charles remained in Great Yarmouth and Leah is recorded in the 1911 census as still living with her parents (her mother being Margaret Cable) at number 19, Row 45, Great Yarmouth, while she was working as an outfitter's assistant. By this time, her brother, Arthur, had moved to London -

living in Islington - and it was presumably through him, or while visiting him, that she became acquainted with Albert Wootten.[198] The most astonishing fact about Wootten's marriage to Leah in 1915 is that, two years earlier, on 16 August 1913 - while working as a barmaid - she had given birth to a boy called George in Clacton.[199] The spaces for the father's name and occupation on George's birth certificate are blank.

Wootten attempted (successfully) to join the army again in May 1916, this time as a private, and when he listed his offspring, as he was required to do on the enlistment report, he included 'George (Cable)' as one of his children, stated to be born before his second marriage. This is not conclusive evidence of Wootten's parentage; he might have regarded George as an adopted son and, in any case, he probably needed to include him in the list for financial reasons because the government paid an allowance for each child of any serving soldier.[200] Nevertheless, it does raise the possibility that Wootten was George's father and, if so, it would obviously mean that Wootten was conducting an adulterous relationship with Leah in late 1912 or early 1913. It is just about possible that Wootten only met Leah after his wife's murder and that, as she had an illegitimate son to look after, she was the perfect person to look after Wootten's children too, but it is difficult to see how he could have formed any kind of relationship with another woman between 23 March and 9 July, considering that for most of that time he was involved in the various court proceedings and was still in the army.

The consequence of Wootten being the father of Leah's son is that he might have been under severe pressure from Leah (and her parents) to look after her, and her child. Perhaps Leah, like Marie, was deeply in love with Wootten and also desperately wanted to take care of his children as well as her own son. Perhaps Wootten gave her the revolver and she killed Annie, causing all her dreams to come true as Wootten married her soon after.

The revelation of Wootten's marriage and the possibility that he might have been the father of Leah's illegitimate son, which would mean that he had been having an affair with Leah long before his wife's death, certainly provides food for thought when considering whether Wootten murdered his wife. Yet we come back to the simple fact that it was 'Mrs Higson's friend', i.e. Marie, not Leah, who visited Annie on the night of the murder and that alone tends to rule out Leah as being the murderer.

True, it is only an assumption that the woman who was heard speaking to Annie by her children on the night of the murder was the person who fired the revolver. Perhaps the woman who visited Annie had a male accomplice who entered the house and pulled the trigger. However, we know that it could not have been Wootten himself because he had a (reasonably) solid alibi, as discussed below.

At some point in July 1915, probably on their honeymoon, the newly married Leah Wootten became pregnant with Albert's baby and she gave birth to Leonard Wootten in April 1916. The Woottens were now living at 4 Florence Street in Islington, the same run down street in which Daisy Williams had killed Dolly Steer a few years earlier. At the time of the birth, Albert was working as a clothing manager but, on 31 May 1916, he rejoined the army with the 2nd Battalion, Royal West Kent Regiment, being promoted immediately to sergeant.[201] In September 1916, he was sent with a draft of men to Iraq (then known as Mesopotamia) where he had a fainting fit on arrival at Basra. He soon recovered and, in

November, joined up with his battalion which was then camped at Khamisayah in Southern Iraq about 215 miles to the South-East of Baghdad in readiness for battle against the Turkish Army.[202] However, it did not see any action but marched instead to Nasiriyah where Wootten again became sick, being admitted to hospital in June 1917 with sandfly fever, a very nasty virus common to the region, although a later diagnosis appears to record the illness as a recurrence of rheumatic fever.[203] No sooner had he recovered from that than he was back in hospital with malaria. Then, in August 1917, after his battalion had reached Karradah, a suburb of Baghdad, he suffered from palpitations, shortness of breath and debility. He was invalided to India and admitted into the Victoria War Hospital, Bombay, in September 1917, where he was diagnosed with valvular disease of the heart, before returning to England and being discharged from the army in December on the basis that he was 'no longer physically fit for war service'.

Consequently, Wootten never engaged with the enemy at any time during his military career. Had he remained fit with the Royal West Kents he would no doubt have been involved in the final battle of the war with the Turks, at Sharqat in October 1918, when 430 soldiers from 2 Battalion distinguished themselves under heavy fire, capturing over 160 prisoners, while taking heavy casualties. The Turkish Army subsequently surrendered and sixteen members of the battalion were awarded medals for their part in the engagement. Wootten would simply have read about it all in the newspapers.

Wootten's medical report from the Victoria War Hospital in Bombay contains one astonishing claim. It states:

> *In March or April 1915 Patient went to France where*

he was only for three weeks when he was invalided to England with Rheumatism…

This statement is clearly and blatantly untrue. In the weeks after his wife was murdered on 23 March, Wootten spent most of his time in and out of both the Islington Coroner's Court and the North London Police Court and he most certainly wasn't slipping across the Channel to fight the Germans in France for a few short weeks. In respect of the period before the murder, it is true that, when Ivy was asked what her father did for a living at the coroner's court, she said: 'He now sees men dig the trenches', which might in theory support the notion that he had been to the front line in France, but there were plenty of practice trenches in England – many parks in London had them - so there is no need for him to have left the country for Ivy's answer to have been correct. In any event, we know that the 10th Bedfordshire was training in the White City during March 1915 following which, on 10 April, it was constituted as a reserve battalion to be utilized only for training and providing reinforcements. It was not a fighting force and soldiers from that battalion were attached to other regiments (or other battalions within the Bedfordshire regiment) before being sent abroad.[204] The battalion never left the country and it is certain that the then Lieutenant Wootten never did either.

We don't have any record of Wootten's movements in the period between 22 February 1915 (when we know he was in London ensuring that Marie left Higson's house to return to Horsted Keynes) and 19 March (when he said he met Marie at the White City) but we can say with confidence that he could not have gone to France during this time. The reason is that, after being given sick leave on 4 February, he should have been re-examined by a Medical Board on 11 February but there was an extraordinary oversight and he remained off sick for longer than the week's leave he was allowed. As a result, on 27 February 1915, Staff Captain H. Lloyd wrote on behalf the War Office to the General Officer Commanding, Eastern Command, as follows:

> *I am directed to transmit to you the annexed medical document relating to Lieutenant A. Wootten 10th Service Battalion, Bedfordshire Regiment, and to enquire how this officer is now situated, having in view the fact that he should have been re-examined by a Medical Board on the expiration of his sick leave on the 11th February 1915.*
>
> *There is no trace of the receipt in the war office of the proceedings of a Medical Board reporting this officer fit for general service.*

However, this letter was forwarded by the General Officer Commanding of the Eastern Command to the General Officer Commanding of the London District on the basis that the 10th Bedfordshire Battalion (which normally fell under the jurisdiction of Eastern Command) was now based in the White City, thus coming under the jurisdiction of the London District. As a consequence, the issue of Wootten's sickness fell between two stools and nothing was done until a chaser from the War Office on 25 March.

In the event, Wootten was not examined by a Medical Board, and certified as fit for duty, until 31 March 1915, a week after his wife had been murdered. This brings into focus the realisation that we do not have independent confirmation that Wootten even rejoined his regiment at any time after 23 February and before 23 March. We only have his word that he was on duty at the White City on 19 March when Marie visited him there and that, on 23 March, he was carrying out exercises with his regiment at Richmond Park all day.

If he was not certified as fit for duty until the end of March, what was he doing back with his unit in the period 19 to 23 March?

It will be recalled that no identified person actually spoke to Wootten at the White City on 23 March. He claimed that he returned to White City that night, having visited Marie at Richmond Road, and was told that there was a message for him about his wife. He supposedly obtained permission from a superior officer to go home but the name of the officer who gave this permission was not stated although, as his rank was said to be a major, this can only have been Major William Coote-Brown, the sole officer with that rank in the 10th Bedfordshire Battalion at the time. The only person who gave evidence that he actually saw Wootten at the White City on 23 March was Second Lieutenant Caldwell-Cook and this was never tested under cross-examination to ensure that he had not mistaken the date. Furthermore, there was never any evidence presented in court to corroborate Wootten's account that, on the night of the murder, he went to the hairdresser's, the name of which, incidentally, he corrected during re-examination at the police court from 'Everett' (which is what he said in the coroner's court) to 'Everest'. A hairdresser called Herbert Everest features in the Post Office London Directory for 1915 and ran his barber's shop at 136 Uxbridge Road, near Shepherd's Bush, so it certainly did exist. Wootten said that he pointed it out to Detective Inspector Davis but there is no record that Davis checked out the story, let alone that the hairdresser remembered him.

On the other hand, there was no dispute that Marie met Wootten at the White City on 19 March. She agreed in the witness box that she did turn up there on the Friday albeit that she claimed he told her that he had expected her the previous day. Had there been any doubt about Wootten's alibi on 23 March, one would certainly have expected it to have been challenged by the defence, even if the police might have failed to corroborate it. The assumption must be that Wootten reported back for duty at the White City at some point between 23 February and 19 March despite not having been properly certified as fit.

Perhaps the most extraordinary aspect of Wootten's claim to have been in France in 1915 is that he affected an inability to recall whether it was before or after the murder of his wife, which one would have expected to have been a definite reference point. For him to have said that he was uncertain if he had gone to France in March 1915 or April 1915, surely the most memorable period in his entire life, is bizarre and demonstrates that he was capable of telling the most brazen of lies. He appears to have been banking on the fact that no-one at the military hospital would remember the murder and that the army did not have, or would not consult, any record of his military history showing that he never left England in 1915. The lie, which may well have been recorded on his report with the connivance of the medical officer, was almost certainly concocted to ensure that Wootten would receive a disability pension after the war. For this purpose, he needed to show that he became sick during the course of overseas service, ideally in France. Thus, his medical report stated: 'His condition is not caused, but aggravated by Active Service conditions in France and Mesopotamia in my opinion' while the medical officer in charge at the Victoria War Hospital went even further, declaring : 'I consider there is a presumption that disability is due to service in France'. It seems that this did the trick and Wootten was awarded a pension; he would describe himself after the war as an 'army pensioner'. Ironically, considering the blatant untruth in his medical report, his army discharge form dated 22 December 1917 described him as 'honest and intelligent.'

When Wootten was before the Medical Board in September 1917 he claimed to have been a dentist prior to joining the army. At the time, one did not need any qualifications to become a dentist and it is just about possible that Wootten had attempted to join this profession after resigning from the 10th Bedfordshire in July 1915 although, when his son Leonard was born in April 1916, he described himself as a 'clothing manager' on the birth certificate. As he rejoined the army in May 1916, it is difficult to see how he could have done much dentistry work. Yet, when he left the army in December 1917 and was asked to: 'State what qualifications you have for employment in civil life', Wootten said that he had been: 'In business as a Dentist on my own accord' and was also a 'clothing manager'. In fact, when he left the army, he became a clerk with the Holloway Medical Board. It was in this role that Wootten found himself in trouble again. Incredibly, in October 1918, he was back at the Old Bailey. This time in the dock!

In a prosecution initiated by the War Office, Wootten was charged before a magistrate at Brentford Petty Sessions on 7 October 1918 with forging a security for payment of money in June of that year.[205] He was sent for trial at the Central Criminal Court with bail set at £50 and appeared as a defendant at the Old Bailey on 25 October 1918 with the full charge on one count being that, contrary to Section 4(1) of the Forgery Act of 1913, 'Albert Wootten on the 21st day of June 1918 in the County of Middlesex with intent to defraud forged a certain document purporting to be a request for the Secretary of Sec R of the War Office National Reserve for the payment of £10'.[206] The document he was accused of forging was an army form to which he had access in connection with his employment at the Holloway Medical Board. Apparently, he filled out the form and initialled it on behalf of the Secretary of State for War, directing the Hounslow Paymaster's Department to pay him a bounty of £10 for his service in the Royal West Kent Regiment. He had already been paid a bounty of the same amount for his brief service in the Middlesex Regiment and a representative from the Paymaster's Department at Hounslow gave evidence that no soldier was entitled to more than one bounty. The form was, nevertheless, presented for payment at Hounslow but it was quickly discovered that it was a forgery. Wootten admitted filling in the form but denied any intent to commit a fraud, believing (wrongly), he claimed, that he was entitled to a £10 bounty for rejoining the army. He said that he only used the form to expedite its payment.[207] Despite this terribly weak defence, he was found not guilty of the charge before the Common Sergeant at the Central Criminal Court.

Following his acquittal, Wootten continued to try and extract money from the War Office. Shortly after the armistice was signed on 11 November 1918, the government announced that soldiers who served during the war would be paid a gratuity.[208] In February 1919, it was further announced that the minimum payment for a lieutenant would be £40.[209] The War Office stated that soldiers and officers should not contact them but that they would communicate with everyone who qualified for such an award in due course. There were some exceptions in the small print which stated that the gratuity would not be issued to any officer: 'Whose services are dispensed with or who resigns his commission for misconduct or other causes which, in the opinion of the Army

Council, disqualify him from the grant of the gratuity'
or to any officer who 'prior to November 11 1918,
voluntarily resigned his commission after less than two
years' commissioned service'. Unless one quibbled
over the word 'voluntarily' in respect of the second
clause, this clearly excluded Wootten from the gratuity
for his period of service as a lieutenant in the 10th
Bedfordshire Battalion (he received one for his period
of service as a sergeant in the Royal West Kents) but he
either did not read this or ignored it because he wrote
to the Military Secretary of the War Office on 7 April
1921 from his then home at 26 St John's Villas in Upper
Holloway saying:

> *Sir,*
>
> *Kindly note I have not yet received my War Gratuity
> as a commissioned officer from 22.12.14 to 14.7.15
> inclusive.*
>
> *Gratuity for non commissioned service received.*[210]

The request caused a certain amount of confusion
in Whitehall because the War Office had initially lost
Wootten's file relating to his time in the Bedfordshire
Regiment. However, they found a note in one of
their records stating that he had relinquished his
commission through 'inefficiency'. While his army
file was being searched for, Wootten was becoming
impatient, sending a chasing letter to the War Office
from 106 Essex Road, where he was now living, on 8
November 1921 which stated:

> *Dear Sir,*
>
> *Kindly note I have not yet received my war gratuity
> as an officer period 30/12/14 to 14/7/15 inclusive.*

A memo in the War Office's file dated 21 November
1921 notes:

> *This officer was reported as not being as proficient*

as he should be and was called upon to resign his commission.

It was also noted that Wootten had actually been told in May 1919, and again in July, that he was not eligible for a gratuity in respect of his period of service in the Bedfordshire Regiment. It was concluded that 'any further communication need not be sent to Mr Wootten'.

Before he received any reply, Wootten chased again on 28 November, informing the War Office: 'I have not had a settlement yet...'. A note on the War Office file states: 'I think we will reply to keep him quite (sic)' and, on 9 December 1921, a letter from the War Office to Wootten stated:

you are ineligible for a gratuity in respect of your commissioned service. This must be considered as final and no further communications of the subject can be answered.

That was the end of that.

Wootten's brush with the law in 1918 did not prevent him joining the civil service because the 1920 birth certificate of his daughter, Margaret, records that he was then a clerk at the Office of the Ministry of Munitions. By 1923, when another daughter, Eileen, was born, he was stated to be an Admiralty Clerk in the Accountant General's Department. Wootten continued to work as an Admiralty Clerk up to at least 1925 when he and Leah gave birth to their third daughter, Gladys, and when Ivy married railway carriage cleaner, Ernest Lines, in 1927 she gave her father's occupation as 'Clerk (Admiralty)'. However, Wootten described himself as a 'Commercial Clerk' when their fourth daughter, Kathleen, was born in 1928.[211] He certainly changed career in the 1930s when he returned to the clothing industry and made his living as a drapery salesman.[212] When his daughter, Margaret, married a steel worker, Thomas Tyler, in 1938, he was described as a retired Major of the Royal West Kent Regiment on the marriage certificate, which he signed as a witness, so perhaps he had (falsely) taken to calling himself 'Major Wootten' at this stage. He remained married to Leah, who died in May 1939 at the age of 45, and he died of pancreatic cancer aged 58, in September 1941, having become an auxiliary fireman who no doubt assisted in putting out fires in London during the Blitz. It turned out that his unlucky number was really the rather more traditional 13 because he died on the thirteenth day of September in 1941.

CHAPTER 14

GETTING AWAY WITH MURDER

'Truth will come to light; murder cannot be hid long.'

The Merchant of Venice by William Shakespeare, 1596-8

Evil, like danger, can take many shapes and forms. A man in a mask and cape holding a long knife or axe might be the ultimate nightmare for many but the exact same amount of danger and threat to life can come from an attractive young woman, perhaps wearing a veil, with a hidden revolver. Is that what Annie Wootten saw when she looked out of the window of her children's bedroom on the night of her murder? We will never know for certain but the most likely answer is that it was Marie Wheatley standing outside her house.

Marie's father revealed in evidence that his daughter was out of action for a couple of weeks with a bout of measles shortly after she returned home from London at the end of February. During that period of solitary illness she must have brooded over her defeat by Mrs Wootten for the love and possession of her husband. If only Annie were not in the way, all her dreams could come true. Bert and the children would be hers. According to Marie, in one of her newspaper articles, Annie's killer was 'a woman who had nourished a deadly hatred against her'. The likelihood is that this woman was none other than Marie herself. Almost teasing her reader, Marie had said that she knew 'that no enmity can be more deadly than that of a woman who is torn with jealousy'. Marie certainly knew all about jealousy because she was consumed by it. She most likely did not see Annie as a woman with her own rights and feelings but as a rival for the affections of the man she loved: someone who was blocking her path to happiness, someone who did not deserve Bert, someone who did not deserve four lovely children. In her mind, despite anything he said to the contrary, Bert loved her, not Annie. If he did not, he would not have cheated on Annie and he would not have spent those wonderful days with her at the end of 1914 and beginning of 1915. What follows is a possible reconstruction of events in 1915 although, it hardly needs saying, after all these years the truth can never be known for certain.

Once she had recovered from the measles, and having pawned all but one of her rings, Marie pretended for the benefit of her parents that she had received a letter from Bert summoning her to London. She took her father's rusty pinfire revolver, which she locked safely inside her attaché case, and caught the train to London. There were plenty of trains running to London from Horsted Keynes during the morning. She might have caught the 9:58 arriving at Victoria at 11:31 or, perhaps, the 11:37 arriving at 13:22. Once in London, she needed to purchase some ammunition but had some difficulty in finding the correct size pinfire cartridges. After visiting a number of specialist shops she finally managed to obtain a box of fifty Eley 7mm pinfire cartridges and celebrated her achievement by a sensible test firing of the rusty old revolver, probably in an isolated London park, after which she made her way to Ecclesbourne Road in Islington where she arrived at around 6:45pm. Her subsequent appearance outside 114 Rotherfield Street might have had a practical purpose in establishing what time Fred Dixon came home from work but her knocking at the door to complain about the children, or rather 'Mrs Wilson's' children, was probably just a simple stalking of Annie Wootten with no other reason than a perverse pleasure in the confrontation.

Any precise plans Marie had formed in her mind to eliminate her love rival must have been disrupted by Mrs Alland's demand for her rent in advance and the subsequent confiscation of her attaché case, revolver and cartridges. The murder would have to wait until she could reclaim her weapon which, with Bert's unknowing (financial) assistance, she did on Sunday, 21 March. Knowing that Bert usually visited her at about 8:30pm, Marie calculated that, if she could carry out her diabolical plan in Islington at, or shortly after, 7:30pm, there was a reasonable chance she could get back to Richmond Road before his arrival, thus diverting suspicion from herself. During the afternoon of Tuesday 23 March, Mrs Connor saw Marie writing some letters in the kitchen of 12 Richmond Road. One of these would have been a letter requesting employment at a public house in the Old Kent road. Regarding the others, we can only speculate that Marie was writing out the 'Come at once' telegram to Mrs Dixon and the 'L. Davey' lettercard to Wootten, both in a disguised childlike handwriting, perhaps with her weaker hand. Certainly no other signed letters written by Marie at this time of the day are known to exist.

Shortly after 6pm, Marie walked into the post office at 309 St John Street and handed in the telegram. It's possible she gave it to a child to hand it in for her but, as no child ever came forward to say a woman asked him (or her) to do this, it is more likely she handed it in herself. There was little chance that the postal clerk would remember everyone who handed in telegrams that day. She would then have walked directly to Rotherfield Street, arriving about twenty minutes later. If the 'Come at once' telegram was to have any purpose at all, it required the sender to wait outside 114 Rotherfield Street for the arrival of the boy messenger who would have brought the telegram to the house and then to watch as Mrs Dixon rushed out of the house to visit her father as soon as she received it. Once Marie knew Annie and the children were alone in the house she could then knock at the front door to commence her murderous plot. But Mrs Dixon never left the house. Unknown to Marie, she was not there, having gone to visit her parents much earlier in the day. Mr Dixon was, of course, at work.

During Marie's trial, Mr Pratt speculated that Annie was expecting a visitor, thus explaining her strange behaviour of entering the children's bedroom and looking out of the window. That does not seem likely. Although not expressly stated in the evidence, the impression the children gave was that their mother returning to their room so quickly after putting them to bed, while they were supposed to be asleep, was highly unusual. If Annie really had been expecting a visitor, she would have been waiting for a knock at the door and there was nothing to be gained by looking out of the window of the children's bedroom in the basement which had a very restricted view, being below street level. Although she would have been able to see the path leading to the front door she would not have been able to see the front door itself nor would she have been able to see up or down Rotherfield Street. Moreover, Lily's evidence was that her mother looked out of the window furthest from the path leading to the front door which does not seem to be consistent with someone waiting for a visitor.

Instead, the most likely explanation starts with the fact that the boy messenger must have knocked at the front door to deliver the telegram. The usual practice of messenger boys was to hand over their telegrams and ask if there was to be a reply, rather than simply posting them through the letterbox. It is true that the children never heard any knock at the door but the telegram might have arrived while they were bathing or the knock was not loud enough to catch their attention. The point is that Annie must have opened the door to receive the telegram and, in doing so, she might well have seen the shadowy figure of a woman standing opposite her house. If the telegram arrived before, or around, six-thirty in the evening it would not yet have been fully dark so there should have been sufficient light available for her to see the figure of someone across the street.

As the telegram was found open on the mantelpiece after her death, we know that Annie definitely received and read it. With both Dixons out of the house there was nothing she could do, and no-one to discuss it with, but she must have pondered over its puzzling message of 'Come at once' from 'Father'. The more she thought about the fact that the telegram was addressed to 'Dickson', and was from an unknown 'Popham' of Laker Street, the more suspicious it would have seemed. Perhaps she wondered if the mysterious woman she had seen standing outside her house had anything to do with the telegram. Perhaps she connected the woman in the street with the woman who had knocked at her door on the previous Thursday evening who she believed to be Marie. This might well explain her unexpected entry into the children's bedroom. The bedroom window was the only location available to her in the house from which she could view the street in the front of the building. She would have needed to get a better look to confirm her suspicions that it was Marie. If she concluded that it was indeed Marie standing in the street she would probably have believed there was no threat. After all, she knew Marie and what possible harm could she do to her?

The chances are that Annie went up the stairs

and opened the front door, inviting Marie into the house where a conversation between the two women ensued. It is, of course, true that Lily thought the voice of the visitor sounded like her Auntie Mabel and it appears that Auntie Mabel's voice was different from Marie's normal speaking voice. However, it would be quite wrong, in this instance, to place any reliance on Lily's understanding. While an eight-year-old child can be expected to state basic facts from her memory accurately it is quite another matter to expect a child so young correctly to interpret a complex situation such as the sudden appearance of a complete stranger.

Lily's frame of reference in respect of visitors to her home would have been extremely limited. Only a small number of women were likely to arrive unannounced at the front door of her house. She would have recognized Mrs Higson's voice and that of Lily Dixon who lived in the house but there is no evidence that Annie had any female friends other than Mrs Higson, so anyone else arriving at 114 Rotherfield Street in the evening would probably be a family member. Thus, when Lily heard a woman's voice at the door she would have called upon her own limited experience of female voices to assume it must be her Aunt Mabel. Her assumption does not mean that the visitor actually sounded anything like Aunt Mabel. It was just a small child's instant deduction and she did not state during the criminal proceedings that she still believed that the visitor sounded like Aunt Mabel. It cannot be relied upon as any form of identification and, equally, cannot begin to eliminate Marie from being the visitor.

Lily's description of the visitor's voice as 'soft' also does not help us very much. Any woman appearing at the door in the evening intent on murder is likely to have spoken softly and we also have to bear in mind the pressure an eight-year-old girl would have been under when asked by the coroner in the witness box if a voice was 'deep' or 'soft'. Presented with those two options, would anyone describe a woman's voice as 'deep'? Almost by definition, male voices are deep while female voices are, certainly in comparison with men, soft. It was almost a leading question by the coroner and Lily's answer is not helpful in narrowing down the type of female voice that she heard, especially when we consider that a woman with a deep voice could still speak softly. In any event, Marie's own grandson, who was 30 years old when she died, and thus knew her very well during the latter part of her life, has informed the author that she was 'softly spoken' and there is, therefore, no inconsistency between Lily's evidence about the sound of the visitor's voice and the actual sound of Marie's voice.[213]

Lily's own choice of words, that the woman had a 'nice voice', is also uninformative and while it is true that Marie's voice was described by Mrs Higson as 'peculiar' (although we have no idea what she meant by that – Marie's grandson can only think that it may be something to do with his grandmother being asthmatic[214]), it is nowhere near enough to rule her out as being the visitor. Lily was never asked directly if Marie, whose voice she would not have known at the time of the murder, sounded like the visitor and no attempt was made for her to listen to Marie's voice during the legal proceedings. That being so, the evidence relating to the voice gets us nowhere.

From the fragments overheard by the children it seems that Marie complained of her treatment by Annie's husband. No doubt the focus was on the fact that she had no money, despite Bert having promised to support her, and that, as a result, she was 'thin and hungry'. As the children heard Marie ask for some coppers and Annie's purse was found on the stairs next to her body, it seems that Annie gave Marie some money. Marie's comment 'I don't know the bar' might have been in response to Annie suggesting possible employment for her at a local drinking establishment. Clearly, Marie asked for a glass of water and Annie walked down to the kitchen to fetch one: in the process telling Lily and Ivy, as per the protocol agreed with her husband, that it was only Mrs Higson's friend at the door so that (in effect) there was no need for them to worry.

We can only guess as to whether Marie came to Rotherfield Street with her attaché case or whether she had the revolver hidden somewhere about her person. If the former, she would probably have taken advantage of Annie's temporary absence to remove the weapon from the case and conceal it in her coat. It might, indeed, have been the very reason she asked for the water. From the fact that a half drunk glass of water was found inside the locked parlour, we can assume that Annie invited Marie into the parlour to sit down, drink the water and continue the conversation. By this time, Marie would have been comfortable that neither of the Dixons were in the house and that Annie was the only other adult there. With her loaded revolver ready, Marie would, no doubt, have been keen to move towards her ultimate goal. Having sipped some of the water she would have indicated it was time for her to leave. The two women would have emerged from the parlour and Annie would have turned her back to lock the parlour door. While she did so, Marie would have taken the opportunity to pull out her revolver. Although the key of the parlour was normally kept in the lock, it seems that Annie must have removed it on this occasion and had it in her hand when she was shot because it was later found on the floor. When she turned round and saw Marie pointing her weapon directly at her she would have suddenly understood her terrible fate. It was probably at this point that she said 'Oh don't there are four children downstairs' to which Marie replied 'Oh I wouldn't for the world', meaning that she wouldn't harm the children. Marie then fired once, the bullet penetrating Annie's chest below the left collarbone, passing through her lung and lodging in her spine.

A mystery, which was never apparently addressed during Marie's trial, or at any of the earlier hearings, was that the children were adamant they heard not one but two loud bangs, with a pause between them, whereas it seems that only one bullet was fired from the revolver: there being only one bullet found inside Annie's body and none inside the house. It is possible that one of the bangs was the sound of a door banging, which is what the children thought it was, and, if so, with the parlour door being found locked, it can only have been the sound of the killer dashing out of the house and slamming the front door.

A more likely explanation, however, is that Marie pulled the trigger of the revolver a second time in order to finish off Annie but the bullet was not expelled through the barrel. It will be recalled that Harry Wheatley's evidence was that the gun had a cracked barrel and he thought it liable 'to explode if fired'. Having been fired twice by Marie, one assumed test fire and one shot at Annie, it may be that the barrel of the revolver had become so deformed that the third bullet could not be discharged and remained in the chamber. In such event, the revolver would not have exploded as such – the black powder used by an Eley cartridge would have been too weak to cause an explosion sufficient to shatter the weapon - but there would certainly have been the sound of an explosion as the hammer of the revolver struck the pin on the cartridge, igniting the black powder inside the cartridge causing it to be transformed into a gas. The escaping gas would have produced a noise exactly like normal gunfire – a loud bang in other words – no different, to the untrained ear, to the shot which penetrated Annie's body. With the useless weapon in her hand (and perhaps with her attaché case into which she then hid it), Marie fled from the house, pausing only to post her 'L. Davey' letter card. There were plenty of post boxes in the area, including one in Rotherfield Street itself, so the posting of the card would not have held up her escape for any length of time. Without further delay she raced from Islington back to 12 Richmond Road where she was lucky enough to return before Bert's visit.

If she had not got rid of it already, Marie had the whole morning and most of the afternoon on Wednesday 24 March to dispose of the revolver and Mrs Connor said that she went out in the morning between the hours of nine and ten and again between ten and eleven. All Marie had to do then was wait until Bert's visit when he would no doubt inform her of the tragic death of his wife and she could comfort him and magnanimously offer to look after his children. She was not expecting Joe Higson to be accompanying Bert and she could immediately tell from Bert's angry face and hostile posture that her plan was not working. As no-one had seen her come and go from Rotherfield Street, and unaware that Annie had spoken to her girls when she fetched the glass of water, she probably did not expect to be the prime suspect and must have been surprised by the aggressive tone of the questioning. When she fled the scene of the crime she had no idea that Annie had positively identified her to her daughters as 'Mrs Higson's friend'. It was the flaw of her entire plan which she had neither anticipated nor prepared for.

Without any alibi for the evening of 23 March, Marie was unable to offer any account of her movements when questioned by Higson. She made an obvious mistake in telling Higson that she did not know Annie's sister was called 'Dickson' when shown the telegram which did not state that it was addressed to Annie's sister. She was at least able to offer a genuine denial when it was alleged that she had pushed Annie down the stairs. She must have been astonished that no-one had yet worked out Annie had been shot. However, she knew it would not take the police long to work out what had really killed Mrs Wootten, hence her eagerness to show Higson the contents of her attaché case or rather the absence of a revolver inside it.

Once Bert and Higson had left Richmond Road, Marie must have realised that the murder had been for nothing. Bert's harsh words, not to mention him throwing her out of her lodgings into the street without a penny, had made it perfectly clear to her that, despite the loss of his wife, he was not interested in her looking after him or his children. Her attempt at damage limitation, in respect of maintaining the fantasy world she had created, was to write to her mother to explain why she was never going to see Bert Wootten again: the story being that he was off to the front. There was still a chance she would never be arrested for the murder so that her parents would never know the truth. However, she could not count on that and her one clever action was to write to Higson to let him know her new address so that no-one could claim she was fleeing from justice.

Marie also did well not to say much to the police after her arrest. Once lawyers became involved, her complete silence was on legal advice but it is clear that she had not worked out what story she would tell. By her own admission, she did not inform her legal representatives that she had given the revolver to Wootten until shortly before her evidence at the Old Bailey. It is clear, therefore, that while Mr Pratt was cross-examining Wootten at both the Islington Coroner's Court and the North London Police Court, he did not know what his client's full defence to the charge of murder would be. Marie made good use of the advantage enjoyed by defendants at criminal trials of carefully listening to all of the prosecution evidence and then coming up with a story consistent with that evidence to explain her actions which could not be disproved. By the close of the prosecution case she knew that no-one could say she was not having tea in Oxford Street on the evening of 23 March or that she was not walking home to Richmond Road at the time of the murder. Equally, she knew that no-one could prove that she had not given the revolver to Wootten.

After her trial, Marie was, despite her fears of eternal infamy, quickly forgotten - unlike George Joseph Smith who became a waxwork in Madame Tussaud's Chamber of Horrors shortly after his execution in August 1915: a fate which might also have awaited Marie had the verdict of her jury been different. When Wootten was back in the news in October 1918, due to his arrest for fraud, his connection with the murder of his wife was not even mentioned in the press and thus Marie was not mentioned either.

In the summer of 1920, Marie quietly married a plumber and decorator, Ernest Habgood, who, at 24, was three years younger than her, showing that she was not only attracted to older men. Ernest and Marie Habgood lived in Oxted, Surrey, for the rest of their lives, giving birth to two boys. Ernest died in the Oxted

& Limpsfield Hospital in 1964 while Marie lived on until the ripe old age of 97 until she died of a stroke in 1990 at the East Surrey Hospital, Redhill. No-one who knew her during her later years was aware, or even suspected, that the nice little old lady, Mrs Alice Mary Habgood, was once a prisoner in the dock at the Old Bailey, a nationally famous accused murderess. She told her children and grandchildren that she had been engaged to an officer who had been killed during the First World War (which was, of course, not true) but mentioned nothing else about her past life.

That she killed Annie Wootten is almost certain but the official verdict is that she was not guilty of the crime and we have seen why this was the case. If the verdict was wrong and she was guilty it is nevertheless fair and right to say that she was not an evil woman. She certainly committed an evil act, murdering a defenceless woman within hearing distance of her four young children, but that moment of madness, of what the law would then have described as 'temporary insanity', does not in any way encompass her entire being. For a short time in her life she was madly in love with Lieutenant Wootten and that overpowering love caused her to act in a way which was totally and utterly out of character.

There was, nevertheless, an unfortunate miscarriage of justice in this case. Justice for Annie Josephine Mary Wootten and her two poor daughters, who saw their mother die before their eyes, was never done and sadly never will be.

Alice Mary Habgood, aged 87

AFTERWORD BY SIMON LAWRENCE

(MARIE'S GRANDSON)

When the author contacted me about my late
Grandmother informing me of his research it was like
a proverbial bolt out of the blue. My Grandmother was
in her late sixties when I was born although I did know
something of her earlier life, but clearly not all. Nor
do I think my own immediate family knew anything
of the events of 1915. It was known in the family that
she had been engaged to an army Officer whom we
believed had been killed during the Great War. We
certainly knew of her father being in the Police and on
retirement keeping a Public House, and other pieces of
scant information and family legend and that was the
full extent of our knowledge.

The Grandmother I knew was elderly, had not
enjoyed good health for the majority of her life. She
had married after the First World War, had a daughter
lost in childbirth, then had a son born prematurely,
who was subsequently to be killed in action during
the Second World War in the North Atlantic aged 19 in
September 1943. His death and loss she never came to
terms with and there was always a sadness about her.
My own late father was the youngest son and had a
good relationship with his mother, and would I believe
have been horrified to have known of his mother's
early years.

I realise that when we see people in their latter
years we can only envisage how they may have been
in their early days. In one sense none of the events
that are detailed in the book can I equate with the
lady I knew, but of course I cannot negate them either.
Only she could do that. I would certainly like to ask
her, sadly that opportunity has now gone, as she died

at 97 some twenty odd years ago. For me I think the saddest thing about all this is that she kept her secret of the events for some 75 years and must have lived in an almost perpetual state of worry as to whether that secret would be found out and she would be exposed to family and friends and have to be put on trial in the press a second time, that was her life sentence from which there was no escape.

Whether she was guilty or not, and the truth of that she has carried to her grave, she was found to be not guilty, but she will I believe face a higher court, where truth will prevail and justice will have its day. I leave it the reader to make up their own mind and draw their own conclusions.

Simon Lawrence

October 2011.

Alice Mary Habgood in 1950

Note on Sources

As you may have gathered, putting this story together has not been without its frustrations. After dominating the home news pages in the weeks after the murder during late March, April and early May 1915 when the sensational facts emerged from the coroner and police courts, by the time of the trial at the Old Bailey in June much less space was allotted in the newspapers to reports of the case. This was partly due to the fact that editors did not want to regurgitate all the same facts for a third time but also, as I have mentioned, because of the more exciting trial of George Joseph Smith running concurrently in number one court. Most newspapers only had one crime reporter and he (because it invariably was a man) was sitting in Court No.1 to report the extraordinary story of the Brides in the Bath murders, or more particularly the story of the prosecution's attempt to prove that the deaths of Smith's wives was murder, against Marshall Hall's attempts to demonstrate they were accidental. Smith's frequent outbursts from the dock also provided great copy for the reporters. Most newspapers therefore relied on a single agency reporter for their reports of Marie's trial which means that we are largely dependent on one person to establish what was going on during that hearing. At the same time, the newspapers were short of space because of so much news of the war being carried. Reporting of the trial of Rex v Wheatley was often squeezed to only a few paragraphs. Mr Muir's cross examination of Wheatley followed on the same day as her examination-of-chief in which the only new details of the case were revealed. For this reason, Marie's examination-in-chief by Mr Pratt was reasonably well reported but her cross-examination was not and it seems that a number of questions Muir must have asked are lost to history, together with Marie's answers. Until 1913, detailed summaries of proceedings from the Old Bailey were published but after that date we are totally dependent on newspaper reports. A shorthand reporter was in court and made notes of the entire

trial but these would only have been typed up into a full
transcript in the event of a guilty verdict (because it would
be needed for any appeal). The judge also made notes (and
Justice Lush's typed up notes of the 1914 murder trial of
Charles Longmore at Stafford Assizes can be found in a file
in the National Archives) but his notes of the Wheatley trial
do not appear to have survived. All this has, unfortunately,
led to gaps in our knowledge of the evidence presented in
the Old Bailey. To make matters worse, the Metropolitan
Police files on the case were not selected for preservation in
the National Archives, so the entire police investigation is
now lost to us.

Of all the main players in the case, there has only been a
biography written about one of them: Richard Muir.
However Muir's biographer, Sidney Theodore Felstead, does
not mention the Wheatley trial at all, no doubt because it
was a major defeat for Muir, whereas Felstead wanted to
present his subject as the greatest criminal barrister who
ever lived. Frustratingly, Felstead makes reference to
Muir's manuscript cross-examination notes, which he clearly
had access to while writing his book, but these now appear
to be lost. No biography has been written about the judge or
the defence barrister or about either of the investigating
police officers. Sir Bernard Spilsbury, who cannot be
described as a major player in this particular case, has a
number of biographers but none of them mention his role in
the Wheatley investigation: not surprising given the
uncontroversial nature of the cause of death. What is rather
more surprising is that, to the best of my knowledge, only
one book of the many written about murders of the period
even mentions the murder of Annie Wootten. This is a
passing reference in a 1967 book about the Smith case, The
Life and Death of a Ladykiller, in which the author, Arthur
La Bern, noted the 'astounding coincidence' that Smith and
Wheatley were both living in Richmond Road at the time of
their arrest and he commented that for neighbours in a
London street, both accused of committing unrelated
murders in Islington, to find themselves neighbours in the
first and second courts at the Old Bailey was just about 'the

most amazing coincidence' he had ever come across - although, in describing them as 'neighbours' he appears to have been under the impression that they resided there at the same time, which was not the case.

Thankfully we do have in the National Archives the original transcripts of the depositions provided at both the coroner's court and the police court during the period March to May 1915 which provide us with first hand testimony on which most of this book is based. The files in the National Archives also contain a typed up version of the depositions and typed up copies of the letters which form part of the exhibits plus two or three bonus witness statements prepared specifically for the criminal trial (but not, it seems, a complete set of statements). Additional information about the case, however, is very hard to find.

The same is true of the life of Albert Wootten. The short (and largely inaccurate) biography in the *Islington Daily Gazette*, published when he was promoted to the rank of lieutenant, reveals very little other than that he worked as a shop boy in a department store. His war records are held at the National Archives but there is precious little additional documentation about him in existence relating to the years before 1914. I thought I made a breakthrough at one point when I established that the person who signed the educational reference on his 1914 application for a commission, 'Francis Lambourn C.M.' (C.M. standing for 'Certificated Master'), was recorded in the 1891 census as being a teacher at the Orphan Working School at Haverstock Hill, London NW3. With Wootten having been born in North London an orphan, on account of his father being dead, I felt certain he must have been a pupil at the school. Detailed school records are held at the Surrey History Centre and would have provided very useful information had Wootten indeed been a pupil there but, to my disappointment, when I attended the centre to inspect the records, the first file I examined revealed that Lambourn resigned from the school in October 1893, when Wootten was 10 years old - an age at which boys tended to join the school. The 1901 census has Lambourn living with his mother in Brentford (and presumably teaching in the area) while the 1911 census has him living in Kew, teaching at the Chiswick Council School. Lambourn died in 1939 and his obituary in the Brentford & Chiswick Times does not mention the Orphan Working School but states only that he taught at both the Richmond British School and the Hogarth School in Chiswick. It is not clear where he taught between 1893 and 1901. Interestingly, he joined the army at the start of the war in August 1914, at the ripe old age of 52, serving in the Middlesex Regiment, which was the very same regiment Wootten was serving in at the time he made his application for a commission in late 1914. Thus, the educational reference might have had nothing to do with the school Wootten went to but might have been a favour from an army colleague.

Somewhere there probably does exist some record of Wootten's attempt to prosecute pub landlord William Davy for assault in a local police court but, frustratingly, I have not been able to find it. It is not known which year this was or even which police court it was heard in and there were a number of candidates in the Islington/Clerkenwell area.

Of Marie's early life there is equally little documentation – surprising for a major murder suspect. Was her ex-boyfriend 'Lanteri' real or a figment of her imagination? What was her actual involvement in a supposed betting ring for which she was supposedly arrested in Victoria? On the other hand I was very lucky, and grateful, to be provided with a lot of valuable information about her by her grandson who was extremely generous with his time and memories – almost unbelievably so considering I confessed to him that I suspected his grandmother of being a murderer. He has also kindly given me permission to reproduce some family photographs in this book. To him I offer my sincere thanks.

I was pleased to find plenty of information about the police careers of Harry Wheatley and Charles Cable at the East Sussex Record Office and Norfolk Record Office respectively. To what extent their work had any influence on their daughters it is impossible to and can only be a matter of speculation. A strange coincidence though that they were both policemen and rather ironic too.

Finally, my thanks to the staff at the various libraries and archives I have attended, or used the services of, including the National Archives, the London Metropolitan Archives, the British Library, the British Newspaper Library, the Islington Local History Centre, the East Sussex Record Office, the Norfolk Record Office, the Bedfordshire and Luton Archives, the Surrey History Centre, the Tyne & Wear Archives and Museums, the British Postal Museum and Archive and the Wellcome Library. I am also indebted to the members of the International Ammunition Association Forum for helping me locate an Eley Brothers price list and for explaining the workings of pinfire revolvers and to the members of the Great War Forum for assistance with protocol in an Officers' Mess.

Update - December 2014

Shortly after publication of this book, I discovered that Albert Wootten was arrested, for a second time, on 16 November 1926 for a serious cheque fraud committed in August of that year.

The circumstances of this were that a nurse called Alice Crowther had been run over at Oxford Circus by an omnibus operated by the London General Omnibus Co. and taken to the Middlesex Hospital where she had her leg amputated. The company accepted responsibility and sent the poor woman a banker's cheque in the sum of £150 for damages while she was still at the hospital but she never received it. Somehow it got into the hands of Albert Wootten who, accompanied by an unknown woman pretending to be Alice Crowther, presented it, with a forged endorsement, at the National Provincial Bank in Gray's Inn Road on 19 August 1926 and opened an account in Ms Crowther's name. The next day, Albert Wootten withdrew £104 from the account but the police eventually uncovered the fraud and he was arrested by Detective Sergeant Ball of the Metropolitan Police's 'D' Division.

At Marlborough Street Magistrates Court in December, Wootten was committed for trial at the Central Criminal Court and so it was that, once again, Albert found himself at the Old Bailey! He was tried in January 1927 before the common sergeant, Sir Henry Dickens KC, and found guilty of forgery and of 'conspiring with other persons to obtain money from the National Provincial Bank by false pretences with intent to defraud'. He was, however, cleared of stealing the cheque and it remains a mystery as to how he obtained it in the first place. At his trial, Detective Sergeant Ball said that a total of four postal orders sent to the Middlesex Hospital had not arrived but were forged and 'presented in the locality where the accused lived'. There may nor may not be a connection with the fact that, in November 1926, James Freeman, a 47-year-old sorter from the Northern District Post Office in Upper Street, who had worked for the Post Office since 1907, was convicted at Clerkenwell Police Court of stealing two letters in the course of transmission and sent to prison for six months. Wootten had formerly worked for the Post Office and perhaps his old friends there were part of the conspiracy. Detective Sergeant Ball suggested at his trial that 'others were concerned in the theft', and that Wootten 'was brought in through want of money'. Wootten was convicted in January 1927 and sentenced to eight months imprisonment.

From private family information received after publication, I can say that it is now clear that Albert Wootten was not the father of George Cable. In fact, the identity of George's biological father is known to me. Furthermore, from the same information, I am also satisfied that Leah Cable did not know Albert before 23 March 1915 and only became acquainted with him following the murder of his wife.

Finally, it has been suggested that perhaps the killer shot Annie through the letter box (so that the first bang was the front door shutting). I think it unlikely but mention it for completeness.

Select Bibliography

Primary Sources

National Archives ("NA")

CRIM 1/133/6 – Central Criminal Court: Depositions - Sargent Philip
CRIM 1/139/3 – Central Criminal Court: Depositions - Elizabeth Florence Pettifer
CRIM 1/134/1 – Central Criminal Court: Depositions - Daisy Williams
CRIM 1/156-157 – Central Criminal Court: Depositions - Alice Mary Wheatley
CRIM 4/1403 - Records of the Central Criminal Court: October 1918
CRIM 6/24 - Records of the Central Criminal Court: First Court
CRIM 6/62 - Records of the Central Criminal Court: Second Court
CRIM 9/64 – Calendar of Prisoners 1918
DPP 3/47 - Director of Public Prosecutions: Registers of Cases, 7 June – 18 December 1918
DPP 9/1 - Department of Director of Public Prosecutions: Central Criminal Court Prosecution Books Volume 1: 9 January 1905 to 7 February 1911
DPP 9/3 – Department of Director of Public Prosecutions: Central Criminal Court Prosecution Books, 7 June – 18 December 1915
HO 45/24645 – Pardons: Johnson, Mary
HO 45/9668/A46382B – Dalston Police Court
HO 146/15 – Home Office: Miscellaneous Criminal Entry Books, 8 August 1914 – 17 May 1915
HO 151/10 - Home Office: out letter books, 8 September 1913 - 21 May 1919
MEPO 3/189 - Criminal libel: "The Sutton Libel Case" (Mrs Annie Tugwell)
MEPO 3/235 - Murder of Bernard Balod by John Albis on the high seas
MEPO 4/346 - Registers of Leavers
MEPO 7/54-77 - Police Orders 1892 - 1915
MEPO 21/48 - Pension records in numerical order
RAIL 950/41 London, Brighton and South Coast Railway: public timetables
WO 123/56 – Army Orders 1914
WO 123/57 – Army Orders 1915
WO 123/58 – Army Orders 1916
HO 144/1284/241805 - CRIMINAL - LIST OF CRIMINAL CASES, INCLUDING EXTRADITION CASES: Morse, Emily COURT
T1/11801 - Home Office. Payment of compensation to Miss E.M. Morse for wrongful conviction and imprisonment for desertion of minor children.
WO 95/5208 - 2 Battalion Queens Own (Royal West Kent Regiment)

WO 162/3 – New Armies – Organisation

WO 293/2 – Instructions Issued by the War Office Jan-June 1915

WO 339/15467 - Lieutenant Albert WOOTTEN. The Worcestershire (sic)
Regiment

WO 339/41049 – Lt E.A. Caldwell Cook

WO 364/4852 - War Office: Soldiers' Documents from Pension Claims, First
World War: Wootten, Albert - Wootten, Green

London Metropolitan Archives ("LMA")

CLA/003/PR/05/027, Printed Calendar of Prisoners, Central Criminal Court,
1915

LCC/EO/DIV03/ROT/AD/004 – Rotherfield Street School Admission &
Discharge Register for Girls

LCC/EO/DIV03/ROT/LB/002 - Rotherfield Street School Log Book - Girls

LCC/EO/DIV03/ROT/LB/005 Rotherfield Street School Log Book - Infants

LCC/PC/COR/02/20 – Appointment of Coroner for the Central District of the
County of London

LCC/PC/COR/03/018 – Coroner's Courts – Islington

PS/NLO/A/01/015-016 – Court Register 1915

PS/B/B/01/104 – Brentford Petty Sessional Division Register 12.09.18-19.02.19

X098/429 – St Pancras Workhouse South Infirmary Admission and
Discharge Register Feb 1926-May 1926

Norfolk Record Office ("NRO")

Y/TC 3 29-33 – Watch Committee Minutes of the Yarmouth Police 1878-1904

East Sussex Record Office ("ESRO")

PA/3/1/9-10 Chief Constable's Report Books

SPA 3/17/2-3 Defaulters Books

DB/B/12/7-23 Minutes of Watch Committee Meetings

PTS6/4 – Register of Licences granted in the Division of Hailsham, Sussex

TAM 1/2/4-6 – Board Minute Books of Tamplin & Sons Ltd 1902-1915

TAM/1/29/2 – Tamplins Brewery Ltd House Specifications Book 1909

Bedfordshire and Luton Archives and Record Service ("BLA")

X/550/11 - Digest Services of the 10th Battalion, Bedfordshire Regiment
(Service Battn)

British Postal Museum & Archive ("BPMA")

POST 92/146 – Post Office Guide 1915 Jan

Wellcome Library: Spilsbury Collection

PP/SP1/2 (2/164 & 164a) – Notes relating to the post-mortem of Annie Josephine Wootten

Main Newspapers from 1915

Argus, Daily Call, Daily Chronicle, Daily Citizen, Daily Express, Daily Graphic, Daily Mail, Daily Mirror, Daily News & Leader, Daily Sketch, Daily Telegraph, Echo and London Evening Chronicle, Evening News, Evening Standard and St James's Gazette, Globe, Guardian, Illustrated Sunday Herald, Islington Daily Gazette and North London Tribune, Lloyd's Weekly News, Morning Advertiser, News of the World, Observer, People, Reynolds Newspaper, Star, Sunday Pictorial, Sunday Times, The Times, Weekly Dispatch

Secondary Sources

Bellah, Kent, *The Book of Pistols and Revolvers*, The Stackpole Company, 1965

Browne, Douglas G., *Sir Travers Humphreys: A Biography*, George G. Harrap & Co, 1960

Browne, Douglas G. and Tullett, Tom, *Bernard Spilsbury: His Life and Cases*, George Harrap & Co, 1980

Cosh, Mary, *A History of Islington*, Historical Publication Ltd, 2005

Cosh, Mary, *The Squares of Islington Part II*, Islington Archaeology & History Society, 1993

Crew, Albert, *The Old Bailey*, Ivor Nicholson Watson Ltd, 1933

Draper, Chris, *Islington's Cinemas & Film Studios*, London Borough of Islington, 1989

Eddlestone, John J, *Foul Deeds in Islington*, Wharncliffe Local History, 2010

Eden Hooper, W, *The Central Criminal Court of London*, Eyre and Spottiswoode, 1909

Eden Hooper, W. *History of Newgate and the Old Bailey*, Underworld Press, 1935

Fairfield, Sheila, *The Streets of London*, Macmillan, 1983

Felstead, Sidney Theodore, *Famous Criminals and Their Trials*, George Doran Company, 1926

Harding, C.W., *Eley Cartridges*, Quiller Press, 2006

Harris, Seymour F., *Principles of the Criminal Law*, 12th edition, Stevens and Haynes, 1912

Bibliography

Hodge, Harry, *Famous Trials,* Penguin, 1954

Jackson, Robert, *Coroner: The Biography of Sir Bentley Purchase,* George G. Harrap Co Ltd, 1963

La Bern, Arthur, *The Life and Death of a Ladykiller,* Leslie Frewin, 1967

Lewis Jnr, S., *The History & Topography of the Parish of St Mary of Islington,* J.H. Jackson, 1843

Money Barnes, Major R., *The British Army in 1914,* Seeley Service & Co, 1968

Mullen, Paul E., Pathé, Michele, Purcell, Rosemary, *Stalkers and Their Victims,* Cambridge University Press, 2nd edition, 2009

Murphy, Theresa, *The Old Bailey: Eight Centuries of Crime, Cruelty & Corruption,* Mainstream Publishing Co Ltd, 1999

London Tramways History Group, 1991

O'Donnell, Bernard, *The Old Bailey and its trials,* Burke Publishing Co., 1950

Poulson, Neville, Rumble, Mike & Smith, Keith, *Sussex Police Forces: A Pictorial history from 1836 to 1986,* Middleton Press, 1987

Richardson, John, *Islington Past: A Visual History of Islington,* Historical Publications Ltd, 1988

Rinaldi, Richard A., *Order of Battle of the British Army 1914,* General Data LLC, 2008

Roberts, Sonia, *The Story of Islington,* Robert Hale & Co, 1975

Sainsbury, J.D., *A Guide to the History of the Bedfordshire and Hertfordshire Regiment,* Hart Books, 1987

Shields, Pamela, *Essential Islington: From Boadicea to Blair,* Sutton Publishing Ltd, 2000

Simkins, Peter, *Kitchener's Army: The Raising of the New Armies 1914-1916,* Manchester University Press, 1988

Smith, Gavin, *Islington,* Chalford Publishing Co, 1995

Names of the Streets of Places in the Administrative County of London, London County Council 4th Edition, 1955

Willats, Eric A., *Streets With A Story: The Book of Islington,* 2nd edn, Islington Local History Trust, 1988

Wills, William, *An Essay on the Principles of Circumstantial Evidence,* 6th edn, edited by Sir Alfred Wills, 1912

Websites

www.ancestry.co.uk

www.oldbaileyonline.org

Endnotes

1.   Lily went to Rotherfield Street School. Her sister, who was in a lower year at the same school, returned earlier - at midday according to Ivy – although their aunt, Lily Dixon, said that when she left the house at 4pm to visit her father, 'The two little girls hadn't come home from school' NA: CRIM 1/156 & CRIM 1/157.

2.   Their full names being Lily Josephine, Ivy Elsie, Doris Elizabeth and Edwin Bernard.

3.   The children normally went to bed at 6:30pm and there is nothing to suggest this evening was any different (CRIM 156/1, 157/1). Sunset on 23 March 1915 was at 6:15pm with lighting up time at 7:15pm (*Whittaker's Almanack* for 1915).

4.   Annie sometimes kissed her children goodnight and sometimes she did not (NA: CRIM 156/1, 157/1). Tonight she did not - but there does not appear to be any significance in this.

5.   According to her father, this was a couple of weeks before her murder. He said she was taken to St Bartholomew's Hospital where her leg was bandaged (NA: CRIM 1/156 and CRIM 1/157). The hospital archives have no surviving record of this – probably because she was not formally admitted as a patient.

6.   Ivy was reported in some newspapers to have said that the story told at school was about 'a mother and a bee'. It has not been possible to establish what this story was about.

7.   A service battalion was a battalion created for the duration of the war.

8.   The newspaper was actually quoting from *The Diocesan Gazette*.

9.   *Worthing Mercury*, 3 October 1914; additional information on Shoreham during the period from *The Hove Gazette & Sussex County Mirror*, *Brighton & Hove Times* including '*A Shoreham Recruit's Experience: My Life in Camp*' by an unnamed recruit, *Hove Gazette & Sussex County Mirror*, 3 October 1914.

10.   *Hove Gazette & Sussex County Mirror*, 19 September 1914.

11.   The proprietor is stated by *Kelly's 1915 Directory for Sussex* to be one Thomas Bushby.

12.   *Hove Gazette & Sussex County Mirror*, 21 November 1914.

13.   Ibid, 28 November & 19 December 1914.

14.   The 10th Bedfordshire Battalion was originally part of the 106th Infantry Brigade in the 35th Division of Kitchener's Fourth New Army (NA - WO 162/3).

15.   See e.g. *The Times*, 25 October 1909, 'The Special Reserve Infantry'.

16.   Lily's birth certificate states that her father's occupation was an Electrician's Labourer as at July 1906 although Wootten's army applications for temporary commissions in 1914 and 1915 state that he had worked at the Stores Department of the GPO for 9 years, quitting to start in business, which is not entirely consistent with the certificate.

17.	Information on Harry Wheatley's police career comes mainly from the Chief Constable's Report Books (ESRO - SPA/3/1/9-10), the Default Register (ESRO - SPA3/17/2) and from the Watch Committee Minutes (ESRO -DB/B/12/7-23) held at the East Sussex Record Office. It is interesting to note that Harry was evidently not comfortable with being known as a police constable in the early years of his career. In the 1881 census, at which time he was living in a boarding house, so probably did not want fellow lodgers to know what he did for a living, he lists his occupation as 'carpenter'. Oddly, but by no means uniquely, he is recorded twice in the 1881 census; the second occasion living with his parents in Kent where his occupation is again recorded as a carpenter, like his father.

18.	*Brighton Guardian*, 19 August 1891.

19.	ESRO - DB/B/12/15. The fire was at 21 German Place in Brighton and the unfortunate 13-year-old was Ethel Sarah Ann Thirkettle. The superintendent of the fire brigade was Louis Victor Le Croix.

20.	The lodging house keeper being Mrs Elizabeth Holderness of 31 Marlborough Place (the scene of the fire) although the letter commending Harry's conduct was written on her behalf by a Mr Cushion - presumably James C. Cushion, a local wine merchant who ran a store nearby (ESRO – DB/B/12/15; *Kelly's 1895 Directory for Sussex*).

21.	He was appointed Engineer on 20 February 1890 and Chief Engineer on 22 July 1891 (ESRO - DB/B/12/14).

22.	*Brighton Times*, 12 January 1894.

23.	*Brighton Gazette & Sussex Telegraph*, 8 February 1894.

24.	*Brighton Times*, 4 April 1894 and 26 May 1894.

25.	The likelihood is that this 'Sweeney' was Julia Sweeney who, in the early 1890s, was keeping a lodging house at 17 Wyndham Street in Brighton (*Kelly's 1890 Directory for Sussex*; 1891 Census). Contrary to what seems to have been believed by the police, Mrs Sweeney was a genuine widow. Her husband, Lieutenant John Robert Glover Sweeney of the 20th Hussars, who she had married in 1865, died in 1866 of inflammation of the liver while on service in India (*Times of India*, 30 May 1866). At the same time, she seems a little old to have been a woman Harry was (allegedly) conducting some form of sexual relationship with. In 1894 she was 51 while Harry was 37. However, she had a 28-year-old daughter, Mary Rose, stated in the 1891 census to be 'living on her own means' (the same description applied to her mother) and it may be that she was involved in some way in this scenario.

26.	ESRO - DB/B/12/15.

27.	ESRO - DB/B/12/16. It could all have been worse. In November 1898, PC William Henry of the Brighton Police Force felt the need to tender his resignation after he was reported to the Watch Committee for 'gross misconduct' simply because he had been living with a woman, despite being a single man (ESRO - SPA 3/1/10). In August 1902, PC David Miller was discharged for misconduct when he was reported for consorting with a married woman one night, having spent the evening with her in a music hall (ESRO - DB/B/12/21).

28.	*Sussex Daily News*, 27 September 1898. There were some questions raised by a local councillor who believed that Harry had been badly treated by a negligent Fire Brigade and the Watch Committee felt the need to pass a resolution on 12 October 1898 that the councillor be informed 'that Wheatley was not burnt by the chemical fluid used on the occasion in question and that….he is receiving full pay during his incapacity' (ESRO -DB/B/12/18).

29.   There was, however, a small supplement for Harry. On 29 July 1891 the Watch Committee resolved that the Chief Engineer of the Fire Brigade be paid a further sum of 16 shillings per quarter on top of his police salary. Harry remained Chief Engineer until February 1905 when he had to step down, having reached the age limit for the fire service of 48 years old.

30.   A few examples: Samuel Jupp had joined the Brighton Police Force three years before Harry in 1875 and was appointed superintendent on 14 February 1894 on £155 per annum, his salary being increased to £165 per annum on 11 July 1900. His career advanced nicely, despite having been found asleep in his first year in the force, and he was appointed detective inspector on the same day that Harry was promoted to detective. When Jupp retired due to ill health in 1903 he was replaced as superintendent by Henry Reene who had joined the force on 29 November 1883, nearly five years after Harry. Had Harry avoided the temptation of Mrs Sweeney he would surely have been elevated to the rank of superintendent instead of Reene, assuming he had wanted the job. Thomas Holloway, the man whose promotion from sergeant to detective created a vacancy for Harry to become sergeant in 1889, was appointed superintendent in 1891 (and, as Holloway had been Chief Engineer until that point, this created a promotion for Harry in that year in the fire brigade). Another colleague of Harry's, William Hale, joined the force in March 1889, more than ten years after Harry, and was appointed detective on 14 February 1894. Detectives Wheatley and Hale worked together between February and May 1894, until Harry's demotion. Hale gained promotion to detective inspector only two years later in 1896 and was appointed superintendent in July 1900 on a salary of £145 per annum.   In short, there was no reason why Harry should not have been on the way to promotion to a superintendent by 1901, if not having already been promoted, had he kept out of trouble. There were no examinations; promotions in the Brighton Police Force at the time were dependent on 'intelligence and good conduct…a diligent discharge of…duties and strict obedience to the command of….superiors' (ESRO - DB/B/12/11).

31.   Under the terms of the Police Act 1890, a police officer could retire on full pension, i.e. two thirds of pay, on completion of 26 years service, *Police Chronicle* 26 June 1901 & 20 April 1911.

32.   *Brighton Gazette,* 14 June 1906, *Brighton & Hove Times*, 15 June 1906, *Police Review & Parade Gossip,* 29 June 1906.

33.   The 'mile from nowhere' quote is by John Curtis, a local of Maynard's Green, who was giving evidence at the East Sussex Licensing Sessions in favour of the Runt-in-Tun's licence being renewed in 1908 - reported in the *East Sussex News* of 13 March 1908. Harry Wheatley gave evidence and provided information about the pub's clients and sales.

34.   An unnamed daughter died after 10 hours in April 1894. Another

daughter, Florence Adelaide Wheatley, was born in August 1900 but died after 20 days of Epidemic Diarrhoea. In the 1911 Census, Harry indicates that three of his children had died. I have not managed to identify the third child who presumably died in infancy.

35. Tamplins' House Specifications Book 1909, ESRO – TAM1/29/2.

36. *East Sussex News*, 10 March 1911 and ESRO - PTS6/4.

37. *Islington Gazette*, 25 June 1864 (for date of re-naming) and 25 July 1863 (for reasons for name change).

38. A number of alternatives were considered by the members of the Islington Vestry. St Matthew's Road was rejected as too 'Romish' and Northumberland Road (suggested because the road was on the Northampton estate) was rejected because there was already a road with that name in Clerkenwell. Raleigh Road, after Sir Walter Raleigh, was patriotically suggested but Essex Road was preferred, with one member of the Vestry commenting to laughter that this would 'no doubt have the support of those who recommended Raleigh-road for the names were connected and it was impossible to think of one without also thinking of the other insomuch as they both had their heads chopped off' (*Islington Gazette*, 17 July 1863). He was, of course, referring to the Second Earl of Essex, beheaded in the Tower of London in 1601.

39. *The Times*, 19 November 1858.

40. *Islington Gazette*, 4 August 1898.

41. Ibid, 12 September 1898 (for both letters).

42. Ibid, 20 June & 25 July 1876.

43. Ibid, 21 November 1876.

44. *Islington News* 13 November 1914.

45. *Daily Call*, 6 February 1915.

46. *Daily Call*, 20 March 1915.

47. *Aberdeen Weekly Journal*, 3 March 1882; *Cheshire Observer*, 4 March 1882; *North Eastern Daily Gazette*, 4 March 1882; *Reynolds Newspaper*, 5 March 1882.

48. *Sheffield & Rotherham Independent*, 16 April 1889.

49. There is a slight discrepancy in the evidence here. Constable Masson was certain that the revolver was fully loaded with five cartridges in the chambers and one spent. However, Sergeant Hewitt believed it was only loaded in three chambers with one spent cartridge. Mrs Alland mentioned seeing three cartridges. Horace Mitchell said that he saw four loaded chambers and one spent cartridge Marie herself was to say that she loaded three chambers but she might have simply been adopting Hewitt's recollection for her own purposes. Overall, I prefer the evidence of Masson. Hewitt said he was not an expert in revolvers and asked Masson to handle the weapon. It was Masson who examined it and who physically removed the cartridges. He is thus the person most likely to know how many were in it. However, nothing turns on this point.

50. *Daily Mirror*, 22 March 1915.

51.   There were, in fact, a small number of post offices open in the London district on Sundays for telegraph business and the sale of postage stamps (*Post Office Guide Jan 1915* – BPMA POST 92/146).

52.   The advertisement read as follows: 'WANTED as BARMAID, a respectable willing young lady, for good business house – chance for improver – good home and wages – permanent station. Apply after ten, at the Gun Tavern, Lupus Street, Victoria' – *Morning Advertiser*, 24 March 1915.

53.   A letter posted in London before midday for someone in Horsted Keynes would actually arrive later on the same day. It would reach the main post office at East Grinstead at 4:40pm and from there it would be dispatched to Horsted Keynes, arriving at 6:15pm. All letters posted before 1:45pm in London would get to East Grinstead at 7:15pm and arrive in Horsted Keynes in time for the first delivery of the following day at 6:00am. Letters posted between 1:45pm and 10:15pm would reach East Grinstead at 8:00am while those posted before 6:30am would be there by 11:15am, all arriving together at Horsted Keynes at 11:30am (*Post Office Guide for 1915* and *Kelly's 1915 Directory for Sussex*). In other words, a letter posted by Marie late in the evening would have been expected to arrive at its destination either shortly before or shortly after noon of the next day (depending on the speed of dispatch from the Horsted Keynes sub-post office). It is quite conceivable, therefore, that Marie, with local knowledge of the delivery times by her postman, could have expected her letter from Tooting, posted very late on a Wednesday evening, to be with her mother on Thursday morning. If Marie had posted a letter to her mother between noon and 1:45pm on Wednesday then she would have expected it to have reached her mother first thing in the morning so it cannot be said to be impossible that there were two letters received by Mrs Wheatley that morning.

54.   On balance, I would suggest, the likelihood is that there was only one letter – the one sent from Tooting - and that Marie was anticipating her mother's surprise in receiving it, as opposed to remarking on her likely surprise at the contents of an earlier letter. Presumably Marie had not written any other letters from London to her mother since she departed from Horsted Keynes on 18 March (none were produced in evidence) so that it came out of the blue on 25 March, hence the reference to a surprise. This notion is partially supported by the evidence of Harry Wheatley who said at the inquest: 'My daughter Alice occasionally wrote to me and addressed the letter to me. I have not received one for probably the last 3 weeks or months' (CRIM 157/1).

55.   When Davis was asked why he went to the Gun Tavern he said: 'Because I had been making inquiries with a number of officers. I had good reason to go there' *North London Guardian*, 23 April 1915.

56.   Examples can be found in NA - HO 151/10.

57.   He joined the Bethnal Green force (J Division) on 25 July 1892, transferring to Islington (N Division) on 8 March 1898, at which time he was promoted to detective-sergeant (NA - MEPO 21/48; MEPO 4/346).

58.   *The Times*, 28 November 1899.

59.   *Ipswich Journal*, 9 January 1869.

60.	Information on the murder from *Norwich Mercury*, 28 June, 5, 12, 19 & 26 July 1851 *Daily News* 30 June & 2 July 1851, *Lloyds Weekly Newspaper* 6 July 1851, *Nottinghamshire Guardian* 10 July 1851, *Morning Post* 18 July 1851.

61.	e.g. *The Times*, 30 June 1851.

62.	*Standard*, 31 March 1869.

63.	*Morning Post*, 4 February 1898, *Times*, 4 February 1898.

64.	*Islington Gazette*, 25 January & 7 February 1898.

65.	*Lloyds Weekly News*, 7 April 1912.

66.	*Police Chronicle and Constabulary World*, 27 March 1942 and Wesley's birth certificate.

67.	www.oldbaileyonline.org.

68.	www.oldbaileyonline.org.

69.	*Daily Mirror*, 22 June 1936.

70.	*The Times*, 5 & 6 February 1937 and 12 March 1942.

71.	*The Times*, 23 October 1874.

72.	*Morning Post*, 4 May 1874.

73.	*St Pancras Chronicle*, 8 June 1906.

74.	*The Times*, 20 December 1909.

75.	*British Medial Journal*, 13 August 1910.

76.	*Islington News* 16 September 1910.

77.	*The Times*, 24 November 1910.

78.	LMA – LCC/PC/COR/02/020.

79.	The public control committee of the L.C.C. initially recommended that Samuel Oddie, deputy coroner for West London, be appointed but this was overturned on amendment and Schröder was appointed instead (*The Times*, 31 October & 2 November 1910).

80.	Schröder appears to have privately claimed that he was not satisfied at the time about the result of the Lofty inquest and would have preferred an open verdict. This notion appears in *Famous Trials*, second series, ed. Harry Hodge, Penguin, Harmondsworth, 1954, supposedly based on confidential police communications between Highgate, Blackpool, Aylesbury, Bath, Bristol and the CID. No reservations of the coroner were mentioned by the press when they reported the inquest.

81.	*Islington News & Hornsey Gazette*, 16 July 1915.

82.	*Islington Gazette*, 27 April 1877.

83.	LMA - LCC/PC/COR/03/018.

84.	NA – HO 45/9668/A46382B; *Lloyds Weekly Newspaper*, 27 October 1889 and 18 May 1890; *Daily News*, 28 February 1890.

85.	*Islington News & Hornsey Gazette*, 11 February 1910.

86.	*Islington Daily Gazette and North London Tribune*, 11 February 1918; *Police Chronicle* 15 February 1918.

87.	A curious fact about the case was that Hedderwick had supposedly taken his boots off because he was not wearing them when found in the morning.

88. The photograph was, I believe, taken by Bernard Alfieri, a former Daily Mirror journalist and keen photographer, who had recently established his own photographic press agency, Alfieri Picture Services.

89. Mrs Alland also identified Marie in a line-up but not until Wednesday 7 April. The stress of that situation might help to explain Marie's apparent illness and absence from court the next day.

90. *The Times*, 11 December 1882.

91. *Brighton & Hove Times*, 12 & 19 June 1914, *Sussex Daily News*, 10 June 1914.

92. *Evening News*, 29 June 1915.

93. *Daily Call*, 6 April 1915.

94. *Daily Express*, 6 April 1915.

95. It seems that Lily was never asked what she understood by the expression 'Mrs Higson's friend' or whether she had ever previously heard it mentioned (nor was Ivy).

96. Newspaper reports suggest that Marie was usually referred to as 'the prisoner', sometimes as 'Wheatley', by counsel and witnesses during court hearings. For consistency and simplicity, I have changed this to 'Miss Wheatley' throughout when reproducing cross-examinations.

97. *Islington News*, 6 January 1911.

98. Ibid, 5 May 1911.

99. *The Weekly Dispatch*, 28 April 1915.

100. A contemporary advertisement for Dr J. Callis Browne's Chlorodyne described it as 'The Best Remedy known for coughs, Colds, Neuralgia, Toothache, Rheumatism. It acts like a charm in curing Diarrhoea and other bowel complaints. At all chemists', *Thomson Weekly News*, 27 March 1915.

101. *John Bull*, 21 December 1907. Kane's failure to caution his prisoner did not affect the verdict and Wooltorton was convicted at Hertford Assizes on 5 November 1907 and sentenced to seven years penal servitude (*The Times*, 6 November 1907).

102. *Morning Advertiser*, 10 January 1911.

103. *The Times*, 3 April 1911.

104. See *Police Chronicle*, 10 September 1910, reporting an article in the *National Review* of Washington in respect of the arrest of Crippen, although the words 'You do not have to say anything' are not here mentioned.

105. *Islington News*, 21 February 1913.

106. Ibid, 1 October 1913.

107. *The Times*, 8 May 1905.

108. See *Police Chronicle*, 3 July 1914.

109. *The Times*, 16 December 1912.

110. *Police Chronicle*, 6 August 1915.

111. *People*, 28 May 1915; *Daily Express*, 29 September 1910.

112. *Daily Mirror*, 28 September 1911.

113. Ibid, 18 February 1913.

114. *Daily Express*, 4 April 1913.

115. According to Stanley Jackson, author of *The Old Bailey*, writing nearly fifty years after the judge's death, Justice Lush, being a religious Baptist, preferred to say 'May you be led to seek and find salvation' instead of 'May the Lord have mercy on your soul'. However, contemporary local newspaper reports of the sentencing to death of Charles Longmore, found guilty of murdering his wife, at Stafford Assizes on 17 February 1914 record that Lush J. used the traditional form of words, following which Longmore fainted to the floor of the dock (see cuttings in HO 144/4234).

116. Not all of them were actually hanged. They were Frederick Albert Robertson (Old Bailey, executed), Jon Albis (Old Bailey, respited), Sargent Philp (Old Bailey, executed), Josiah Davies (Stafford Assizes, executed) and Charles Longmore (Stafford Assizes, respited). For Old Bailey decisions see NA - DPP 9/1.

117. *The Times*, 3 April 1912.

118. NA – CRIM 1/134/1. Dolly Steer's real name was Annie Elizabeth Marianne Miller but she was known as Dolly.

119. Thomas appears to sign his name as 'Thomas Andrew' in his deposition but he is referred to by Daisy in some of her letters to him as 'Thomas Andrews' (but on one occasion as 'Theo Andrew'). His age is not stated in any of the depositions in the National Archives or in any newspaper reports I have seen but he is presumably the same Thomas Andrews who gave his occupation as 'professional violinist' in the 1911 census when he was staying with his parents in Liverpool. If so, he was 39 years old in 1911 and thus much older than Daisy.

120. If I have correctly identified Thomas Andrews, then his father was 76 years old but he must have moved from Liverpool to Sheffield because he is stated to have been living there in the deposition evidence.

121. On the way to her home with Dolly, Daisy spoke to a policeman to ask what action she could take against Theo for assault and she was advised to take out a summons against him.

122. When sentencing Daisy, Justice Lush said: 'If I had thought that the prisoner had premeditated the death of Steer, I would not have sanctioned the course I have taken in this case. My view is that the prisoner, in a moment of anguish, committed this unlawful act against the girl which was followed by consequences she did not anticipate or realise'. He added that Theo's conduct was 'so bad that one could not help expressing a wish that he should to some extent be made answerable for the consequences' (*The Times*, 13 September 1912).

123. NA – CRIM 1/139/3.

124. *Daily Mirror*, 8 April 1913.

125. Another factor in the jury's thinking might have been that the couple's 14-year-old son, Frederick Henry Pettifer, would have lost both

his parents if Elizabeth was found guilty of the murder. Young Frederick gave evidence in court about this father's brutality towards his mother and he seemed like a nice boy who did not deserve to be in the situation in which he found himself.

126.   NA – CRIM 1/133/6.

127.   After he was arrested and taken to a police station, Philp removed his glass eye and flung it violently on the floor (*Lloyds Weekly News*, 6 October 1912).

128.   NA - MEPO 3/235.

129.   NA – CRIM 1/83/2.

130.   NA - HO 144/4234.

131.   Reduced in 1924 to 12 years (NA - HO 144/4234).

132.   One further option was an appeal from the Criminal Court of Appeal to the House of Lords as per the Criminal Appeal Act of 1907 but this was only allowed if the appeal involved a point of law 'of exceptional public importance' (*The Times*, 31 March 1911).

133.   NA - CRIM 6/24.

134.   *Famous Criminals and their Trials*, Felstead, Sidney Theodore, George H. Doran, 1926.

135.   The earliest mention of the quote appears to be by Sidney Felstead, Muir's biographer, writing in 1926 and he does not mention who told him.

136.   Minutes of Evidence of trial of Louisa Josephine Jemima Masset for the wilful murder of Manfred Louis Masset on 11 December 1889, www. oldbaileyonline.org.

137.   NA - CRIM 6/62.

138.   Other crimes had also grabbed the public's attention, such as the murder of a 7 year old girl, Maggie Nally, whose body was found at Aldersgate Street Station during the evening of Sunday 4 April 1915. This hit the headlines the day after 7 year old Lily Wootten gave evidence at the inquest, and dominated the news for the next few days as theories were discussed as to how little Maggie got from her home in Paddington to the City of London, but the murderer was never caught and the story had fizzled out by the end of the month.

139.   There are no newspaper reports of Mabel's evidence and the fact that she was a witness at the trial is only known from Mr Pratt's mention of her appearance before the judge and jury during his closing speech. That she confirmed she did not visit Rotherfield Street on the night of the murder is inference but must be the case.

140.   NA – WO 339/41049.

141.   Winifred married in 1939 and gave the name of 'Francis William Rufus' as her father, stated to be deceased, on her marriage certificate. This was, however, her brother's name. Her mother's husband was called Francis Henry Rufus but he died almost four years before Winifred was born.

142.   *The Times*, 30 June 1898.

143. Ibid, 6 December 1909.

144. Minutes of Evidence of trial of John Ryan for the wilful murder of James Baldwin on 24 October 1898, www.oldbaileyonline.org.

145. NA - MEPO 3/182.

146. 'The Law and the Man: Psychological Study of the Great Trial' in *Daily Mail*, 20 December 1907.

147. This was the form of wording prescribed by the Oaths Act of 1909 (*The Times*, 28 December 1909) although it may be that the words 'touching the matters in question' were discarded by 1915. There was originally some controversy as to whether the oath needed to be terminated with the words 'so help me God' but the Lord Chief Justice ruled this was unnecessary (see The Lord Chief Justice on the Oaths Act, *The Times*, 1 February 1910).

148. *Famous Criminals and their Trials*, Felstead, Sidney Theodore, George H. Doran, 1926.

149. The evidence being from a buyer of Jones Brothers Ltd of Holloway that pyjamas which wrapped some of the remains found in the cellar of Hilldrop Crescent could not have been purchased before 1906, the Crippens having moved in during 1905. In fairness, this was not a credibility issue and can thus be distinguished from Muir's application in the case against Marie.

150. NA - HO 144/1284/241805.

151. Letter from E. Blackwell of the Home Office to the Secretary to the Treasury dated 15 May 1915, NA - T1/11801.

152. The neighbour she accused was one William Charlwood who, at one time, lived at a residence adjoining the Johnson's house. He gave evidence at Mrs Woodman's trial and said he knew her by sight but had never spoken to her or been in her house.

153. NA - HO 45/24645.

154. *Daily Express*, 6 April 1915.

155. Witness Statements of Arthur Leonard Lawrence, landlord of the Three Brewers Public House, and Charles Hattich, clockmaker, in NA - CRIM 1/157.

156. *Thomson's Weekly News*, 3 July 1915.

157. Ibid.

158. Conversation with the author, February 2011.

159. *The Times*, 3 April 1912.

160. *Daily Mirror*, 22 January 1915; *Daily Express*, 22 January 1915.

161. *The Times* 19 March 1915. There was another connection with the Jack the Ripper murders in that an old sword-bayonet discovered a few days after the murder in a Westminster sewer - possibly the murder weapon, although this was never established - was made in 1888 (Daily Mirror, 19 March 1915).

162. One might reasonably ask if it is correct to say that Marie knew that Wootten was at the White City. Perhaps she thought he was still signed off sick from the army and living in Rotherfield Street. On her own account

of events, however, this cannot be the case. She said she had a letter from Wootten on 18 March (which would have revealed he was at the White City) and agreed that she went straight to Wootten at the White City on 19 March, without calling first at Rotherfield Street. It does, perhaps, beg the question, if her account of events was untrue, of *how* she knew he was back at White City. The simple answer is that he probably told her that he was due to rejoin his unit before she left London at the end of February. We might also note that Marie told Higson she had been writing to Wootten without reply, albeit at a time when she was secretly liaising with the lieutenant, and (if this was true) her letters had obviously not been returned as 'not received by addressee' so she might have assumed he was there. Having said this, we know that one of Marie's letters from January was forwarded to Rotherfield Street when Wootten was absent from the White City so this cannot be the answer unless Wootten had told her that he had made arrangements to ensure that it would not happen again. To some extent, the fact that she knew he was at the White City might offer support to her claim to have received a letter from him on 18 March but, if so, we simply return to the question of why she took a room in Islington in order to see Wootten knowing he was in West London. If she never received a letter on 18 March then perhaps her purpose in observing and calling at 114 Rotherfield Street during the evening of 18 March (assuming she was the veiled lady) was to establish if Wootten was living there. This might provide an innocent explanation for her appearance at Ecclesbourne Road but would mean not only that she was the veiled lady but that she was not called to London by Wootten, thus demolishing key planks of her defence.

163.   NA – RAIL 950/41.

164.   *Daily Mirror*, 8 February 1915; *The Hotel Review*, March 1915 and see *Daily Mirror*, 29 January 1914.

165.   No pawn tickets were found in Marie's possession when she was arrested but there was, apparently, no search of her room in Horsted Keynes and the tickets could have been kept there.

166.   At the opening of the hearing proper at the North London Police Court on 20 April 1915, Mr Boyd for the prosecution stated that Marie 'came to that house [i.e. 114 Rotherfield Street during the evening of 18 March] with a revolver and a box of cartridges'. The prosecution theory at this stage appears to have been that Marie intended to murder Annie but was deterred by the presence of the Dixons. The evidence of Ms Thorn strongly suggests Marie did not have the weapon with her at the time. At the Old Bailey trial, Mr Muir was reported as saying in his opening speech to the jury that, 'on March 18 a woman, believed to be the prisoner, was loitering about outside Mrs Wootten's house, and there was evidence which, [in my submission], left it beyond doubt that the prisoner had in her possession a loaded revolver and a box of cartridges' (*Standard*, 22 June 1915). This was (probably deliberately) ambiguously worded, leaving it unclear as to whether it was being suggested that Marie was actually carrying the revolver when she was loitering outside the house on 18 March. The prosecution never really clarified their case as to why Marie was loitering that evening.

167.   *The Richmond and Twickenham Times*, 30 January 1915.

168.   Minutes of Evidence of Trial of William Whelen for feloniously shooting at Florence Ethel Howard with intent to murder her; feloniously sending, knowing the contents thereof, a letter threatening to murder the said F. E. Howard on 30 January 1912, www.oldbaileyonline.org.

169.   NA - MEPO 3/189.

170.   *The Times*, 1 August 1910. Sir Alfred Wills, the editor of the 1912 edition of the influential book, *Circumstantial Evidence*, written by his late father William Wills, stated that in his experience as judge, unless the jury had the aid of photography to follow the evidence in handwriting cases, 'the mere evidence of expert opinion is of little value'.

171.   For the fee chargeable by a professional expert in handwriting for examining and giving an opinion on documents see correspondence dated 27 January 1915 in NA – HO 146/15.

172.   An innocent explanation could be that she did not want her mother to inform Wootten of her whereabouts but that cannot be what she had in mind because she wrote to Higson to inform him of her new address at the Gun Tavern and it would have been obvious to her that Higson would pass this information to Wootten.

173.   *Daily Express*, 18 March 1915.

174.   He is recorded as Edward Wootten on most official documents including his birth certificate, marriage certificate, death certificate and the birth certificates of all but one of his children. However, on the birth certificate of his daughter, Louisa, in March 1868, his name is given as 'Charles Wootten' and, proving this was not some sort of clerical error, on Elizabeth's death certificate from May 1926 she was stated to be 'widow of Charles Edward Wootten, a French Polisher (pianoforte)' – the informant being 'L. Scott, niece' albeit, as discussed in the text, this must have been his daughter, Louisa. In addition, when another of Elizabeth's boys, Ernest Wootten, married Julia Newington in April 1897, Ernest's father is stated on the marriage certificate to be 'Charles Wootten', albeit a 'Pianoforte Maker', not a French Polisher (of pianoforte), and Ernest, who was 25 years old at the time of his wedding, wrongly states his age as 26, consistent with the age he gave of 19 years and 10 months old when he enlisted with the marines on 24 February 1890 (NA - ADM 157/1498 & ADM 159/44), at which time he was really only 18 years and 14 days old (having been born on 10 February 1892).

175.   *The Hull Packet and East Riding Times*, 3 April 1885.

176.   *The Times*, 16 July 1900.

177.   *The Eastern Mercury*, 23 August 1904. The jury was not impressed by Meade, who was staying at a hotel near London Bridge at the time of the inquest, complaining that his salary was too low. One of the jurors told him: '…you come here giving an address at a swell hotel. You certainly ought to be ashamed of yourself'. It should be noted that the baby's birth and death was registered at the same time.

178.   As late as 1921, *The Times* reported that Mrs Cooper of Margate paid Mrs Holden of Broadstairs £200 to adopt her baby and register it as her own under the name Elinor Mary Cooper. Both women were remanded on a

charge of supplying false information to the Deputy Registrar of Births (The Times, 25 February 1921). Not until the Adoption of Children Act of 1926 did this type of thing come to an end.

179.   See *Daily News*, 12 March 1863; *The Standard* 16 March 186 and *Lloyds Weekly Newspaper* 12 April 1863.

180.   Two men, George Brown and Gerhard Loeber, were remanded in custody at Bow Street Police Court in September 1906 on charges of obtaining money by false pretences in this fashion, at which time it was stated that such a system of fraud had been carried out 'for many years' (*Daily Mirror*, 1 October 1906. See also *The Times*, 22 November 1906).

181.   *The Times*, 12 October 1870.

182.   *Islington Gazette*, 8 January 1884.

183.   *Islington News*, 18 February 1905.

184.   *The Times*, 28 February 1908.

185.   LMA – X98/429 (Elizabeth was admitted to the St Pancras Hospital as 'Elizabeth Wooton').

186.   James Scott died in the summer of 1925. The electoral register shows that Sydney Isaac, and presumably his wife Louisa – Elizabeth's granddaughter – were also living at 19 Liverpool Street at the time of Elizabeth's death.

187.   The St Pancras Hospital was part of the St Pancras Workhouse at 4 Kings Road. Elizabeth's death certificate states only that she died at '4 Kings Road' which was a widely used euphemism for the workhouse and infirmary due to the shame of going into the workhouse. It is not impossible that Louisa wanted to distance herself from her mother for this reason but financial reasons seem rather more likely.

188.   See NA - WO 339/15467 (inaccurately described in the National Archives catalogue as 'Lieutenant Albert Wootten. The Worcestershire Regiment').

189.   Ibid. Brigadier-General Rodwell had been appointed commander of the 106th Infantry Brigade on 29 November 1914 (*Army List, April 1915*). On 10 April 1915, the 106th Infantry Brigade, of which the 10th Bedfordshire Battalion was a part, became the 18th Reserve Infantry Brigade (NA -WO 293/2) and it was as the commander of this brigade that Rodwell was involved in the discussion about Wootten's future.

190.   Wootten's appeal was made under paragraph 446 of the King's Regulations which stated: 'Every officer whose character or conduct as an officer has been impugned, must submit a case within a reasonable time to his C.O. or other competent military authority, for investigation'.

191.   Charles Cable was appointed a police constable for a month on probation on 2 May 1878 and was sworn in on 30 May of the same year (NRO – Y/TC 3/29).

192.   e.g. *Ipswich Journal* 28 March 1888; *Yarmouth & Gorleston Times*, 18 January 1890.

193.   *Yarmouth & Gorleston Times* 12 July 1890; *Yarmouth Independent* 16 August 1890; NRO – Y/TC 3/30. The types of problems that needed to be

dealt with were: loitering and plying for hire off the stands, drunkenness while in charge of a horse & cab, overloading, leaving horse & cab unattended, cruelty to the horse, speeding, unlicensed drivers, failure of drivers to wear a badge, not having table of fares exposed in the cab, refusal to take a fare etc. (NRO - Y/TC 3/31).

194.   *Yarmouth Independent*, 16 August 1890; NRO – Y/TC 3/30.

195.   e.g. *Yarmouth Gazette* 6 July 1895 at which time, ironically, Cable was no longer the Inspector of Hackney Carriages but it obviously took a while for the news to sink in with the local press. When he died in 1929, Leah (who was present at the death) described his occupation as 'Retired Police Inspector' on the death certificate, albeit that this was not strictly accurate.

196.   NRO – Y/TC 3/31.

197.   *Yarmouth & Gorleston Times* 12 January 1895; *Yarmouth Gazette* 12 January 1895; NRO - Y/TC/ 3/31.

198.   Alternatively, with the 10th Bedfordshire based in Colchester from May 1915, not far from Clacton (where Leah was living in 1913), it is not impossible that Wootten met Leah while based out in Essex.

199.   A curious feature about George's birth in Clacton on 16 August 1913 is that it was (illegally) not registered until 10 October – some 55 days later - when Leah (whose occupation is stated on the certificate to be 'Barmaid) is recorded as living at 85 Bolingbroke Street, Newcastle upon Tyne. Why she was in Newcastle is unknown. The resident of 85 Bolingbroke Street at the time was a 46-year-old commercial traveller and tobacconist, William Alexander Ross, a married man with three children.

200.   For a soldier like Wootten, with a wife and over four children, there was an extra two shillings a week allowance for each additional child (Army Order: AO100 1915 WO 123/57).

201.   NA - WO 364/4852.

202.   NA - WO 95/5208.

203.   There is conflicting information in Wootten's papers as to the date he fell ill with Sandfly Fever. His casualty form in WO 364/4852 appears to suggest that he was admitted with Sandfly Fever on 3 August 1917 and then admitted again with valvular disease of the heart on 29 August 1917. However, his medical report is more detailed and I have assumed this to be more accurate. Although at first sight the casualty form looks like it was filled in contemporaneously, on close inspection his latter illnesses all appear to have been recorded at the same time in September 1917 while Wootten was in India.

204.   The Digest of Service of the 10th Bedfordshire (BLA - X/550/11) does refer to eight officers of the battalion who went overseas before Wootten resigned his commission, namely: 2nd Lieutenant David George Turner Kerr-Cross who joined the Royal West African Frontier Force, Sierra Leone Battalion, on 5 March 1915, Lieutenant William Walter Keightly Page (himself attached to 10th Bedfordshire) who proceeded to France to join the British Expeditionary Force on 25 March 1915, Captain John Amhurst Tennant and Lieutenant John Thomas Adair (both attached to the 1st Battalion Border Regiment) and 2nd Lieutenants Walter Alfred

Leland (attached to the 1st Royal Dublin Fusiliers) and Alfred Morton (attached to the 2nd Royal Fusiliers) who joined the British Mediterranean Expeditionary Force on 18 May 1915, 2nd Lieutenant George Walker (attached to the Nigeria Regiment) who joined the West African Frontier Force on 29 May and Captain Thomas Clifton Hutchings (attached to the Lancashire Fusiliers) who joined the British Mediterranean Expeditionary Force on 28 June (NA: WO 339/23681, WO 339/16307, WO 339/24630, WO 339/21100, WO 339/75, WO 339/2031, WO 339/29839 and WO 339/19640). So it was possible for an officer in the 10th Beds to go and fight overseas with another force but the point is that Wootten is not listed as such an officer. It should also be pointed out that a draft of 100 non commissioned officers and men from the 10th Bedfordshire went to France in August 1915 to join the 6th Bedfordshire Battalion so the fact that the entire battalion remained stationed in the UK did not prevent some men leaving en masse to fight abroad. This was, of course, after Wootten had left the regiment.

205.   LMA – PS/B/B01/104.

206.   NA - CRIM 4/1403 & NA – CRIM 9/64.

207.   *Evening News*, 7 October 1918, 'A Double Bounty'.

208.   *The Times*, 21 November 1918.

209.   Ibid, 13 February 1919.

210.   This and following extracts from NA – WO 339/15467.

211.   Birth certificate of Kathleen Wootten.

212.   Leah's death certificate states that she was the 'Wife of Albert Wootten Drapery Salesman'. He subsequently became an 'Inspector: Credit Drapers' according to his death certificate.

213.   Conversation with the author, February 2011.

214.   Ibid.

Lightning Source UK Ltd.
Milton Keynes UK
UKHW041127270721
387787UK00014B/783